Note: For the purposes of this book, large sums have been expressed in US dollars

WHAT YOU NEED TO KNOW NOW

The World in Facts, Stats, and Graphics

London, New York,
Melbourne, Munich, and Delhi

Senior editor Jenny Finch
Senior art editor Stefan Podhorodecki

Editors Steven Carton, Niki Foreman,
Ashwin Khurana, and James Mitchem
Designers Sheila Collins, Mik Gates, Jim Green,
Katie Knutton, Philip Letsu, and Hoa Luc

Managing editor Linda Esposito
Managing art editor Diane Thistlethwaite

Category Publisher Laura Buller

Picture researcher Nic Dean
Production editor Andy Hilliard
Senior production controller Angela Graef
Jacket design Smiljka Surla
Jacket editor Matilda Gollon
Design development manager Sophia Tampakopoulos

Additional consultants Keith Lye,
Dr Adrian Campbell, Professor Denise Cush,
and John Woodward

First published in Great Britain in 2010 by
Dorling Kindersley Limited,
80 Strand, London, WC2R 0RL

Copyright © 2010 Dorling Kindersley Limited
A Penguin Company

2 4 6 8 10 9 7 5 3 1
175776 – 04/10

A CIP catalogue record for this book
is available from the British Library

ISBN: 978-1-40535-371-7

Hi-res work flow proofed by MDP, UK
Printed and bound by Hung Hing, China

Discover more at
www.dk.com

WHAT YOU NEED TO KNOW NOW

The World in Facts, Stats, and Graphics

Written by Joe Fullman, Ian Graham, Sally Regan, and Isabel Thomas

Consultant Dr Stephen Scoffham

Contents

Earth

Our world is a 4.5-billion-year-old ball of rock, orbiting the Sun at a distance of 149.6 million km (93 million miles). The Earth is a living planet — not only is it home to about 1.7 million known species of plants and animals, but the planet itself is constantly changing. Over millions of years, its surface has been shaped into the continents and oceans we see today — the crust is constantly shifting, mountains are forged, and rock is being recycled.

Earth in Space

Compared to the vastness of the cosmos, our planet is almost infinitesimally small. Earth forms just a minute part of the Solar System, which itself is just a tiny speck in the Milky Way galaxy. According to scientists, the Milky Way is just one of more than 100 billion galaxies making up the universe, each containing billions of stars.

5. Our supercluster

Even the Local Group is dwarfed by our supercluster, a vast structure some 150 million light years across. At its centre is the Virgo cluster, a group of galaxies surrounding a giant black hole. The universe is thought to be made up of many superclusters, separated by great voids.

Bigger and bigger

Big as it is now, the universe is getting bigger all the time. It was formed about 13.7 billion years ago in a giant explosion known as the Big Bang, and continues to expand outwards in all directions.

2 million light years away

1 million

Ursa Minor

Milky Way

NGC 68222

NGC 185

Fornax

Andromeda (M31)

DDO 210

Triangulum (M33)

Pheonix

250,000 light years away

200,000

150,000

100,000

Pegasus

Sagitarrius Dwarf

4. The Local Group

The Milky Way is part of an even larger structure, the Local Group, which contains around 30 galaxies. These galaxies come in three main types: spiral, elliptical, and irregular. The Andromeda Galaxy, a spiral galaxy, is the closest major galaxy to the Milky Way.

Milky Way

Small Magellanic Cloud

Large Magellanic Cloud

Sculptor

Ursa Minor

3. Our galactic realm

The Sun and its neighbouring stars slowly revolve around the centre of our spiral-shaped Milky Way galaxy. The Milky Way is surrounded by a number of smaller satellite galaxies, the closest being the Sagitarrius Dwarf. The nearby Small and Large Magellanic Clouds are visible only from Earth's Southern Hemisphere.

75 million light years away

50 million

25 million

NGC 5907

NGC 4571 | Ursa Major

Virgo

Virgo W

NGC 4594

Local Group
(Milky Way)

NGC 2903

20 light years away
15
10

GI 628

Procyon A,B

Solar   Alpha
System   Centauri

GI 674

Sirius A,B

Epsilon Indi

Tau Ceti

2. The Sun's neighbourhood

The region stretching for 20 light years
around our Sun is known as the solar
neighbourhood. Travelling at about
300,000 km (186,411 miles) per second,
it takes light 4.2 years to travel from the
Sun to our next nearest star, Proxima
Centauri, part of the Alpha Centauri
triple star system. The binary star system
Sirius A, B is only the ninth closest star
to Earth, yet – after the Sun – it is the
brightest star in our sky.

1. Our Solar System

Our home in the universe, the Solar System, is
made up of eight planets and countless smaller
bodies orbiting the Sun. The farthest planet,
Neptune, lies about 4.5 billion km (2.8 billion
miles) from the Sun. Humans have travelled
only as far as Earth's moon, although
unmanned spacecraft have journeyed
to the system's outer reaches.

Neptune

Uranus

Venus   Sun   Mercury

Mars

Earth

Jupiter

Saturn

Story of the Earth

In the long story of the Earth, human life doesn't start until the last few chapters. The planet formed along with the rest of the Solar System about 4.6 BYA (billion years ago), and the first life forms appeared some 3.8 BYA. However, complex life evolved only 600 MYA (million years ago), while the first humans did not arrive until about 200,000 years ago. If you imagine the whole of Earth's history as a single year, modern humans would not appear until 20 minutes to midnight on 31 December.

The Earth evolves

As this timeline shows, for much of its existence the Earth was largely empty of life. The lush, green planet we know today only began to take shape after life from the oceans colonized the land 475 MYA – nearly 4 billion years after the birth of the planet.

Oceans form, 4.2 BYA

4 BYA

3 BYA

2 BYA

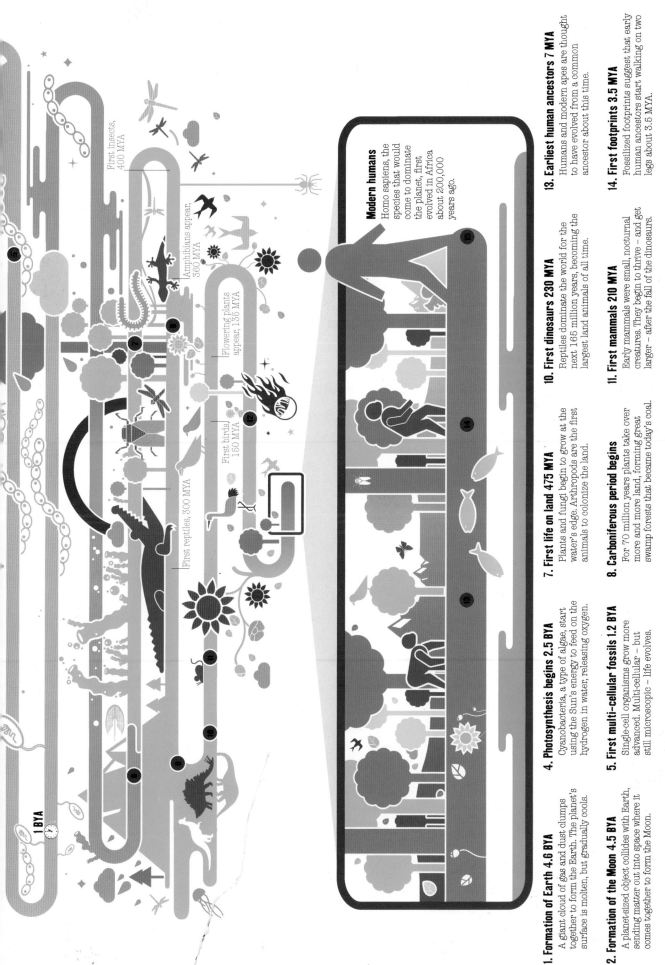

First insects, 400 MYA

Amphibians appear, 360 MYA

Flowering plants appear, 135 MYA

First birds, 150 MYA

First reptiles, 300 MYA

Modern humans
Homo sapiens, the species that would come to dominate the planet, first evolved in Africa about 200,000 years ago.

1 BYA

1. Formation of Earth 4.6 BYA
A giant cloud of gas and dust clumps together to form the Earth. The planet's surface is molten, but gradually cools.

2. Formation of the Moon 4.5 BYA
A planet-sized object collides with Earth, sending matter out into space where it comes together to form the Moon.

3. First life 3.8 BYA
The first single-cell life forms appear in the oceans. Life remains microscopic for more than 3 billion years.

4. Photosynthesis begins 2.5 BYA
Cyanobacteria, a type of algae, start using the Sun's energy to feed on the hydrogen in water, releasing oxygen.

5. First multi-cellular fossils 1.2 BYA
Single-cell organisms grow more advanced. Multi-cellular – but still microscopic – life evolves.

6. First known animals 570 MYA
The first large soft-bodied animals were the Ediacarans. They lived in the sea and looked a bit like modern jellyfish.

7. First life on land 475 MYA
Plants and fungi begin to grow at the water's edge. Arthropods are the first animals to colonize the land.

8. Carboniferous period begins
For 70 million years plants take over more and more land, forming great swamp forests that became today's coal.

9. Mass extinction 251 MYA
Earth's history is punctuated with mass extinctions. This one wiped out more than 90% of all species.

10. First dinosaurs 230 MYA
Reptiles dominate the world for the next 165 million years, becoming the largest land animals of all time.

11. First mammals 210 MYA
Early mammals were small, nocturnal creatures. They begin to thrive – and get larger – after the fall of the dinosaurs.

12. Extinction of the dinosaurs 65 MYA
An asteroid impact destroys around 75% of the world's species, ending the dinosaurs' reign.

13. Earliest human ancestors 7 MYA
Humans and modern apes are thought to have evolved from a common ancestor about this time.

14. First footprints 3.5 MYA
Fossilized footprints suggest that early human ancestors start walking on two legs about 3.5 MYA.

15. Out of Africa 100,000 years ago
Modern humans begin to migrate from Africa to other continents, kickstarting the human colonization of Earth.

Planet Earth

Our home planet is a ball of rock 12,740 km (7,916 miles) in diameter. At its centre is an iron core, surrounded by a large mass of moving rock known as the mantle. Above this is the thin rocky crust that supports all of the planet's life. If planet Earth were the size of a peach, the part humans inhabit would only be the thickness of the fruit's skin.

Inside Earth

This cutaway diagram shows the layers that make up Earth's internal structure. The blue ring represents the narrow blanket of gases held in place by Earth's gravitational pull that protects the planet from extremes of temperature.

Earth's atmosphere

Although the atmosphere technically extends thousands of kilometres up, about three-quarters of the gases it contains are within a thin layer next to the surface called the troposphere. Relatively speaking, you don't have to go very far to get into outer space – NASA considers anyone who travels above 80 km (50 miles) an astronaut.

Troposphere

The lowest layer of the atmosphere is the troposphere, and it rises to around 17 km (10.5 miles) from the surface. It is where most weather occurs, and the only part of the atmosphere that supports human life. Above the troposphere, the ozone layer protects the Earth from the Sun's harmful ultraviolet radiation.

15 KM (9.3 miles)

10 KM (6.2 miles)
Commercial airliner

5 KM (3.1 miles)
Cirrus clouds
Migrating birds
Cumulus clouds

0 KM (0 miles)
Birds
Hot-air balloon
OCEAN

5 KM (3.1 miles)
CONTINENTAL CRUST

8,000 KM (4,971 miles)
7,500 KM (4,660 miles)
7,000 KM (4,350 miles)
6,500 KM (4,039 miles)
6,000 KM (3,728 miles)
5,500 KM (3,417 miles)
5,000 KM (3,107 miles)
4,500 KM (2,796 miles)
4,000 KM (2,485 miles)
3,500 KM (2,175 miles)
3,000 KM (1,864 miles)
2,500 KM (1,553 miles)
2,000 KM (1,243 miles)
1,500 KM (932 miles)

700 KM (435 miles)
600 KM (373 miles)
500 KM (311 miles)
400 KM (248 miles)
300 KM (186 miles)
200 KM (124 miles)
100 KM (62 miles)

Hubble Space Telescope
International Space Station
Meteor
Aurora

Crust

The surface of the planet is covered in a rocky crust. The crust beneath the oceans is about 5–10 km (3–6 miles) thick and made from basalt. Continental crust (the rocks that form the continents) is made from lighter rock, such as granite, and can be up to 50 km (31 miles) thick. The deepest borehole ever dug is just over 12 km (7.4 miles) deep – around a third the depth of the continental crust.

OCEANIC CRUST

MANTLE

15 KM
(9.3 miles)

20 KM
(12 miles)

25 KM
(15 miles)

30 KM
(18.6 miles)

35 KM
(21.7 miles)

INNER CORE

OUTER CORE

MANTLE

300 KM
(3.1 miles)

SURFACE: 0 KM
(0 mi)

500 KM
(311 miles)

1,000 KM
(621 miles)

1,500 KM
(932 miles)

2,000 KM
(1,243 miles)

2,500 KM
(1,553 miles)

3,000 KM
(1,864 miles)

3,500 KM
(2,175 miles)

4,000 KM
(2,485 miles)

4,500 KM
(2,796 miles)

5,000 KM
(3,107 miles)

5,500 KM
(3,417 miles)

6,000 KM
(3,728 miles)

CENTRE: 6,370 KM
(3,958 miles)

Core

The Earth's iron-and-nickel core is made up of two parts: a liquid outer core 2,260 km (1,404 miles) and a solid inner core 1,228 km (763 miles) thick. The inner core can top 7,000°C (12,632°F) – hotter than the surface of the Sun.

Mantle

The mantle is a vast interior volume (around 84% of the Earth's volume). Heat from the core makes the mantle move in slow convection currents that move the crust, which can create earthquakes and cause mountains to form.

Plate Tectonics

We tend to think of the continents as permanent and immovable, but nothing could be further from the truth. Earth's hard outer crust is divided into a number of large pieces called tectonic plates, which move constantly on top of a layer of softer molten rock, known as the mantle. Carried along these moving plates are the seven main continents we know today: Asia, Africa, Europe, Australia, Antarctica, North America, and South America.

Transform boundary

The San Andreas Fault is part of a transform boundary that slices across California's coastal region. A transform boundary is where plates move sideways past each other. Sometimes the plates get stuck, creating an immense amount of stress. The longer the plates remain stuck, the more energy builds up, eventually to be released as an earthquake when the plates finally pull free.

A giant jigsaw

Earth's tectonic plates fit together like the pieces of a giant rock jigsaw. Geological events, such as earthquakes, volcanoes, and mountain formation, may occur on the plate boundaries, depending on whether they are coming together, pulling apart, or slipping past one another.

200 MILLION YEARS AGO

100 MILLION YEARS AGO

TODAY

FUTURE: 150 MILLION YEARS

PACIFIC PLATE

NORTH AMERICAN PLATE

COCOS PLATE

CARIBBEAN PLATE

NAZCA PLATE

ANTARCTIC PLATE

Changing continents

Around 200 million years ago, Earth's continents were fused together in a giant supercontinent known as Pangaea. Since that time they have gradually drifted apart, and will continue drifting to new positions in the future.

NORTH AMERICAN PLATE

EURASIAN PLATE

CARIBBEAN PLATE

COCOS PLATE

NAZCA PLATE

PACIFIC PLATE

EURASIAN PLATE

SOUTH AMERICAN PLATE

SOUTH AMERICAN PLATE

ANTARCTIC PLATE

Plates move between **2–20 cm**
(0.8–8 in) per year – the rate at which fingernails grow

Divergent boundary

When oceanic plates diverge (pull apart) magma wells up from the mantle into the gap to form new crust. This process is known as seafloor spreading. Continental plates also sometimes diverge, which can create a line of volcanoes, or even cause the continent to break in two. This type of boundary is evident at certain parts of the Cocos Plate, located under the Pacific Ocean near the west coast of Central America.

Convergent boundary

The world's longest continuous mountain range, the Andes in South America, is a result of an oceanic plate converging with a continental plate. When these two plates collide, the thinner oceanic plate sinks into the mantle and eventually melts. This leads to the creation of an ocean trench and a chain of volcanic mountains on land.

Mountains

A mountain is formed by slow but extremely powerful movements of the Earth's crust, which gradually push rocks up above the surrounding landscape. Though definitions vary across the world, peaks above about 600 m (2,000 ft) are usually considered mountains, while those below that are hills. Asia has the world's highest mountains, while Australia is the flattest and lowest continent.

Highest mountains

Here, you can see the highest mountains on each of the seven continents. The 10 highest mountains in the world are all in the Himalayas, and are all still growing at a rate of around 6 cm (2.5 in) a year, as the Indian tectonic plate continues to push into the Eurasian plate.

First ascent
In 1953, the New Zealander Edmund Hillary, and Tenzing Norgay from Nepal became the first people to set foot on the summit of Mount Everest.

160 km

From the top of Mount Everest, you can see for more than **160 km** (100 miles), and you can even make out the curvature of Earth's surface

10,000 M (32,800 ft)

9,500 M (31,170 ft)

9,000 M (29,530 ft)

Aeroplane
Most commercial aeroplanes cruise at altitudes of between 9,100 m (29,850 ft) and 12,100 m (39,700 ft). Air at that altitude is thinner, allowing the planes to fly faster while using less fuel.

8,500 M (27,890 ft)

Geese
Bar-headed geese are among the world's highest-flying birds. Every year they migrate right over the top of Mount Everest.

8,000 M (26,250 ft)

Mount Everest
8,850 M (29,035 FT) ASIA

7,500 M (24,600 ft)

Death zone
Above 7,000 m (23,000 ft), there is too little oxygen to sustain human life. Climbers must bring their own oxygen supply if they venture up this high.

7,000 M (22,960 ft)

Aconcagua
6,962 M (22,841 FT) SOUTH AMERICA

6,500 M (21,320 ft)

Spiders
The tiny jumping spider has been found up to 6,700 m (22,000 ft) above sea level on the slopes of the Himalayas, making it one of the world's highest-living creatures.

Mount McKinley
6,194 M (20,321 FT) NORTH AMERICA

6,000 M (19,680 ft)

Kilimanjaro
5,892 M (19,331 FT) AFRICA

Elbrus
5,642 M (18,510 FT) EUROPE

5,500 M (18,040 ft)

5,000 M (16,400 ft)	
4,500 M (14,760 ft)	
4,000 M (13,120 ft)	
3,500 M (11,480 ft)	
3,000 M (9,840 ft)	
2,500 M (8,200 ft)	
2,000 M (6,560 ft)	
1,500 M (4,920 ft)	
1,000 M (3,280 ft)	
500 M (1,640 ft)	
0	**SEA LEVEL**

Vinson Massif
4,892 M (16,050 FT) ANTARCTICA

Unseen summit
Much smaller than the world's tallest mountains, the Vinson Massif – located in the frozen heart of Antarctica – wasn't discovered until 1958. Its summit was first scaled in 1966 by a US team.

Mountain goat
Mountain goats live high above the reach of most predators, using specially adapted hooves to help keep their footing on the rocky terrain.

Cold cuppa
It's difficult to enjoy a cup of tea on a mountain. Water boils at a lower temperature the higher you get, so the further up the mountain you are, the colder your tea will be.

At a length of almost **16,000 km** (10,000 miles) the world's longest mountain range is the mid-Atlantic ridge, which runs below the Atlantic Ocean

Kosciuszko
2,228 M (7,310 FT) AUSTRALIA

Scenic convenience
Situated just below the summit of Mount Kosciuszko, one of the world's highest flushable toilets serves some of the mountain's 30,000 visitors every year.

Tallest tower
The tallest structure ever built is dwarfed by even the smallest mountains. The Burj Khalifa in the United Arab Emirates is 828 m (2,717 ft) tall and has 160 floors.

EVEREST

MAUNA KEA

UNDERSEA GIANT
Everest is the tallest mountain on dry land, but the biggest mountain on Earth is Mauna Kea, which rises to about 10,203 m (33,500 ft) from the floor of the Pacific Ocean. Just 4,205 m (13,796 ft) pokes above the ocean's surface. This diagram shows how the two would compare if lined up.

TYPES OF MOUNTAIN

Fold mountains
The most common type of mountain is formed when two tectonic plates collide, pushing the rocks on their borders up into a series of high folds.

Block mountains
Sometimes tectonic plates pull apart, creating giant cracks in the Earth's crust and splitting rock into giant blocks, some of which are pushed up to form new mountains.

Volcanoes
Volcanoes occur in places where molten rock rises to the surface, most commonly on the borders between tectonic plates. Over time, the lava may build up to form a cone-shaped mountain or, at sea, a volcanic island.

Quakes and Shakes

Earthquakes are sudden, unpredictable shocks to Earth's surface. They can range from tiny, barely noticeable vibrations to enormous rolling ground waves that crack roads, flatten buildings, and break bridges in half. Most are caused by the movements of the Earth's tectonic plates. Where two plates move past one another, parts sometimes get stuck. The pressure then builds up until the plates finally break free, creating a ground tremor.

Earthquake-resistant architecture

Most deaths following earthquakes are caused by falling buildings. Scientists can predict where but not when a quake will strike. People can protect themselves against harm by constructing buildings that can withstand the tremors. The 49-storey Transamerica Building in San Francisco, USA, a well-known earthquake zone, is designed to sway by up to 30 cm (12 in) either side. In 1989, its design allowed it to survive, unscathed, a 7.1-magnitude earthquake.

Richter scale

The magnitude (size) of an earthquake can be calculated using a number of different methods. The best known is the Richter scale, which measures the amount of ground motion caused by a quake using an increasing number scale, with 1 being the weakest. The top of the scale is currently 9.5, but stronger earthquakes in the future could push the scale into double figures.

Seismographs

The instrument that measures the magnitude of earthquakes is called a seismograph. It records an earthquake's strength in the form of a wavy line: the more the line wiggles up and down, the stronger the earthquake.

Measuring the shakes

A seismograph consists of a base, which shakes during a quake, and a weight, which does not. Measuring the contrast between the two gives the quake's magnitude.

Aftershocks

Earthquakes are usually short-lived. Even the biggest ones typically last less than a minute, although they are often followed by smaller quakes known as aftershocks.

1   **2**   **3**   **4**   **5**

1.0
These tiny tremors take place deep underground. They can be detected by seismographs, but not usually by people.

2.0
You might just about be able to feel a 2.0 earthquake if you were sitting still, upstairs in a house.

3.0
Though hardly serious, a 3.0 quake is certainly noticeable, with enough force to make hanging objects swing.

4.0
You might easily mistake a 4.0 quake for a large truck passing by your house, causing trees to sway and windows to rattle.

5.0
A size-5.0 quake may cause liquids to spill from glasses, windows to break, doors to swing open, and (some) people to fall over.

Tsunamis
A really big quake on the seafloor can cause a series of large waves to form, known as a tsunami. These waves can travel at speeds of up to 700 km/h (435 mph), causing huge levels of destruction when they hit land.

Top 10 earthquakes
The earthquakes listed are the biggest to occur since records began. Larger quakes probably took place in the past, but went unrecorded by science. The largest quakes are not necessarily the most destructive, however, as this depends on how built-up the area is and how prepared for an earthquake it is.

1	Chile	9.5	22/05/1960
2	Price William Sound, Alaska	9.2	28/03/1964
3	West Coast of Northern Sumatra	9.1	26/12/2004
4	Kamchatka	9.0	01/11/1952
5	Off the coast of Equador	8.8	31/01/1906
6	Rat Islands, Alaska	8.7	04/02/1965
7	Northern Sumatra, Indonesia	8.6	28/03/2005
8	Assam Tibet	8.6	15/08/1950
9	Andreanof Islands, Alaska	8.6	09/03/1957
10	Southern Sumatra, Indonesia	8.5	12/09/2007

Predicting earthquakes
Although scientists can measure the size of earthquakes and identify the regions most likely to suffer from future quakes, they cannot predict exactly when an earthquake will strike.

Great Chilean Earthquake – 9.5
The biggest earthquake since detailed records began struck Chile in 1960. It triggered landslides, tsunamis, and caused a volcano to erupt, killing thousands.

6

6.0
It can be difficult to stand during a 6.0 earthquake. The walls in some buildings may crack and tiles may fall from roofs.

7

7.0
A size-7.0 earthquake can cause a great deal of damage, cracking roads and moving houses on their foundations.

8

8.0
Typical damage from an 8.0 quake can include twisted railway lines, broken roads and bridges, burst pipes, and collapsed buildings.

9

9.0
These intense quakes send out undulating waves across the surface, which unleash total destruction and cause large-scale loss of life.

Earthquake frequency
Although we tend to think of earthquakes as rare events, an estimated 2,500 happen every day – which is nearly a million a year. Most, however, are too weak to be felt.

MAGNITUDE	ESTIMATED NUMBER EACH YEAR
2.5 or less	900,000
2.5–5.4	30,000
5.5–6.0	500
6.1–6.9	100
7.0–7.9	20
8 or greater	One every 5 to 10 years

There are about **1,500** active volcanoes in the world. Up to **20** of them will be erupting at any one time.

1

2

3

4

VOLCANO MAP

▲ Volcano

△ Volcano featured in panel (right)

— Plate boundary

— Pacific Ring of Fire

Volcanoes

A volcano is an opening in the Earth's crust through which lava (molten rock), ash, and gases can escape from beneath the surface. in some places the lava gently oozes out, while in others it is flung clear with explosive force. One in 10 people in the world lives close to an active volcano.

World volcano locations

Most volcanoes are found on the boundaries between tectonic plates, caused by plates colliding or moving away from each other. Sometimes, however, a volcano will burst through the middle of a plate over a hotspot in Earth's mantle.

More than **75%** of the world's volcanoes are located in a ring around the Pacific Ocean known as the "Ring of Fire"

1. Surtsey, Iceland

In 1962 the island of Surtsey didn't exist. It was formed by a volcanic eruption on the seabed, 130 m (426 ft) below the surface, which built layers of lava that emerged above the waves in November 1963. The eruption ended in 1967.

2. Etna, Italy

Etna is continental Europe's largest volcano and one of its most active, sending out great plumes of ash, which make the surrounding soils extremely fertile. Despite the risk of lava flows, farms and villages cover its lower slopes.

3. Krakatoa, Indonesia

Heard more than 5,000 km (3,100 miles) away, the 1883 eruption of Krakatoa killed more than 35,000 people. The blast demolished the old volcano, but since then a new one – Anak Krakatoa, or "child of Krakatoa" – has emerged.

4. Pinatubo, Philippines

Mount Pinatubo's 1991 eruption was one of the most explosive of the 20th century. It destroyed nearly 5,000 homes and sent a thick cloud of ash and gas into the air that lowered global temperatures by 0.5°C (0.9°F).

5. Kilauea, Hawaii

The Hawaiian island chain was formed from lava bubbling up through a hotspot in the ocean floor. Kilauea lies on the south side of Hawaii's Big Island and is one of the most active volcanoes on Earth.

6. Yellowstone, USA

Though its forested landscape looks serene, Yellowstone National Park is the site of a huge network of ancient volcanoes. A giant cauldron of magma 60-km (37-miles) across heats the park's many geysers.

Inside an eruption

Pressure deep inside the Earth forces molten rock towards the surface where it breaks through a weak point in the crust. Over time, layers of lava may build up to form a cone-shaped volcanic mountain.

Surface rocks

Most surface rocks are just visitors. They will eventually be worn away by the weather or dragged down into the bowels of the Earth by tectonic plate movements. Replacement rocks are brought to the surface through the processes of uplift and volcanic eruptions.

Igneous intrusion

Magma doesn't always break the surface. Sometimes it collects in an underground reservoir, or magma chamber. Here, it will gradually cool and harden to form a mass of solid rock known as an igneous intrusion. Uplift may then bring this intrusion to the surface.

Subduction

When two tectonic plates come together, one may get pushed down (or subducted) beneath the other into the Earth. As the plate is dragged deeper, and the temperature and pressure increase, it will begin to melt.

Igneous extrusion

In some places, rising magma will escape through a volcano on to the Earth's surface – when it becomes known as lava. Sometimes this lava contains gases that make it erupt with explosive force. Surface rocks formed from cooled lava are known as extrusive igneous rocks.

The oldest rocks on the Earth's surface are thought to be more than

3.8 billion years old

UPLIFT

Magma

Magma is molten rock that that forms deep below the Earth's surface. It can reach temperatures of 1,300°C (2,372 °F). As magma rises and cools it solidifies to form igneous rock.

Melted rocks

Rock that has been pushed deep into the Earth at a subduction zone may melt, forming magma. This happens to all three types of rock – igneous, sedimentary, or metamorphic – although different rocks melt at different temperatures.

Metamorphic rocks

Both sedimentary and igneous rocks can transform into metamorphic rocks. Tectonic plate movements may drive these rocks deep underground where they melt, or push them up to the surface via uplift.

Weathering

The rocks on Earth's surface are gradually broken down into smaller pieces by a number of processes. These include the action of rain and ice, extreme temperature changes, and the growth of tree roots.

Transportation and deposition

Small, weathered pieces of rock are transported away by wind, ice, and water. Rivers carry rock particles all the way to the sea where they are dropped, forming layers of sediment on the seabed. This is known as deposition.

Rock Cycle

About **75%** of Earth's surface rocks are sedimentary

Although you wouldn't know it to look at them, Earth's rocks are constantly — but very slowly — changing. On the surface, weathering breaks large rocks into little pieces, which may be compacted together to form new rocks. Underground, the movement of tectonic plates draws rocks deep into the Earth where they melt, and this also pushes new rocks on to the surface — where the cycle begins again.

Compaction and cementation

As an increasing amount of sediment is deposited, the layers on the seabed get packed more and more tightly. Pressure compacts the particles together, squeezing out any water. The rock grains are then cemented together by minerals, forming new sedimentary rock.

Uplift

Just as tectonic plates can drive rocks down into the Earth, they can also push them up to the surface where they will begin to weather and erode. This process is known as uplift.

Sedimentary rocks

There are several different types of sedimentary rock. Some, such as sandstone, are made of eroded rock particles, while others, such as chalk, are formed from the compacted remains of tiny sea creatures.

Transformation

Deep beneath the surface of the Earth, rocks are subjected to intense heat and pressure. Below a certain temperature, this can change the texture and mineral composition of the rock, transforming it from one type of rock into another via a process called metamorphism.

Rock melts

Above a certain temperature, sedimentary rocks can no longer transform into metamorphic rocks, but instead melt, turning into magma.

Water Cycle

Constantly on the move, water falls from clouds and flows along in rivers to oceans, before the Sun's rays evaporate it back into clouds. The journey water goes on as it circulates between the atmosphere, land, rivers, and oceans is known as the water cycle. it may move around a lot, but the amount of water in the world remains exactly the same and has done since the planet was formed.

Precipitation

The water that falls from the air as rain, snow, sleet, or hail is called precipitation. It happens when small, light water droplets in clouds gather together to become larger, heavier ones, which then drop down to Earth under the force of gravity.

Ice and snow

Just 3% of the Earth's water is fresh, of which two-thirds is frozen in the form of ice and snow, found in glaciers and ice caps. The remaining 97% is held in the oceans. This water is salty and therefore not suitable for humans to drink.

On the ground

A proportion of the water that falls on the ground soaks into the soil. If the underlying rock is permeable, it will become saturated. Water stored in this way emerges on the surface in marshes and springs. Springs are common at the point where a layer of permeable rock meets a lower layer of impermeable rock.

Water is the **only** substance found naturally on Earth as a solid, liquid, and gas

Condensation

As water vapour rises into the air, it cools and turns into tiny droplets of water in a process called condensation. This is the opposite of evaporation. The suspended water droplets gather together to form clouds.

Lake Baikal, Russia, contains roughly
20%
of the world's surface freshwater

A drop of water can spend as little as
9 days
or as long as
40,000 years
moving through the water cycle

Evaporation

The heat of the Sun's rays causes the liquid water to turn into a gas called water vapour. This process is called evaporation. Across the world the amount of water falling to Earth as precipitation is about the same as the amount entering the atmosphere via evaporation.

Streams and rivers

In places where water doesn't seep into the ground – perhaps because the ground is waterlogged or made of impermeable rock (rock that does not allow liquids to pass through it) – it will start to flow downhill and may find its way into streams and rivers, which will eventually carry it back to the oceans.

Rivers

Earth has more than a million rivers. They can be found on every continent except for frozen Antarctica. There are more than 150 rivers in excess of 1,000 km (620 miles) long. Of the world's five longest rivers, shown below, two — the Yenisey-Angara and the Yangtze — are found in Asia while the Mississippi-Missouri is in North America, the Amazon is in South America, and the longest river of all, the Nile, flows through Africa.

5,550 KM (3,449 miles)

5,971 KM (3,710 miles)

6,380 KM (3,964 miles)

Missouri River

Lake Baikal

Angara River

More than **1.2 million** people's homes were flooded during the construction of the Three Gorges Dam on the Yangtze River, creating a reservoir some 600 km (375 miles) long

Lined up end to end, the five longest rivers would stretch **three-quarters** of the way around the world

Yenisey River

Mississippi River

Arctic Ocean

Atlantic Ocean

Pacific Ocean

Yenisey-Angara

Beginning as a trickle in Mongolia, the Yenisey-Angara enters Russia, where it flows through Lake Baikal – the world's largest freshwater lake. It then heads north through Siberia to the Arctic Ocean.

Mississippi-Missouri

On its journey from northwest to southeast USA, the mighty Mississippi-Missouri River is crossed by more than 170 bridges. Its drainage basin – the total area drained by the river and its tributaries – encompasses some 3.2 million sq km (1.23 million sq miles).

Yangtze

About 350 million people live near this great Chinese river, which flows through more than 30 cities. The Yangtze deposits 170 million m³ (6 billion ft³) of fertile silt every year onto the Jiangsu Plain, one of the world's major centres of rice production.

BIGGEST RIVERS
[sq m (sq ft) per second]

The Nile may be the longest river, but the Amazon is by far the largest in the world, carrying more water than the next four longest rivers combined and holding about 20% of the planet's flowing fresh water. The volume of water each river carries is measured by how much they discharge into the oceans every second.

5,100 (54,896)	16,200 (174,375)	19,000 (204,514)	31,000 (333,681)	219,000 (2,357,296)
Nile	Mississippi-Missouri	Yenisey-Angara	Yangtze	Amazon

6,696 KM (4,161 miles)

6,450 KM (4,008 miles)

The Amazon is by far the widest river on Earth – in the wet season its lower stretches can be up to

40 km (25 miles) wide

❹

Atlantic Ocean

Mediterranean Sea

❺

Amazon

This massive river drains water from 40% of the South American continent and has thousands of tributaries feeding into it. It is home to 2,500 different species of fish – more than are found in the entire Atlantic Ocean.

Nile

Passing through 10 African countries, the Nile is a thin ribbon of water for much of its great length, carving its way through the dry Sahara Desert. In Egypt, where the Nile reaches the sea, most people rely on its water and live near the river's banks.

❶ Yenisey tributaries

A river usually begins as a thin stream flowing quickly over steep ground. It slows as it reaches flatter terrain, and gradually grows in volume as it is joined by smaller streams and rivers, known as tributaries.

❷ Lake Carter

In its middle course a river will often flow in giant loops, known as meanders. Occasionally, the river may change its course, leaving behind a C-shaped body of water known as an oxbow lake.

❸ Three Gorges Dam

Around the world people build dams across rivers, creating huge artificial lakes that can be used to generate electricity. The Three Gorges Dam in China is the world's largest electricity-generating plant.

❹ Amazon floodplains

Many rivers flood as part of their natural annual cycle. Every wet season the Amazon River rises by more than 9 m (30 ft), deluging the surrounding area and depositing valuable nutrients back into the ground.

❺ Nile Delta

A river carries huge amounts of sediment, which help it to gouge out its course across the land. When the river meets the sea, this material is dropped and may form a low, triangular-shaped area of land known as a delta.

Ocean Depths

From the surface to the seafloor, the ocean can be divided into four zones, each colder than the last. The inky black waters of the ocean's lowest reaches are largely unexplored by people. It is often said that we know more about the surface of the Moon than we do about the ocean depths.

Ocean sizes

Water covers 71% of the Earth's surface. Most of it can be found in five interlinked oceans. The Pacific is by far the biggest, covering some 180 million sq km (69 million sq miles) or about one-third of the Earth's entire surface area. This diagram shows how much of the world's total ocean cover is taken up by each body of water.

ARCTIC 4%
SOUTHERN 6%
INDIAN 20%
ATLANTIC 23%
PACIFIC 47%

200 M (656 ft)

CONTINENTAL SHELF

1,000 M (3,281 ft)

CONTINENTAL SLOPE

SUBMARINE RIDGES

Some **90%** of all the ocean's water is contained in the midnight zone

Blue shark · Sting rays · Sperm whale · fish · Haddock · Elephant seal · Dolphins · Plankton · Great white shark · Sea lions · Flying fish · King penguins · Anchovies · Bluefin tuna · Comb jelly · Johnson Sealink submarine · Scuba diver · Man o' war · Jellyfish · Nuclear submarine · Sea turtles · Angler fish · JIM atmospheric diving suit · Black smokers · Leatherback turtle · Deep-sea squid

VOLCANIC ISLAND

Sunlit zone
At the top layer of the ocean, plants and microscopic organisms use the abundant sunlight for photosynthesis. The energy they create forms the basis of an intricate food chain involving a variety of wildlife, including plankton, fish, crustaceans, marine mammals, and aquatic birds. Some 90% of marine life can be found in this zone.

THE VENOMOUS MAN O' WAR JELLYFISH HAS 10-M (30-FT) LONG TENTACLES

Twilight zone
The murky blue waters of the twilight zone receive some faint sunlight, but not enough for photosynthesis. No plants can live at these depths, but plenty of animals do. Many boast special adaptations to cope with the darkness. Some use a process called bioluminescence to produce their own ghostly light to lure prey, attract mates, or distract predators.

ANGLER FISH EMIT A BRIGHT GLOW

Midnight zone

Not even a glimmer of light filters down to the midnight zone. Although much of this zone is barren, thriving ecosystems are found living around hydrothermal vents, known as black smokers. These vents spew forth superheated water rich in minerals, providing sustenance to a whole array of creatures, including giant worms, clams, crabs, and shrimp.

THE WATER FROM A BLACK SMOKER CAN REACH 300°C (570°F)

Hadal zone

Creatures in the hadal zone eke out an existence as best they can amid the darkness, cold, and crushing pressure. Many are scavengers, feasting upon the bodies of dead animals that float down from above. People have visited the Mariana Trench, the deepest point in the ocean just once, in 1960, aboard the submersible Trieste.

TRIESTE CARRIED A CREW OF TWO PEOPLE TO A DEPTH OF ALMOST 11 KM (6.8 MILES)

Island Formation

An island is an area of land smaller than a continent that is completely surrounded by water. The Earth is home to well over 100,000 islands, ranging from tiny patches of sand to giant, almost continent-sized landmasses. It is estimated that one in every 10 people lives on an island. The majority of islands are formed either by volcanic activity, changes to continental plates, or the growth of coral.

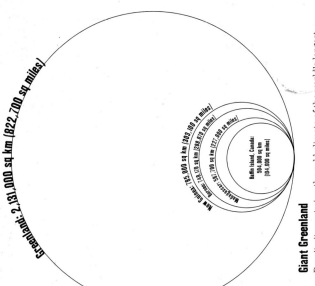

Greenland: 2,131,000 sq km (822,700 sq miles)

New Guinea: 785,000 sq km (303,100 sq miles)
Borneo: 748,170 sq km (288,870 sq miles)
Madagascar: 587,700 sq km (227,000 sq miles)
Baffin Island, Canada: 504,000 sq km (194,000 sq miles)

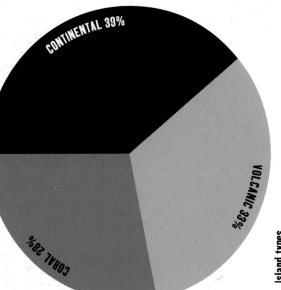

CONTINENTAL 39%

VOLCANIC 33%

CORAL 28%

Giant Greenland

Despite its vast size, the cold climate of the world's largest island, Greenland, means that it is home to just 55,000 people. The next three largest islands – New Guinea, Borneo, and Madagascar – could all fit inside it with a bit to spare.

Island types

There are three main types of island. Continental islands fringe the world's major landmasses, volcanic islands are formed by molten rock welling up from beneath the Earth's crust, and coral islands are slowly built up by tiny creatures living in warm tropical waters.

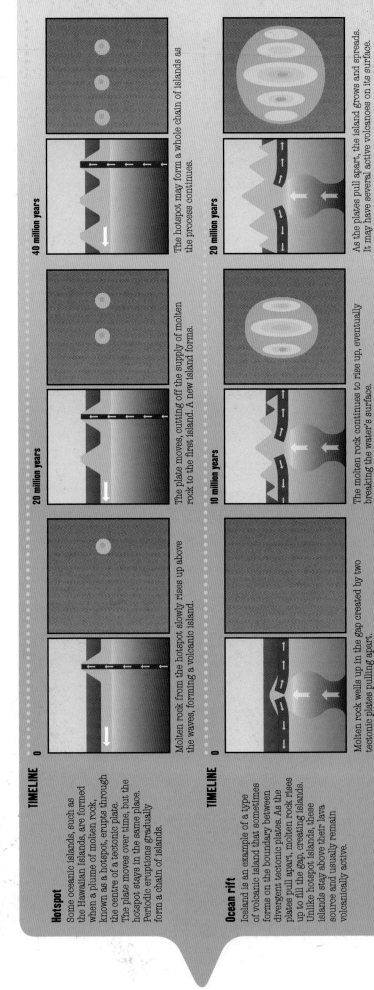

VOLCANIC

Hotspot

Some oceanic islands, such as the Hawaiian Islands, are formed when a plume of molten rock, known as a hotspot, erupts through the centre of a tectonic plate. The plate moves over time, but the hotspot stays in the same place. Periodic eruptions gradually form a chain of islands.

TIMELINE

0

20 million years

40 million years

Molten rock from the hotspot slowly rises up above the waves, forming a volcanic island.

The plate moves, cutting off the supply of molten rock to the first island. A new island forms.

The hotspot may form a whole chain of islands as the process continues.

Ocean rift

Iceland is an example of a type of volcanic island that sometimes forms on the boundary between divergent tectonic plates. As the plates pull apart, molten rock rises up to fill the gap, creating islands. Unlike hotspot islands, these islands stay above their lava source and usually remain volcanically active.

TIMELINE

0

10 million years

20 million years

Molten rock wells up in the gap created by two tectonic plates pulling apart.

The molten rock continues to rise up, eventually breaking the water's surface.

As the plates pull apart, the island grows and spreads. It may have several active volcanoes on its surface.

Shifting plates

When a divergent plate boundary runs through a continent, the gradual separation of the plates may force a portion of the landmass to break off. In time, this will form a new island known as a microcontinent. Madagascar, off the east coast of Africa, is an example of this.

TIMELINE 0

A continent sits above the boundary between two tectonic plates.

1 million years

The plates slowly pull apart, eventually dividing the landmass in two.

2 million years

The sea fills the gap left by the landmass dividing, forming the island.

Oceanic convergence

Where oceanic plates come together, one may get drawn down beneath the other in a process called subduction. As the lower plate is pulled under, it melts, sending molten rock breaking through the upper plate to form a lava island. Islands may emerge all along the plate boundary, creating an island arc known as an archipelago, such as Japan.

TIMELINE 0

One tectonic plate is gradually drawn down beneath the other into the mantle.

100,000 years

The molten rock pushes through the top plate and gradually builds up to form an island.

200,000 years

The island continues to grow and may have several active volcanoes, fuelled by the molten rock below.

Rising sea levels

Many of the world's largest islands, including Great Britain, were formed by rising seas. During the last Ice Age, much of the world's water was frozen and sea levels were much lower than today. When the ice melted as the climate grew warmer, water levels rose and separated land that was previously joined.

TIMELINE 0

Two mountains, one slightly higher than the other, stand amid the frozen Ice Age landscape.

5,000 years

As the ice begins to melt, flooding in low-lying areas of land creates two islands.

10,000 years

The seas continue to rise, covering the smaller island, leaving only one.

CONTINENTAL

Atoll

Coral reefs are limestone structures created by tiny marine creatures called polyps. When a reef breaks the surface of the water, sand may begin to accumulate upon it, turning it into an island. An atoll is a type of coral island that forms around a volcanic island.

TIMELINE 0

A coral reef grows around the outside of a volcanic island.

10,000 years

The island begins to sink, but the reef continues to grow upwards around it, breaking the surface of the water. Sand gathers on the top of the exposed reef.

20,000 years

The volcanic island subsides beneath the waves, leaving behind the coral atoll ring. The water inside is called a lagoon.

CORAL

Weather

The word "weather" is used to describe the day-to-day variations in a number of things, including temperature, wind speed, cloud cover, and sunshine. Climate, on the other hand, is the typical weather in a place over a long period of time. The driving force of weather is the Sun's heat, which powers the constant movement of air and water vapour in the atmosphere.

Water vapour and clouds

Clouds form when rising water vapour condenses into water droplets or ice. If the air already holds a lot of vapour, this happens at low altitudes and forms low-level clouds. At high altitudes, where the air temperature is below freezing, the vapour condenses into ice crystals.

Cirrus clouds

The highest clouds are made up of ice crystals. Cirrus look like tufts of white hair, cirrocumulus resemble small puffy grains, while cirrostratus clouds form thin, hazy sheets.

Alto clouds

These are the mid-level clouds. Altocumulus can be white or grey and tend to clump together like a tray of bread rolls. Altostratus are less distinct, forming sheets of cloud that fill the sky and often produce drizzle.

Stratus clouds

All stratus clouds are thick and featureless, and stretch across the sky (stratus means "sheet"). Nimbostratus clouds can produce rain that lasts for days, while stratocumulus produce very little moisture.

Cumulus clouds

Closest to the ground, cumulus clouds look like white cotton-wool tufts Sometimes they gather into giant anvil-shaped clouds known as cumulonimbus, which reach far up into the sky. These can produce heavy rain, hail, and thunder and lightning.

CIRRUS

CIRROCUMULUS

CIRROSTRATUS

ALTOCUMULUS

ALTOSTRATUS

STRATOCUMULUS

CUMULONIMBUS

NIMBOSTRATUS

STRATUS

CUMULUS

9 KM	(5.6 miles)
8 KM	(4.9 miles)
7 KM	(4.3 miles)
6 KM	(3.7 miles)
5 KM	(3.1 miles)
4 KM	(2.4 miles)
3 KM	(1.8 miles)
2 KM	(1.2 miles)
1 KM	(0.6 miles)
0	

The coldest temperature on record is **-89°C** (-128°F), and was recorded in Antarctica – the hottest is **57.8°C** (136°F), recorded in El Azizia, Libya

THE BEAUFORT SCALE

BEAUFORT NUMBER	0	1	2	3	4	5	6
DESCRIPTION	Calm	Light air	Light breeze	Gentle breeze	Moderate breeze	Fresh breeze	Strong breeze
EFFECTS ON LAND	Air is still and calm. Smoke rises vertically from chimneys.	Smoke drifts gently in the wind, but weathervanes do not move.	Wind can be felt on the skin. Weathervanes move slightly.	Light flags extend. Leaves and small twigs are in constant motion.	Wind raises dust, fallen leaves, and loose paper. Small branches move.	Branches of medium-sized trees move and small trees sway.	Branches of large trees move. Umbrella use is difficult.

Falling down

Precipitation is water in the atmosphere, falling from clouds to the Earth under the pull of gravity. Depending on the air temperature and wind, this can take the form of rain, snow, sleet, or hail. Raindrops fall at approximately 6.5 m (31 ft) per second.

SNOW

RAIN

3 KM (1.8 miles)

2 KM (1.2 miles)

1 KM (0.6 miles)

BELOW FREEZING — 0°C (32°F) — ABOVE FREEZING

Rain formation

Air currents move tiny water droplets around in clouds where they collide and merge with each other, forming larger drops. This is known as coalescence. When the drops become too large for the cloud to hold, they will fall to the ground as rain. Coalescence usually only happens at temperatures above 0°C (32°F). The droplets may start off as snow if the temperature is cold enough, before melting if the air below is warmer.

SNOW

SNOW

3 KM (1.8 miles)

2 KM (1.2 miles)

1 KM (0.6 miles)

BELOW FREEZING — 0°C (32°F) — ABOVE FREEZING

Snow formation

At sub-zero temperatures, ice crystals in clouds collide and clump together to form snowflakes. As long as the air temperature between the cloud and the ground is below 0°C (32°F), these flakes will fall as snow. If the air is warm, however, they will melt and turn into rain. All snow crystals are six sided.

SNOW

PARTLY MELTED SNOW

SLEET

3 KM (1.8 miles)

2 KM (1.2 miles)

1 KM (0.6 miles)

BELOW FREEZING — 0°C (32°F) — ABOVE FREEZING

Sleet formation

When falling snow reaches a layer of warmer air that partly melts the flakes, sleet forms. The flakes then continue downwards into a layer of colder air, which partly refreezes them, forming soft, ice pellets. These are different from hailstones, which are ice crystals that become encased in layers of ice as they are moved around inside clouds by air currents.

A lightning bolt can heat the air around it to **20,000°C** (36,030°F), which is more than three times hotter than the surface of the Sun

Stormy weather

The Sun doesn't warm the Earth's surface evenly, which creates areas of warm air and areas of cold air. Where two masses of air with different temperatures meet, high winds and thick clouds develop, creating thunderstorms.

Lightning

A lightning strike occurs when thunderclouds become electrically charged. A negative charge at the bottom of the cloud jumps towards a positive one on the ground, travelling at a staggering 209,200 km/h (130,000 mph) and generating around 300,000 volts of static electricity.

7	8	9	10	11	12
Moderate gale	Fresh gale	Strong gale	Whole gale	Storm	Hurricane force
Large trees sway. It is hard to walk against the wind.	Twigs and small branches break off. Moving cars veer on the road.	Small trees blown over. Chimney pots and slates blown from roofs.	Medium-sized trees broken and uprooted. Damage caused to some buildings.	Large trees broken and uprooted. Widespread damage to property.	Severe damage to property and the land. Rarely experienced on land.

Measuring wind speed

Wind is the movement of air from areas of high pressure (where the air is cold) to areas of low pressure (where the air is warm). The bigger the difference in pressure, the stronger the wind will be. Wind speed is measured by the Beaufort scale.

Fiery mountain

Volcanoes erupt in several different ways. Some gently ooze lava, while others send it spurting out like a fiery river. Some of the deadliest volcanoes shoot out a vast cloud of superheated gas and rock, known as a pyroclastic flow, along with volcanic ash. When Mount Tambora, Indonesia, erupted in 1815, the ash sent into the atmosphere blotted out the Sun for several days.

Lava flows can reach temperatures of
1,000°C
(1,832°F)

Hurricane

These violent storms (also known as typhoons) are fuelled by warm sea water. The water evaporates into the air, forming dense clouds that begin to spin around with tremendous force, capable of causing great damage if they reach land. In 2005, Hurricane Katrina became the costliest hurricane on record, causing an estimated £114 billion ($181 billion) worth of damage to the southern coast of the US.

Drought

Not all natural disasters are sudden events. Droughts usually take hold gradually as the available water in an area slowly runs out. However, the impact of a severe drought can be catastrophic and may be felt for a long time. In China, more than 25 million people are estimated to have died in the 20th century as a result of droughts.

Natural Disasters

The natural world can be a dangerous place. Every year about 75,000 people die, and some £40 billion ($65 billion) of property and land is destroyed as a result of natural disasters. According to the United Nations, about 75% of the world's population live in areas that have recently been affected by earthquakes, hurricanes, flooding, or drought. Often striking without warning, the effects of these catastrophes can last for years.

Shocking shakes

When Earth's tectonic plates collide with each other, it can lead to an earthquake. A really bad one, such as the 2010 Haiti quake, can lead to widespread destruction, ripping apart roads and bridges, collapsing buildings, and causing hundreds of thousands of deaths. In Haiti, the effects were particularly devastating because many buildings were not secure and the emergency services not equipped to deal with the crisis.

Giant wave

When a giant earthquake takes place on the seafloor, it can create a series of huge waves known as a tsunami. These waves spread out in all directions like giant ripples, travelling at speeds of up to 700 km/h (435 mph). Where they hit land, the waves can inflict immense devastation. The deadliest tsunami in recorded history swept across the Indian Ocean in 2004, killing more than 225,000 people in 11 countries and leaving millions homeless.

Tsunami waves can be
30 m
(98 ft) high by the time they hit the coast

Twisting times

Tornadoes are giant columns of rapidly spinning air that occasionally form over land during thunderstorms. When a tornado touches the ground, the consequences can be lethal. They can rip the roofs off of houses and toss cars into the air like toys. The US experiences around 1,000 tornadoes a year, more than any other country. Most form in a central region known locally as "Tornado Alley".

Tornado winds have been clocked at speeds of up to

500 km/h

(311 mph)

Wildfire

These fast-spreading natural hazards occur wherever there are expanses of dry vegetation, such as grasslands and forests. Most are started naturally by lightning strikes, but some are the result of human carelessness. In 1997-98, the largest wildfire in recorded history laid waste to more than 60,000 sq km (23,200 sq miles) of Indonesian forest.

Air temperatures of

800°C

(1,470°F) are possible during a wildfire

Avalanche

Snow can come loose and slide down a mountainside at any time. Avalanches usually occur on steep slopes where thick snow has become unstable. In 1970, an earthquake off the shore of Peru sent a 900-m (0.6-mile-) wide mass of ice, snow, and rock from Mount Huascarán crashing onto the nearby village of Yungay, killing more than 17,000 people.

Flood

Of all the natural disasters to afflict the Earth, flooding is by far the most common. The most severe floods deluge huge areas of land, forcing people from their homes, ruining crops, and spreading diseases. Around the world people build defences alongside rivers and coasts in an attempt to hold back the rising waters.

An estimated **4 million** people were killed when China's Yellow River flooded in 1931

There are about **500,000** earthquakes per year, but only **100** cause damage

Life on the Land

Regions that share the same climate and support similar types of plants and animals are known as biomes. Earth's land can be divided into 10 major biomes, ranging from almost barren deserts to fertile rainforests teeming with all manner of life.

71%

Water world
The land biomes shown on this page make up just 29% of the Earth's surface. The other 71% of the globe is water, which has its own wide variety of different biomes.

29%

Earth's terrestrial biomes

The pie chart on the right shows the percentage of land covered by each biome. The type of biome in an area is not fixed but may change over time due to climate change or human activities.

Boreal forest: 8.5%
Also known as taiga, boreal forest is a cold environment with long, harsh winters and short summers. The landscape is dominated by conifer trees, such as firs and pines.

Cultivated land: 9.5%
The only biome created by people, this environment is made up of areas that have been adapted to grow crops or rear animals. Prior to their cultivation, these areas would have formed parts of other biomes.

Savannah: 10%
Remaining warm throughout the year, these great rolling grasslands support huge herds of grazing animals – and their predators. They experience only two seasons: a dry season and a very wet one.

Ice: 11%
The ice caps of the North and South poles, along with the world's snow-topped mountain peaks, make up the coldest biome. Ice is also one of the most barren environments, supporting few plants or animals.

Tropical rainforest: 17%
These rain-soaked jungles are the world's most fertile biome. They enjoy warm temperatures all year round and support more species of animal and plant than any other environment. The plants here produce much of the Earth's oxygen.

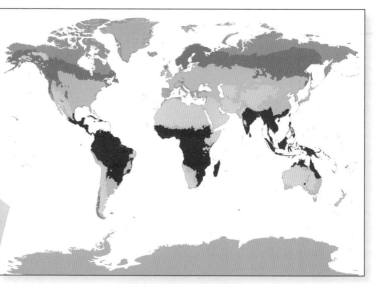

Where in the world?

This map shows how nine of the 10 major terrestrial biomes are distributed across the planet in a series of giant bands sharing the same climate and conditions. As cultivated land takes up parts of other biomes, it has not been shown here.

Temperate forest: 7%
Unlike rainforests, which thrive all year round, temperate (or deciduous) forests have distinct seasons – the trees lose their leaves in autumn and regrow them in spring.

Temperate grasslands: 6%
Cooler than the savannah, these great seas of grass are home to burrowing animals, grazing animals, and animals that prey on both. They have hot summers and cool winters.

Mediterranean: 6%
Also known as chaparral, this is a coastal biome that has extremely hot summers and cool, rainy winters. The landscape tends to be dry and parched, with vegetation made up mainly of shrubs.

Tundra: 5.5%
Despite its inhospitable appearance – it consists mainly of frozen, treeless plains – tundra provides homes to a wealth of wildlife adapted to the extreme conditions, including foxes, hares, caribou, and polar bears.

Desert: 19.5%
Any portion of the Earth's land that receives less than 25 cm (10 inches) of rain a year is considered desert. Here, plants and animals are few and usually small in size. The Sahara in Africa is the world's biggest desert.

PRODUCERS

PRIMARY
CONSUMERS

SECONDARY
CONSUMERS

TERTIARY
CONSUMERS

Trophic pyramid

A trophic level is the position an organism occupies in a food web. Each time an organism is eaten, it only passes on about 10% of its energy to the organism eating it. This is why the number of organisms in each trophic level is smaller than the one before it – giving it a pyramid shape – as there is less energy passed on from level to level.

Food Webs

From the tiniest bacterium to the biggest elephant, every organism needs energy to survive. The way energy is passed from organism to organism in an environment is known as the food web. Plants (producers) get their energy from the Sun. Part of this is then passed on to plant-eating animals (primary consumers), who in turn pass part of their energy on to carnivorous animals (secondary and tertiary consumers). Eventually, all these organisms will be broken down by decomposers, and the process will start again.

African Savannah food web

Organisms often have several different food sources, which means that food webs can be very complicated. The diagram to the right shows how organisms living in the African Savannah combine to form an intricate ecosystem. The arrows show the direction energy travels, and the colours show each organism's role in the web.

GAZELLE

CHEETAH

VULTURE

LION

DUNG BEETLE

Decomposer
When an organism dies, those parts that aren't eaten by animals are broken down by decomposers, such as bacteria and fungi. They return the organism's nutrients to the soil – ready to be reused by producers.

Secondary consumer
Next in the web are the animals that eat herbivores, known as secondary consumers. All species of dog and cat are secondary consumers, with some also being tertiary consumers, depending on the environment.

Producer
All plants, like grass and acacia trees here, are producers and form the basis of most food webs. Producers make their own food using energy from the Sun and nutrients from the ground (or from the water in marine environments).

Tertiary consumer
Some carnivores eat other carnivores as well as herbivores. These are tertiary consumers. A carnivore that has no natural enemies, such as a lion, is known as a "top predator" as it is not hunted by any organism.

Primary consumer
Gazelles, giraffes, and termites are known as primary consumers (or herbivores) as they eat producers. Animals that eat both plants and animals are omnivores. The vast majority of the world's animals are herbivores.

Scavenger
Animals that eat only animals that have already died are called scavengers. They can be primary, secondary, or tertiary consumers. Anything they don't consume will be recycled by decomposers.

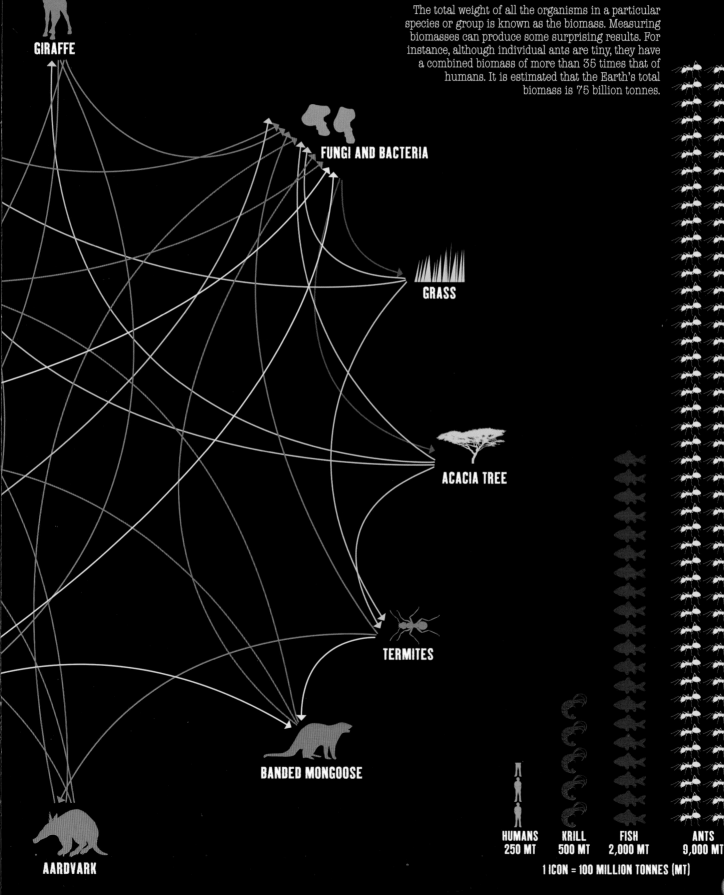

Biomass

The total weight of all the organisms in a particular species or group is known as the biomass. Measuring biomasses can produce some surprising results. For instance, although individual ants are tiny, they have a combined biomass of more than 35 times that of humans. It is estimated that the Earth's total biomass is 75 billion tonnes.

GIRAFFE

FUNGI AND BACTERIA

GRASS

ACACIA TREE

TERMITES

BANDED MONGOOSE

AARDVARK

| HUMANS | KRILL | FISH | ANTS |
| 250 MT | 500 MT | 2,000 MT | 9,000 MT |

1 ICON = 100 MILLION TONNES (MT)

HEIGHT

115 M (377 ft)
110 M (361 ft)
105 M (344 ft)
100 M (328 ft)
95 M (312 ft)
90 M (295 ft)
85 M (279 ft)
80 M (262 ft)
75 M (246 ft)
70 M (230 ft)
65 M (213 ft)
60 M (198 ft)

Box jellyfish
This jellyfish's stingers have killed more than 5,000 people in the past 50 years.

King cobra
The deadly 1.25 cm (0.4 in) fangs deliver venom capable of killing 20–40 humans.

Marbled cone snail
The snail uses a harpoon-like appendage to inject a toxin, strong enough to kill 20 humans.

Blue-ringed octopus
Although its bite is painless, the octopus carries enough venom to kill 25 humans within minutes.

Fastest and slowest

Below, an imaginary race is taking place between the fastest and slowest members of the animal kingdom. Capable of a top speed of about 44 km/h (27 mph), even the swiftest human would quickly be left behind by the speed merchants of the wild.

FASTEST

PEREGRINE FALCON
(When diving)
440 KM/H (273 MPH)

SPINE-TAILED SWIFT
(Straight-line flight)
171 KM/H (106 MPH)

CHEETAH
(Fastest land animal)
113 KM/H (70 MPH)

SAILFISH
(Fastest sea animal)
110 KM/H (68 MPH)

PRONGHORN ANTELOPE
(Fastest, herbivore)
98 KM/H (61 MPH)

SLOWEST

AMERICAN WOODCOCK
(Slowest bird)
8 KM/H (5 MPH)

GIANT TORTOISE
(Slow-moving reptile)
0.27 KM/H (0.17 MPH)

THREE-TOED SLOTH
(Slowest mammal)
0.16 KM/H (0.01 MPH)

SEAHORSE
(Slowest sea animal)
0.016 KM/H (0.01 MPH)

GARDEN SNAIL
(Slowest animal)
0.003 KM/H (0.002 MPH)

Lifespans long and short

From the humble mayfly to the ancient bristlecone pine, this scale shows the planet's longest – and shortest – living organisms. Above, the red arrows identify record-breaking feats of longevity, while below are the average lifespans of the shortest living creatures.

Bristlecone pine
5,000 years

Ocean quahog
410 years

Koi fish
226 years

Bowhead whale
210 years

Giant tortoise
188 years

Geoduck clam
160 years

Human
122 years

450 YEARS
400 YEARS
350 YEARS
300 YEARS
250 YEARS
200 YEARS
150 YEARS
100 YEARS

55 M (180 ft)
50 M (164 ft)
45 M (147 ft)
40 M (131 ft)
35 M (115 ft)
30 M (98 ft)
25 M (82 ft)
20 M (65 ft)
15 M (49 ft)
10 M (32 ft)
5 M (16 ft)
0

Record Breakers

Life comes in every shape and size imaginable, from bacteria so small that more than a million could fit onto the head of a pin, to giant trees weighing thousands of tonnes. Some creatures have lived for more than 200 years, while others buzz through their entire life within a single day.

Blue whale vs jumbo jet

The mighty blue whale is the largest animal ever – and weighing in at 150–170 tonnes, it is as heavy as a Boeing 747. These enormous creatures have hearts the size of cars, and blood vessels so wide a person could swim along them.

Dangerous creatures

There are two types of animals that kill through the use of powerful toxins. Poisonous ones cause harm only if touched or eaten, while venomous ones inject their prey by biting, stabbing, or stinging. Both can be deadly.

Inland taipan
The venom from a single bite by "most poisonous snake in the world" can kill 100 humans.

Poison dart frog
The frog secretes its toxin from skin glands. Just 1 milligram is enough to kill 10 humans.

Biggest and tallest

Below, you can compare some of the giants of the living world – past and present. To the right, and towering above them all, is the mighty redwood, the largest known living organism. The biggest specimens can weigh in excess of 1,800 tonnes.

Titan flower
Height: 3 m (10 ft)

Ostrich
Height: 3 m (10 ft)

African elephant
Height: 3.3 m (11 ft)

Giraffe
Height: 5.2 m (17 ft)

Blue whale
Length: 33 m (108 ft)

Argentinosaurus
Length: 35 m (115 ft)

Giant redwood
Height: 115.5 m (379 ft)

Dragonfly
4 months

Bees and flies
1 month

Drone ants
3 weeks

Gastrotrich
3 days

Mayfly
0.5–24 hours

16 WEEKS
15 WEEKS
14 WEEKS
13 WEEKS
12 WEEKS
11 WEEKS
10 WEEKS
9 WEEKS
8 WEEKS
7 WEEKS
6 WEEKS
5 WEEKS
4 WEEKS
3 WEEKS
2 WEEKS
1 WEEK

41

There are about **200 million** insects for every human

INSECTS
1,000,000 SPECIES

PLANTS
372,775

MOLLUSCS
85,000

FISH
31,300

BIRDS
9,998

REPTILES
9,084

MAMMALS
5,490

AMPHIBIANS
6,493

Bursting with life

Scientists still don't know the total number of species there are in the world. To date, some 1.7 million plant and animal species have been identified – the majority of which are shown here – but there may be twice that many still awaiting discovery. What is certain is that insects are the most abundant life forms, accounting for more than two-thirds of Earth's species.

Under Threat

Extinctions have always been part of the cycle of life on Earth. It is estimated that more than 99% of all the species that have ever lived are now extinct. Most of these were killed off by natural causes, such as volcanic eruptions, asteroid impacts, and changes in climate. Today, however, thousands of species are endangered as a result of human interference, through hunting, fishing, and the destruction of natural habitats.

Lonesome George

George is believed to be the last surviving Pinto Island tortoise. Discovered in 1971, long after the rest of his kind had succumbed to hunting and habitat depletion, his unique status has led to him being called the rarest creature in the world.

AMPHIBIANS 32% With nearly one-third of species classified as endangered, amphibians are under the greatest threat.

MAMMALS 21% More than one-fifth of mammals are on the red list, and almost half of these have declining populations.

BIRDS 12% The destruction of forests for farmland and timber has reduced bird populations around the world.

REPTILES 5% The low figure for reptiles could be because many species have not yet been fully studied.

FISH 4% Large-scale commercial fishing has driven many fish species to the brink of extinction.

PLANTS 3% With their amazing biodiversity, the destruction of rainforests has placed plant species under threat.

MOLLUSCS 1% Of all the species to have recently become extinct, 41% were molluscs.

INSECTS 0.06% Of all the classes of life, insects have proved the most successful, although not all have been fully assessed.

The red list

Every year the International Union for the Conservation of Nature (IUCN) produces an ever-expanding red list of threatened species. Amphibians and mammals are the classes of life forms with the highest proportion of endangered species. Insects, however, are faring much better. Although this is the group containing the greatest number of species, only a fraction is considered under serious threat. These pie charts identify the proportion of species that are considered endangered.

About to go

The major causes for the shrinking numbers of animals include commercial development and clearing land for livestock farming. There are programmes being put in place to increase the population of threatened species and, hopefully, to ensure their future survival. However, will it help the animals to the right that are on the brink of dying out?

Siberian tiger
Today, there are just five subspecies of tiger, compared with eight at the start of the 20th century. The rare Siberian tigers live in the forests of eastern Russia, and there may be just 400 of them left in the wild.

Panamanian golden frog
The Panamanian golden frog currently stands on the brink of extinction as a result of a deadly fungus. They have not been seen in the wild since 2007, although some remain in captivity.

Echo parakeet
The destruction of their native Mauritian forests had reduced the echo parakeet population to 12 in 1990. Captive breeding and habitat regeneration have restored the number to about 300 birds today.

Six Degrees of Change

According to the majority of scientists, Earth's average global temperature is steadily rising, owing to a build-up of carbon dioxide (CO_2) in the atmosphere. They believe this is the result of burning fossil fuels, such as coal, gas, and oil. No one is certain exactly what might happen, but the effect of this global warming could be huge, with extreme weather systems leading to flooding and desertification. Many people think individuals and governments need to take action to avert catastrophe.

The greenhouse effect

Earth's atmosphere prevents some of the Sun's heat from escaping back into space, helping to warm the planet. However, the more carbon dioxide there is in the atmosphere, the more heat it absorbs and radiates back to Earth, and the hotter the planet gets. This is known as the "greenhouse effect".

Sun's rays

About 20% of the radiation bounces off the Earth and back into space

30% of the energy is radiated back to Earth, but this figure is rising

Roughly 50% of the energy is absorbed by the Earth

Atmosphere

Hotting up

The chart to the right spells out the worst case scenarios – both on land and at sea – for every degree of temperature rise. A 6°C (10.8°F) average rise may not sound all that much, but scientists believe that it would be enough to unleash a global disaster from which the human race might never recover. It took only a 5°C (9°F) temperature rise to end the last Ice Age.

6°C (10.8°F)

Methane fireballs

As oceans get warmer they become less able to dissolve oxygen, destroying marine life. Stagnant seas release hydrogen sulphide that poisons the land. If flammable methane rising from the seabed is ignited (by lightning, for example), huge fireballs would sweep across the land, causing further destruction and loss of life.

5°C (9°F)

Migrating people

All rainforests have become deserts and growing crops is now all but impossible in much of the world. Migrant populations spread out across the globe in a desperate hunt for food and safe land. Their hunger leads to increased conflict and indiscriminate hunting, destroying the dwindling food resources.

4°C (7.2°F)

Runaway global warming

Desertification spreads across the globe, causing areas around the Mediterranean to be abandoned. In northern latitudes, the melting permafrost raises sea levels still further. Should temperatures reach this point, some scientists believe that the changes will be irreversible. The Earth will face runaway global warming.

3°C (5.4°F)

Lungs of the world collapse

The Amazon rainforest, producer of 10% of the planet's oxygen (and often called "the lungs of the world"), is killed off by a combination of drought and fire. Its demise releases huge amounts of CO_2 into the atmosphere. Elsewhere, billions starve as crop yields dwindle. Swathes of Africa, India, and China are now effectively wastelands.

2°C (3.6°F)

Heat waves across Europe

Glaciers feeding India's rivers melt, causing flooding for a time and then drought as the rivers dry up. Europe suffers heat waves, forest fires, drying riverbeds, and failing crops. Plants are becoming heat-stressed, emitting CO_2 rather than storing it, thereby speeding up the global warming process.

1°C (1.8°F)

Ever-stronger hurricanes

As the sea warms up, hurricanes of the strength of 2005's Hurricane Katrina are more frequent. Freshwater disappears from a third of the Earth's surface and is replaced by lifeless deserts. Low-lying areas of coastline are flooded, and many people are affected by heatstroke.

6°C
(10.8°F)

5°C
(9°F)

Maximum sea levels

At this stage, all of Earth's ice will have melted into the oceans, and sea levels will have increased by more than 60 m (197 ft). Across the planet, the sea has taken over large tracts of land. Methane, an even more potent greenhouse gas than carbon dioxide, is released from the seabed, speeding up the greenhouse effect.

4°C
(7.2°F)

Florida covered

Both poles are melting fast, releasing tonnes of stored carbon and raising sea levels by 1 m (3 ft) a year, meaning a state of constant flooding. The UK is reduced to an archipelago of small islands, while much of the southeastern United States, including Florida, is now underwater. Supplies of drinkable water are dwindling fast.

UNITED STATES
Houston
New Orleans
Florida
BAHAMAS
CUBA

3°C
(5.4°F)

Bangladesh under water

Some 80% of the Arctic sea ice has now melted, raising global sea levels by an average of 25 m (82 ft). Vast areas of several low-lying countries, including Bangladesh, Myanmar (Burma), and Thailand are now underwater. Storms get ever fiercer as the seas grow warmer. The US and Australian coasts are battered by super-hurricanes.

INDIA
BANGLADESH
Kolkata (Calcutta)
Dhaka
MYANMAR (Burma)
Rangoon
THAILAND
Bangkok

2°C
(3.6°F)

Shanghai submerged

Melting Arctic glaciers raise sea levels by 6 m (20 ft). Water is encroaching onto the land in more and more areas across the globe. Shanghai, China's largest city, lies submerged, as does much of eastern China, forcing its population inland. A third of all marine species face extinction.

Jiangsu
Nanjing
Changzhou
CHINA
Wuxi
Suzhou
Shanghai
Shanghai Shi

1°C
(1.8°F)

Flooding in northern Europe

The Arctic starts to melt, threatening the survival of the region's wildlife and raising sea levels. Areas of low-lying land around the world, including the Maldives and northern Europe (in blue) are the first to be lost to the rising waves. The Great Barrier Reef, the world's largest coral system, dies.

Amsterdam
NETHERLANDS
GERMANY
BELGIUM

45

THE World IN ONE Day

EARTH

In the space of just 24 hours, some amazing things are going on in the natural world.

The Sun beams down enough energy to power a **60-watt bulb** for **1.2 million years**

109 tonnes of **cosmic dust** falls to Earth – more than the weight of the **International Space Station**

There are **87 earthquakes**, and about **78** of them happen around the edges of the Pacific Ocean – an area known as the **Pacific Ring of Fire**

The amount of **forest** land lost is equal to **2,822** football pitches – most is **lost** due to human activity

Bamboo is the fastest growing plant, capable of growing **60 cm** (24 in)

Koala bears sleep for about **21** hours, and eat about **500 g** (18 oz) of eucalyptus leaves in the remaining 3 hours

zzzzz

The United States suffers about **3 tornadoes** – one happens in **Texas** every 3 days, mostly during the warm summer months

A single **tree** releases enough **oxygen** to support **two people**

The Earth travels **2.6 million km** (1.6 million miles) around the Sun

Mosquitos infect about **684,900** people worldwide with **malaria**, causing roughly **2,740** deaths

If you were to **stand completely still** at any point on the Earth's equator, you would still travel **40,080 km** (24,912 miles) due to the **Earth's spin**

An area the size of **Malta** turns into **deserts**

The adult **mayfly** has at most **one day to live**, but may only survive for **30 minutes**

There is only **1 habitable** planet discovered so far in the universe: **Earth**

Enough **freshwater** flows from the Amazon into the Atlantic Ocean to fill **10,368,000** Olympic-sized **swimming pools** – it's about 20% of the total freshwater flowing into oceans worldwide

A swarm of desert **locusts** can **munch** through **192,000 tonnes** of **food** a day – the same weight as **1,027** blue whales

An adult **elephant** eats about **204 kg** (450 lbs) of food, and washes it down with **189 litres** (50 gallons) of water – that's the same as **1,021 burgers** and **305** regular-sized **fizzy drinks**

The Indian **tectonic plate** is moving into the Eurasian plate, causing **Mount Everest** to push up by **0.016 mm** (0.006 in)

Enough **rain** falls on the Earth for every person to have **1,414 showers**

The **wettest place** on Earth is Mawsynram, India, which receives an average of **3.3 cm** (1.3 in) of rain

Lightning strikes about **8.6 million** times – each strike carries enough energy to power a **city** of **200,000** people for one minute

People

As the world's population approaches 7 billion, people are living longer, healthier lives than ever before. But people's life chances are still strongly influenced by where they live. Those living in wealthy Western countries have a massive advantage over those living in poorer countries. This section takes a look at the diversity of the world's people — from the food we eat and the languages we speak, to our beliefs and what makes us happy.

Who lives where?

Does this map look strange, or has your brain been bamboozled by all the facts in this book? It's actually a cartogram, showing each country at a size proportional to its population. (To compare with the continents' true sizes, turn to pages 230–231). The cartogram is top-heavy because the northern hemisphere contains about 90% of the world's total population.

Just **11** countries are home to
61% of the world's population

China

The world's most populous country has a staggering 1.3 billion inhabitants – one-fifth of the people in the world. Thirty years ago, it introduced a policy limiting urban couples to one child each. This is thought to have prevented at least 250 million births.

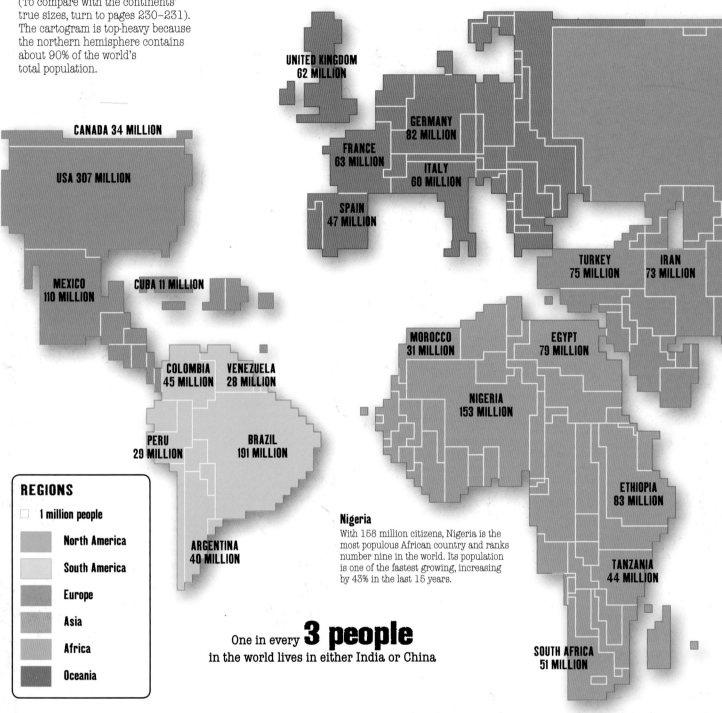

CANADA 34 MILLION

UNITED KINGDOM 62 MILLION

USA 307 MILLION

GERMANY 82 MILLION

FRANCE 63 MILLION

ITALY 60 MILLION

SPAIN 47 MILLION

TURKEY 75 MILLION

IRAN 73 MILLION

MEXICO 110 MILLION

CUBA 11 MILLION

MOROCCO 31 MILLION

EGYPT 79 MILLION

COLOMBIA 45 MILLION

VENEZUELA 28 MILLION

NIGERIA 153 MILLION

PERU 29 MILLION

BRAZIL 191 MILLION

ETHIOPIA 83 MILLION

Nigeria

With 158 million citizens, Nigeria is the most populous African country and ranks number nine in the world. Its population is one of the fastest growing, increasing by 43% in the last 15 years.

TANZANIA 44 MILLION

ARGENTINA 40 MILLION

SOUTH AFRICA 51 MILLION

One in every **3 people** in the world lives in either India or China

REGIONS

☐ 1 million people

- North America
- South America
- Europe
- Asia
- Africa
- Oceania

How many People on the Planet?

The world's population is a colossal 6.8 billion and counting. The number has quadrupled since 1900. All these people are not spread equally around the world – more than 80% live in the developing regions of Africa, Asia, Latin America, and the Caribbean. Every year our numbers swell by 79 million – a growth rate that is stretching the planet's food and resources.

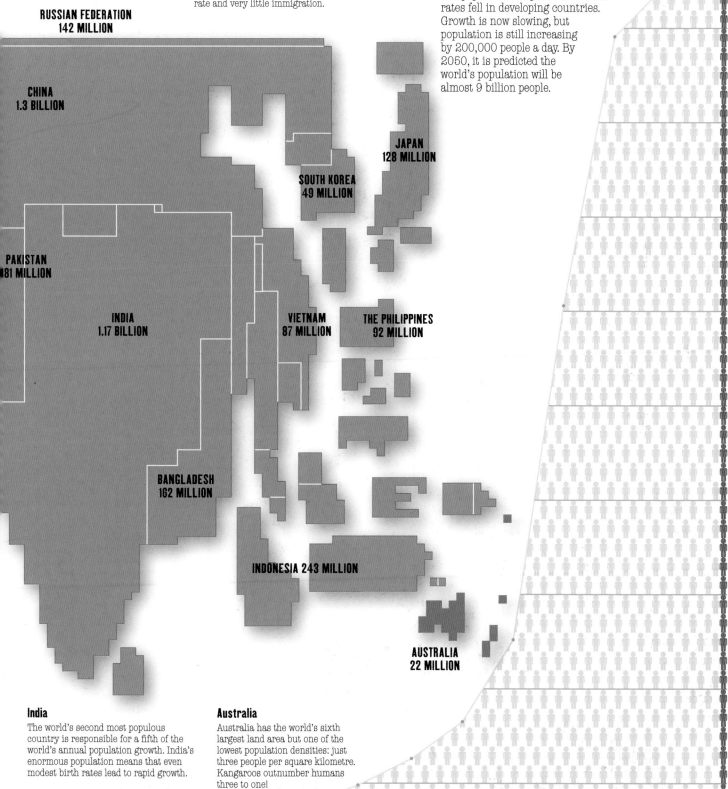

Population growth

The world's population grew slowly for most of human history. The mid-20th century saw the start of a population "explosion" as death rates fell in developing countries. Growth is now slowing, but population is still increasing by 200,000 people a day. By 2050, it is predicted the world's population will be almost 9 billion people.

Japan
Despite having only the 61st greatest land area, Japan is home to the world's 10th largest population. Unlike most nations in the top 10, who are struggling with a growing demand for resources, Japan's population is shrinking due to a low birth rate and very little immigration.

RUSSIAN FEDERATION 142 MILLION

CHINA 1.3 BILLION

JAPAN 128 MILLION

SOUTH KOREA 49 MILLION

PAKISTAN 181 MILLION

INDIA 1.17 BILLION

VIETNAM 87 MILLION

THE PHILIPPINES 92 MILLION

BANGLADESH 162 MILLION

INDONESIA 243 MILLION

AUSTRALIA 22 MILLION

India
The world's second most populous country is responsible for a fifth of the world's annual population growth. India's enormous population means that even modest birth rates lead to rapid growth.

Australia
Australia has the world's sixth largest land area but one of the lowest population densities: just three people per square kilometre. Kangaroos outnumber humans three to one!

BILLIONS OF PEOPLE

10
9
8
7
6
5
4
3
2
1
0

YEAR

1500 1550 1600 1650 1700 1750 1800 1850 1900 1950 2000 2050 2100 2150

The rise of city living

As the world's population grows, a greater proportion of people are choosing to live in towns and cities. Fifty years ago, 732 million people lived in a city or town. Now the figure is 3.2 billion. This is expected to double by 2050 to 70% of the world's population.

2010
50%+

2005
49%

1950
29%

Percentage of the world's population living in urban areas

Trams

Light rail vehicles, usually called trams, were common in many industrialized cities in the early 1900s, but fell out of favour in the middle of the century. In recent years they have made a comeback, with new systems built in France, Ireland, the US, and the UK, often over the old routes from a century ago.

WORLD'S MOST POPULOUS URBAN AREAS (AGGLOMERATIONS)
(figures given in millions)

1 **Tokyo**, Japan, 33.8	11 **Osaka**, Japan, 16.7	21 **Istanbul**, Turkey, 12.5	31 **Bangkok**, Thailand, 8.75	40 **Johannesburg**, S. Africa, 7.35
2 **Seoul**, South Korea, 23.9	12 **Kolkata**, India, 16.0	21 **Rio de Janeiro**, Brazil, 12.5	32 **Bogotá**, Colombia, 8.6	42 **San Francisco**, USA, 7.3
3 **Mexico City**, Mexico, 22.9	13 **Karachi**, Pakistan, 15.7	21 **Tehran**, Iran, 12.5	32 **Kinshasa**, Dem. Rep. Congo, 8.6	43 **Hong Kong**, China, 7.2
4 **New Delhi**, India, 22.4	14 **Guangzhou**, China, 15.3	24 **London**, UK, 12.3	34 **Lahore**, Pakistan, 8.3	44 **Taipei**, Taiwan, 6.75
5 **Mumbai**, India, 22.3	15 **Jakarta**, Indonesia, 15.1	25 **Lagos**, Nigeria, 11.4	34 **Nagoya**, Japan, 8.3	45 **Baghdad**, Iraq, 6.4
6 **New York City**, USA, 21.9	16 **Cairo**, Egypt, 14.8	26 **Paris**, France, 10.0	36 **Washington D.C.**, USA, 8.25	46 **Chongqing**, China, 6.35
7 **São Paulo**, Brazil, 21.0	17 **Buenos Aires**, Argentina, 13.8	27 **Chicago**, USA, 9.85	37 **Tianjin**, China, 8.2	46 **Dallas**, USA, 6.35
8 **Manila**, The Philippines, 19.2	18 **Moscow**, Russia, 13.5,	28 **Shenzhen**, China, 9.4	38 **Chennai**, India, 8.05	48 **Madrid**, Spain, 6.1
9 **Los Angeles**, USA, 18.0	19 **Beijing**, China, 13.2,	29 **Wuhan**, China, 9.0	39 **Bangalore**, India, 7.6	49 **Philadelphia**, USA, 6.0
10 **Shanghai**, China, 17.9	20 **Dhaka**, Bangladesh, 13.1	30 **Lima**, Peru, 8.85	40 **Hyderabad**, India, 7.35	50 **Santiago**, Chile, 5.95

High ride
New York is the world's busiest helicopter zone, with 70,000 flights over the city every year. Half of these are sightseeing trips. São Paulo has the scariest choice of places to land – 70% of its 300 helipads are perched on top of skyscrapers.

At **33.8 million** people, Tokyo's population is bigger than those of 159 countries, including Canada and Australia

Tokyo **1**

oscow **18**

New Delhi **4**

Seoul **2**

Harbin

Tehran **21**

Karachi

Shenyang **64** Tianjin **37** Beijing **19** **79** Harbin **10** Shanghai **98** Pusan

ara

Lahore **13**

Xi'an **68** Chengdu **61**

Mumbai **5** **34**

95 yonpyang

Osaka **11**

Baghdad **45**

Kolkata **12** **20** Dhaka

Chongqing **46** Wuhan **29** Guangzhou **14** **34** Nagoya

Riyadh **65** Ahmadabad **52** Hyderabad **40**

Shenzen **28** **61** Dongguan **71** Nanjing **88** Hangzhou Manila **8**

Hong Kong **43** Taipei **44**

Surat **85**

Chittagong **75**

Bangkok **31** **67** Rangoon

Ho Chi Minh City **57**

Shantou **85**

Cities by the sea
Ten of the world's 15 largest cities are also sea ports. Shanghai is one of the largest, handling 28 million conainers full of goods every year.

Pune **69** Bangalore **39** Chennai **38**

Kuala Lumpur **71**

Jakarta **15**

Singapore **71**

City Populations

A third of the world's people live in cities. Swelled by the numbers of people moving there, some cities grow so big that they overlap with nearby cities to form sprawling urban areas called agglomerations. These include 7 cities with more than 20 million residents each. So many people living in one place can create problems. Around the world, one billion people live in overcrowded slums – city areas without clean water, proper shelter, or sewerage systems.

Sydney **77**

Melbourne **92**

POPULATION DENSITY
(Number of people per sq km/sq mile)

High
(11,400–85,000 per sq km/ 29,640–221,000 per sq mile)

Medium
(5,000–11,300 per sq km/ 13,000–29,380 per sq mile)

Low
(up to 5,000 per sq km/ 13,000 per sq mile)

51 **Belo Horizonte**, Brazil, 5.85	61 **Chengdu**, China, 5.6	71 **Kuala Lumpur**, Malaysia, 4.7	81 **Abidjan**, Côte d'Ivoire, 4.35	91 **Ankara**, Turkey, 3.925
52 **Ahmadabad**, India, 5.8	61 **Dongguan**, China, 5.6	71 **Nanjing**, China, 4.7	82 **Berlin**, Germany, 4.275	92 **Melbourne**, Australia, 3.9
52 **Houston**, USA, 5.8	63 **Miami**, USA, 5.5	71 **Singapore**, Singapore, 4.7	82 **Porto Alegre**, Brazil, 4.275	93 **Brasília**, Brazil, 3.875
54 **Atlanta**, USA, 5.7	64 **Shenyang**, China, 5.15	74 **Guadalajara**, Mexico, 4.65	84 **Barcelona**, Spain, 4.25	94 **Recife**, Brazil, 3.85
54 **Detroit**, USA, 5.7	65 **Riyadh**, S. Arabia, 4.95	75 **Alexandria**, Egypt, 4.5	85 **Monterrey**, Mexico, 4.075	95 **Athens**, Greece, 3.75
54 **Ruhr**, Germany, 5.7	66 **Caracas**, Venezuela, 4.95	76 **Chittagong**, Bangladesh, 4.5	85 **Shantou**, China, 4.075	96 **Montreal**, Canada, 3.75
57 **Khartoum**, Sudan, 5.65	67 **Rangoon**, Myanmar, 4.85	77 **Phoenix**, USA, 4.4	86 **Surat**, India, 4.075	96 **Pyongyang**, North Korea, 3.75
57 **Boston**, USA, 5.65	68 **Xi'an**, China, 4.825	77 **Sydney**, Australia, 4.4	88 **Hangzhou**, China, 4.025	98 **Pusan**, South Korea, 3.7
57 **Ho Chi Mihn City**, Vietnam, 5.65	69 **Pune**, India, 4.75	79 **Algiers**, Algeria, 4.375	89 **Casablanca**, Morocco, 3.975	99 **Cape Town**, S. Africa, 3.675
57 **Toronto**, Canada, 5.65	69 **St Petersburg**, Russia, 4.75	79 **Harbin**, China, 4.375	90 **Seattle**, USA, 3.95	100 **Fortaleza**, Brazil, 3.65

Changing
Populations

Only births and deaths can change our planet's population. The number of babies being born outweighs the number of people dying, so overall the world's population is growing. But the rate of change is very different from one country to the next. Populations are growing fastest in the developing world. The number of people living in the world's 51 poorest countries will double by 2050. In contrast, the populations of many wealthy countries will shrink as deaths become more common than births.

Fertility rates

Populations are growing fastest where people tend to have large families. Death rates are falling almost everywhere, but fertility (the average number of children per woman) is much higher in some regions than others. Average global fertility is 2.6 children per woman – more than enough to replace both parents when they die.

AFRICA

4.6 children per woman

ASIA

2.3 children per woman

SOUTH AMERICA

2.2 children per woman

NORTH AMERICA

2 children per woman

AUSTRALIA

1.8 children per women

EUROPE

1.5 children per woman

Niger

Niger has the world's fastest-growing population and highest fertility rate. The average woman gives birth to 7.3 children. Each year the number of people increases by nearly 4%.

United States

Natural population growth in the US is 0.99% a year. But the number of people there is increasing more rapidly than that due to immigration. The rate of immigration is 4.3 migrants to every 1,000 people.

In the balance

Comparing the birth rate and death rate of a country reveals how fast its population is growing. This "natural population growth" does not take into account migration. Most less developed countries have many more births per year than deaths. In some richer countries, deaths outweigh births – without immigration from poorer countries their populations would be shrinking rapidly.

India

With more than twice as many births each year as deaths, India's already large population is growing at a rate of 1.3% per year. Some states have reduced population growth by helping women to access education, thereby reducing fertility.

Australia

Australia has a similar rate of natural population growth to Brazil, but the effect of its much smaller population is huge. There are just 290,000 births per year in Australia, compared to 2.8 million in Brazil.

Brazil

With 14.2 births per 1,000 people – an average of 2.3 children per woman – natural population growth in Brazil is just 0.75%. But the large existing population means the population swells by 1.5 million people every year.

Lithuania

Low birth rates mean that many European countries have shrinking populations. With just 10 births per 1,000 people per year, Lithuania has the world's fastest shrinking population.

Every year **137 million** babies are born and **59 million** people die. The world's population is growing at a rate of **9,100 people** every hour.

BiRTH AND DEATH RATES

 5 deaths per 1,000 people

 5 births per 1,000 people

How Long have you Got?

Life expectancy is rising in most countries thanks to improved food, hygiene, healthcare, and education. But lifespan varies enormously around the world. In wealthy Western Europe, North American, Japan, and Australia, deaths before age 60 are unusual. In other parts of the world, people expect to die long before the global average of 69. Many are killed by illnesses that could be treated or prevented if living conditions improved. Look at the lineup below to see how average lifespans differ across the world.

Swaziland

In many African countries, life expectancy is falling due to HIV/AIDS. This disease is the world's sixth biggest killer. In 1990, life expectancy in Swaziland was 60. It is now just 33.

1 2 3 4 5 6 7 8 9 10 11 12 13 14 15 16 17 18 19 20 21 22 23 24 25 26 27 28 29 30 31 32 33 34 35 36 37 38 39 40

Population pyramids

The proportion of people in different age groups within a population can be plotted as a pyramid. The shape reveals whether the population is old or young. The age distribution of a young population produces a pyramid with a wide base and steeply sloping sides. As a population ages, the pyramid gets narrower at the bottom and fatter at the top. It starts to look more like a mushroom.

World population

This pyramid shows age distribution for the world as a whole. Although most people in the world are young, rising life expectancy means that elderly people make up a greater proportion of the population than in the past. Currently, almost 8% of the world's population is older than 65. This will rise to 25% by 2050, putting enormous pressure on health and welfare systems.

90-94
85-89
80-84
75-79
70-74
65-69
60-64
55-59
50-54
45-49
40-44
35-39
30-34
25-29
20-24
15-19
10-14
5-9
0-4

Living to 100

Celebrating your 100th birthday is a newsworthy event, but if life expectancy trends continue, half of all the babies born in wealthy countries today will live to blow out 100 candles. Jeanne Calment (right) was 122 when she died in 1997, making her the longest living person ever.

Russia
Cardiovascular disease is the main cause of deaths before the age of 75 in Europe. Death rates are particularly high in Russia, where life expectancy has actually fallen since the 1970s due to heart attack and stroke.

Japan
Japanese women can expect to live longer than anyone in the world – a huge 87 years. Japanese men have a slightly shorter life expectancy, bringing the average down to 82. A 115-year-old Japanese woman is currently the world's oldest living person. In 60 years' time, the average Japanese girl may live to 100.

Afghanistan
Most Afghans have no access to healthcare or safe drinking water. Just 14% of pregnant women are seen by a health professional – 18 mothers die for every 1,000 babies born.

Democratic Republic of Congo
War in Africa has killed 5.4 million people since 1998. In Democratic Republic of Congo, this has wiped 10 years off the average life expectancy. Many people died from preventable diseases that spread during the conflict.

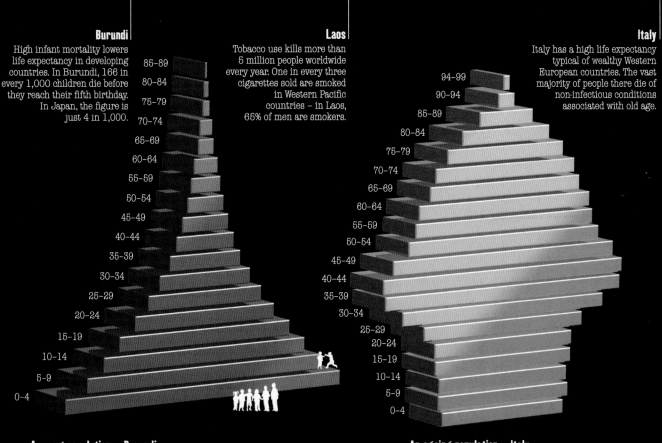

41 42 43 44 45 46 47 48 49 50 51 52 53 54 55 56 57 58 59 60 61 62 63 64 65 66 67 68 69 70 71 72 73 74 75 76 77 78 79 80 81 82

Burundi
High infant mortality lowers life expectancy in developing countries. In Burundi, 166 in every 1,000 children die before they reach their fifth birthday. In Japan, the figure is just 4 in 1,000.

85–89
80–84
75–79
70–74
65–69
60–64
55–59
50–54
45–49
40–44
35–39
30–34
25–29
20–24
15–19
10–14
5–9
0–4

Laos
Tobacco use kills more than 5 million people worldwide every year. One in every three cigarettes sold are smoked in Western Pacific countries – in Laos, 65% of men are smokers.

Italy
Italy has a high life expectancy typical of wealthy Western European countries. The vast majority of people there die of non-infectious conditions associated with old age.

94–99
90–94
85–89
80–84
75–79
70–74
65–69
60–64
55–59
50–54
45–49
40–44
35–39
30–34
25–29
20–24
15–19
10–14
5–9
0–4

A young population – Burundi
In Burundi, high death rates at all ages means that each age bracket has fewer people than the one below. The narrow tip of the pyramid shows that there are relatively few old people. Less than 3% of people in Burundi live past their 65th birthday.

An ageing population – Italy
Populations have aged fastest in developed countries. In Italy, one-fifth of citizens are over 65, and 3.5 million Italians are over the age of 80. By 2050, one-third of Italy's population will be older than 65. This means that for every 100 people of working age there will be 62 elderly people.

Ways to Go

Of the 55 million deaths each year, certain causes are much more common than others. Risk factors are strongly linked to where you live. In developing regions, disease and malnutrition are deadly, whereas in the wealthiest countries, cancer and cardiovascular disorders are the main causes of death. The spinner shows the overall percentage of deaths due to each cause. The warning signs show a few of the less likely ways to go.

WHAT ARE THE CHANCES?

Snakebite
Worldwide, 450 species of snake are dangerous to humans. Venomous snakebites kill an estimated 125,000 people per year. Of those, 100,000 are in Asia, with 20,000 in India alone.

500,000 : 1

Falling down a manhole
Manholes left open in the road are a real hazard. In 2009, an American teenager had a lucky escape after falling into a manhole while texting. She had a soft landing on the sewage below.

1.5 MILLION : 1

Computer game exhaustion
In South Korea, professional online gamers can earn £65,000 ($100,000) per year. Some take gaming too far – in 2005, a 28-year-old man died of heart failure after playing a game almost non-stop for 50 hours.

5 MILLION : 1

Hippopotamus attack
Although they only eat plants, hippos kill more people in Africa than any other mammal. Weighing as much as three cars, they can outrun a person and will attack to protect their territory.

6 MILLION : 1

Infectious illnesses
Every year, 18 million people die from infectious and parasitic diseases. Pneumonia, diarrhoea, and HIV/AIDS claim the most victims, with most of these deaths occurring in developing regions.

Nutritional deficiencies
Malnutrition – not getting the right nutrients – leads to 400,000 deaths annually. A diet lacking enough protein or energy is the biggest killer of children under the age of five, especially in Africa.

Non-infectious illnesses
Non-infectious illnesses are those that cannot be passed on from person to person. Cardiovascular disease (including heart attacks and strokes) is the biggest killer in the world, and cancer accounts for 13% of deaths.

INFECTIOUS ILLNESSES 25%

NUTRITIONAL DEFICIENCIES 1%

NON-INFECTIOUS ILLNESSES 59%

In industrialized countries, **one** in **two** people will die of a heart attack or stroke.

70% of all deaths from car accidents occur in developing countries.

Laughter

15 BILLION : 1

You've got more chance of being hit by a meteorite than you have of dying of laughter. But there have been cases of people with weak hearts for whom laughing has been lethal. Laughter increases heart rate and blood pressure, raising the risk of a heart attack.

Walking into a lamppost

360 MILLION : 1

Some 18,000 lamppost-related injuries are reported every year, with some of those affected dying of their injuries.

Aeroplane ice

815 MILLION : 1

Every year, dozens of people are hit by falling chunks of ice – nowhere near a hailstorm. The ice is likely to form from water leaking from the underside of an aircraft.

Shark attack

256 MILLION : 1

There are around 63 unprovoked shark attacks every year, with more than half taking place in Florida, USA.

Falling coconuts

250 MILLION : 1

It is often claimed that coconut-related deaths are more common than shark attacks. Many tropical resorts warn tourists not to linger under the shady palms, but people who farm the fruit find them harder to avoid.

Lightning strike

10 MILLION : 1

The Democratic Republic of Congo receives the most lightning, with 158 strikes per square kilometre each year. In 1998, one bolt of lightning killed all 11 members of a Congolese football team.

Accidents

Only 6% of deaths are due to accidents, though this adds up to more than 3 million deaths in total. More than a million people die in car accidents alone – two people every minute.

War and violence

Men aged between 15 and 60 years have a much higher risk of dying than women of the same age. This is partly due to the greater risk to men of injuries in areas of war and violent conflict.

Birth complications

Every year, 6.3 million babies die shortly before or after being born. Nearly all of these deaths happen in developing countries where good healthcare is unavailable or unaffordable.

6% ACCIDENTS

3% WAR AND VIOLENCE

6% BIRTH COMPLICATIONS

In sub-Saharan Africa, more than **60%** of all deaths are due to infectious diseases.

Dirty water is thought to be a factor in **80%** of all deaths from diseases.

Disease and Healthcare

Healthcare has improved so much in the last 30 years that the World Health Organization believes the lives of 6.7 million children have been saved. The world now spends a third more on health than it did just five years ago, and on average people are living longer and healthier lives. But progress is not equal around the world. Poorer countries – and even whole continents – are trailing behind.

Across continents

There is an astonishing difference between the rates of infectious diseases in rich and poor nations. In Europe, only 2.5% of deaths are caused by infectious and parasitic diseases. In the developing countries of Africa, the figure is nearer 50%.

Europe

Success in preventing and treating infectious diseases means that most illness and death in Europe is caused by cardiovascular diseases and cancers. These chronic, non-infectious conditions are associated with urbanization, an ageing population, and a lifestyle with plenty of food and little exercise. Lots of these risk factors could be controlled.

CAUSES OF DEATH

Each circle represents 1% of all deaths

NON-INFECTIOUS CONDITIONS

- Cardiovascular diseases
- Cancers
- Digestive diseases
- Respiratory diseases
- Neuropsychiatric disorders
- Diabetes

INFECTIOUS CONDITIONS

- Respiratory infections
- HIV/Aids
- Diarrhoea
- Tuberculosis
- Malaria
- Other infectious or parasitic diseases

OTHER

- Accidental injuries
- Intentional injuries
- Birth conditions
- Pregnancy and childbirth
- Other

EUROPE

Georgia 47

France 34

Australia 25

Canada 19

Brazil 12

Iraq 7

Thailand 4

Kenya 1

Doctors and patients

More doctors don't always mean a healthier population. In Georgia, most doctors are concentrated in the cities. The poorest people living in rural areas have very little access to healthcare. Life expectancy is more than 10 years lower than it is in Canada.

More than **16 million** people in sub-Saharan Africa are living with HIV/AIDS

Africa

In Africa, poor nutrition, unsafe water, and a lack of basic sanitation increase the number of infections and make cases more dangerous than they would be in the developed world. Families often burn wood for cooking and heating, causing a large number of lung infections. Pneumonia is the biggest killer of children.

Cost of care

The USA has one of the world's most expensive healthcare systems. Around 19% of all government expenditure is on health and this is more than doubled by private contributions. Pakistan has the smallest healthcare budget – just 1.3% of government spending.

Pakistan $51
Papua New Guinea $154
Jamaica $240
Namibia $358
Venezuela $396
Jordan $611
Poland $910
Germany $3,328
USA $6,714

AFRICA

TOTAL AMOUNT SPENT ON
HEALTHCARE PER CAPITA

61

Watery Earth

Not all of the water on Earth is suitable for drinking – 97.5% is salty seawater and only 2.5% is drinkable freshwater. Of that 2.5%, the majority is locked up in glaciers, icecaps, and land, leaving just 0.007% in rivers and lakes, readily accessible for us to use.

Water

Water is one of the most important of Earth's resources. Without water to drink, we could not survive for more than a few days. Water is essential for good health, industry, and farming, and we use it to cook with and wash and play in. However, Earth has only a limited amount of this crucial resource, and with the world's population growing, the water is not trickling down to all who need it.

FRESHWATER
2.5%

ACCESSIBLE TO HUMANS
0.007%

SOIL LOCKED
30%

GLACIERS
70%

SALTWATER
97.5%

Global usage

Most of the world's water supply is used for agriculture. The amount that people use in their homes is a mere 8%. However, water usage in different regions varies considerably. In Africa, agriculture consumes 88% of all water withdrawn, while in Europe most water is used in industry.

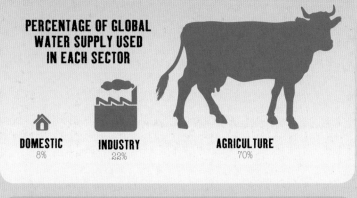

PERCENTAGE OF GLOBAL WATER SUPPLY USED IN EACH SECTOR

DOMESTIC 8%   INDUSTRY 22%   AGRICULTURE 70%

Domestic usage

A person in the US typically uses more water taking a five-minute shower than a person living in a developing country slum uses in a whole day. In developing countries insufficient infrastructure and sanitation prevents people from accessing the water they need. This problem plagues 1.6 billion people worldwide, living predominantly in rural communities.

AMOUNT OF WATER USED BY INDIVIDUALS

SUB-SAHARAN AFRICA
10–20 litres
(21–42 pints)

EUROPE
200 litres
(423 pints)

NORTH AMERICA AND JAPAN
350 litres
(740 pints)

Droplet by droplet

Water is used to produce the food we eat and the products we use. Even the simplest of things requires large amounts of water. Read around the edge of the page to discover how much water is needed to produce different products.

Stressed resources

A country with less than 1,700 m³ (60,035 ft³) of water per capita is said to be experiencing "water stress". One with less than 1,000 m³ (35,315 ft³) is suffering a water crisis. If this drops to below 500 m³ (17,357 ft³), the health of people and economic development in the region is severely compromised.

Greenland

Greenland is covered in glaciers, which hold vast quantities of freshwater. From these, the meltwater provides an immense water supply for very few people – just 55,000 people live in Greenland.

USA

The US uses a huge amount of water each day, but then it has plenty of freshwater to use; the country is packed with reservoirs, dams, wells, huge water towers, and huge lengths of water pipes.

Kuwait

This desert country has the least amount of fresh water in the world. However, its extreme wealth has enabled it to build desalination plants, to make use of the vast amounts of seawater at its disposal, and to buy in water from Iraq.

GREENLAND, 10,767,857 (380,263,281)

USA, 1,563,168 (55,202,756)

FRENCH GUIANA, 812,121 (28,679,782)
ICELAND, 609,319 (21,517,897)
GUYANA, 316,689 (11,183,766)

TOP 5 WATER-SECURE COUNTRIES
m³ (ft³) per capita, 2000

QATAR, 99 (3,496)

BAHAMAS, 66 (2,331)

UNITED ARAB EMIRATES, 58 (2,048)

GAZA STRIP, 52 (1,836)

KUWAIT, 10 (353)

TOP 5 WATER-INSECURE COUNTRIES
m³ (ft³) per capita, 2000

Water for the people

Water and populations are unevenly distributed across the globe; arid regions have little fresh water, yet they account for 40% of global land area across the continents. Nearly three billion people – more than 40% of the world's population – live in water-scarce conditions.

34.8%   60.3%

5.9%   10.9%
EUROPE

ASIA

13.3%   7.7%
NORTH AMERICA

10.6%   14.7%
AFRICA

2.9%   0.5%
OCEANIA

32.2%   5.7%
SOUTH AMERICA

WATER SUPPLY

percentage of world's population

percentage of world's water

Water wars

In the past 50 years, there have been 1,831 water-related disputes, 21 of which have resulted in violence. With continued population growth, increased consumption, and anticipated climate change, this is likely to mean more conflicts in the future between nations that share freshwater supplies.

60 litres (127 pints) to produce 2 microchips

Hunger

We've all felt the unpleasant sensation in our stomach that signals hunger. Some 1.02 billion people battle that feeling every day. It is a huge a barrier to a country's development; hungry people can think of little else beyond their next meal. At the UN Millennium Summit in 2000, world leaders pledged to halve the number of people who suffer from hunger by 2015. They are not on track to do this: whilst undernourishment fell between 1990 and 2006, it is now rising again.

Africa
With 29% of its population undernourished, sub-Saharan Africa has the highest hunger rate per capita in the world. Millions of Africans rely on food aid, and the global economic crisis saw hunger in the region rise further in 2008.

Arctic circle

NORTH AMERICA

EUROPE

AFRICA

Tropic of Cancer

Where hunger hits hardest

Although hunger is a global problem, 65% of the world's hungry live in just seven countries – Bangladesh, China, Congo, Ethiopia, India, Indonesia, and Pakistan. Famine leading to starvation is the most extreme form of hunger, but the long-term effects of a poor diet can be just as serious. Undernourishment describes more than just simple lack of food. One-third of the world's population suffers from chronic malnutrition – a hidden hunger caused by diets that lack the nutrients needed for healthy growth and development. Every day 24,000 people die from hunger-related causes, and a large proportion of these are children.

Equator

SOUTH AMERICA

Tropic of Capricorn

What causes hunger?
It is difficult to understand why so many people go hungry when most people in wealthy countries look forward to long, healthy, food-plenty lives. Less than 60% of our planet's agricultural potential is used to its full capacity, and we already produce enough food each year to feed everyone. But it is not shared out evenly. The main cause of hunger is poverty – a lack of means to buy or grow food. Conflict and natural disasters add to the hunger misery by disrupting food supply, and can turn food shortage into a famine.

EARTH'S AGRICULTURAL POTENTIAL

Utilized

Unutilized

Brazil
Brazil is the world's fourth largest agricultural exporter, yet its number of hungry people keeps rising dramatically. Leaders have tackled the problem for the most vulnerable children, though, through a successful school meals programme.

More than **80%** of the world's hungry live in rural communities in developing countries. They often work in food production, but are not the end consumers

Asia and the Pacific
Nearly two-thirds of the world's hungry live in this region (which includes India). In southern Asia, 48% of children under the age of five are underweight due to an inadequate diet that stunts growth and development, and makes children more susceptible to disease.

ASIA

Global warming and food production

Crops improve
Climate change threatens to increase extreme weather and drought, and to change the seasonal patterns that guide agriculture. While this will devastate the food production of many countries, experts predict that some countries in the mid-latitudes may actually benefit from warmer summers and wetter winters brought about by global warming. In these countries, where fewer people are undernourished in the first place, farms may become more productive.

INCREASE IN CROP YIELDS — THE MID-LATITUDES

The hungrier get hungrier
Countries in this region, already suffering the highest rates of malnutrition, will be worst hit by global warming. Staple crops such as corn and rice are very sensitive to temperature – a rise of just 1°C (1.8°F) could halve crop production in some areas. Combined with population growth, the consequences of global warming could be devastating.

DECREASE IN CROP YIELDS — THE TROPICS

India
Almost 50% of the world's hungry live in India. Malnutrition begins before birth; nine in 10 of India's pregnant women have an inadequate diet. Those who survive the malnutrition of their youth are likely to become hungry adults.

OCEANIA

Food aid
Wealthy countries produce huge food surpluses, a lot of which is donated to poorer, poverty-stricken countries. But it is not always enough. Year upon year developed countries donate billions of dollars to food aid. This goes a long way towards helping many hungry people, but few countries achieve the UN target of donating 0.7% of their national incomes. Food aid is only part of the solution. Providing seeds, tools, and education to help farmers grow their own crops helps build self-sufficiency and reduces the need for food aid.

US $24 billion
Japan $18 billion
UK $13 billion
Germany $12 billion
France $12 billion
Netherlands $6 billion
Italy $4 billion
Spain $4 billion

LARGEST DONORS OF FOOD AID (2006)

Food Waste

Food waste begins on farms, where huge numbers of fruits and vegetables are rejected for being too big, too small, or too ugly. It ends in household bins when we throw away what we can't eat. Wasted food often ends up in landfill sites, where it generates harmful greenhouse gases. By wasting food, we also waste the energy, water, and other resources used to produce, process, and transport it to our tables, further contributing to global warming.

BINNED

EATEN

Worst offenders

UK consumers are among the most wasteful in the world. They spend £12 billion a year buying food that they then throw away. That's about one-third of all the food they buy, and weighs in at a staggering 8.3 million tonnes. Some of this waste is inedible, such as bones or eggshells. But two-thirds – 5.3 million tonnes – could be avoided. Eliminating it would enable a cut in carbon dioxide emissions equivalent to taking a quarter of all the country's cars off the road.

What's in the bin?

Almost a quarter of UK household food waste by weight is vegetable matter. It is estimated that 45% of salad bought in the UK is binned. Rotting vegetables, fruit, and salads are ideal for composting, yet most end up in landfills.

FRESH VEGETABLES AND SALADS 23%

DRINKS 16%

FRESH FRUIT 13%

BAKERY PRODUCTS 10%

READY MEALS 8%

MEAT AND FISH 7%

DAIRY AND EGGS 7%

ALL OTHER 16%

WASTE IN THE FOOD CHAIN: WHERE WASTE HAPPENS IN THE UK

MANUFACTURERS
4–9 million tonnes thrown away every year during the production process

RETAILERS
1.6 million tonnes discarded by shops and restaurants annually

Waste at every stage
Food waste ends in our dustbins, when we miss a "use by" date or cook too much. But your food waste footprint is bigger than you think. Food is lost or thrown away at every stage of the supply chain: during harvesting, processing and distribution, and on the shop floor where "ugly" fruit and vegetables are left on the shelf.

LEFT TO GO OFF
2.9 million tonnes end up in the bin due to not being used in time

SURPLUS TO REQUIREMENTS
2.2 million tonnes are scraped off plates when too much has been prepared. A further 0.2 million tonnes are binned in homes for other reasons.

Rotten rubbish
A fifth of wasted food is tipped down household drains, flooding sewers with a 1.8-million-tonne river of milk, fizzy drinks, fruit juice, and eggs. Around 5.8 million tonnes of food are collected by the local authority. Some councils have composting schemes, but the majority collect food waste with general refuse and send it straight to landfill sites, where it rots and releases methane, a major cause of global warming.

21%
Tipped down drain

72%
Collected with the rubbish

8%
Home composting/ fed to animals

Food mountain
While 1.02 billion people go hungry every day, rich countries waste enough food to meet the world's food needs several times over. The volume of food wasted in one year in the UK alone is more than double the amount all the countries of the world donated to help relieve hunger for those in desperate situations.

8.3 MILLION TONNES
Amount UK consumers throw away each year

4 MILLION TONNES
Amount of emergency food aid donated globally

Eco-friendly options
There are many alternatives to landfills and composting. In some places these options are being explored, but the number of countries, businesses, and individuals taking advantage of them remains small.

Redistribute to the poor
A growing number of charities rescue spare food from supermarkets and restaurants, distributing it to homeless shelters and other people in need.

Generate energy
Rotting food produces methane, which can be burned to generate electricity. Used cooking oil can be made into biodiesel, a renewable fuel used by buses in many cities.

Feed to the pigs
Japan's food industry recycles more than 70% of its waste into animal feed and fertilizer, increasing the supply to agriculture without growing extra crops.

Become a freegan
Supermarkets often discard edible food because the sell-by date has past or the packaging is damaged. Freegans highlight this waste by only eating food they have scavenged.

Globesity

Obesity is a rapidly growing problem around the world. By 2015, 2.3 billion adults will be overweight and 700 million obese. The excess fat stored by their bodies will put them at risk of many serious illnesses. A third of the world's obese people live in the developing world, where healthcare systems are already struggling. Economic growth, urbanization, and the worldwide availability of cheap, imported, processed food all contribute to this modern epidemic.

Body Mass Index

The Body Mass Index (BMI) is used to spot obesity in adults. This chart can be used to find an adult's BMI – using either metric or imperial measurements, plot where weight and height meet on the grid. Measuring children is more challenging because their age and gender must be taken into account. The World Health Organization estimates that there are 22 million obese children worldwide.

HEIGHT IN FEET AND INCHES

Portion sizes

The food portions we eat in restaurants and buy in supermarkets have expanded massively over the past 50 years. Even the weight of a typical slice of bread has increased. The worst culprits are energy-packed fast foods. In the last few years, three US fast-food chains have introduced sandwiches stuffed with 340 g (12 oz) of beef – the amount of meat an adult should eat in two days. Eating more than we need leads to weight gain.

1989

2009

Old portion size – 333 calories
Fast food restaurants in the past offered only one portion size. Now, this portion size is considered "small".

New portion size – 590 calories
Meals today are up to twice as big as they were 20 years ago, and five times larger than they were in the 1950s.

The cost of convenience

Obesity rates are highest in urban populations. Just 5% of Chinese people are obese but this rises to 20% in cities, where people exercise less and are more likely to choose processed food. Factory-made foods tend to be high in energy but low in the nutrients needed for health. The drinks shown here contain similar energy levels (measured in calories) but energy is all that the cola provides.

	COLA DRINK	ORANGE JUICE	MILK
CALORIES	160	168	153
VITAMIN A, IU	0	291	750
VITAMIN C, MG	0	146	3
CALCIUM, MG	0	33	450
MAGNESIUM, MG	0	36	51
POTASSIUM, MG	0	711	352

HEIGHT IN METRES

1.96
1.94
1.92
1.90
1.88
1.86
1.84
1.82
1.80
1.78
1.76
1.74
1.72
1.70
1.68
1.66
1.64
1.62
1.60
1.58
1.56
1.54
1.52

Weight across the nations

Although being underweight is associated with poverty, many people living in poverty are actually overweight. Obesity is rising fastest in low- and middle-income countries, where poverty is rife, as their populations adopt unhealthy Western habits and eat cheap junk foods, imported from Western countries. The World Health Organization is helping governments to tackle the problem by promoting healthy eating in schools.

TOP SIX OBESE COUNTRIES – % OF POPULATION THAT IS OBESE

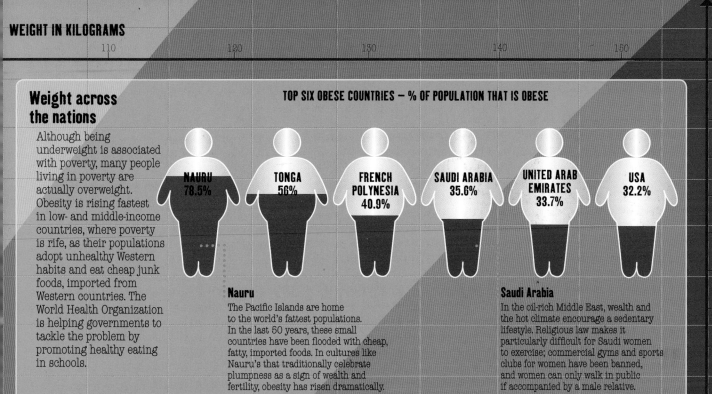

NAURU 78.5%   TONGA 56%   FRENCH POLYNESIA 40.9%   SAUDI ARABIA 35.6%   UNITED ARAB EMIRATES 33.7%   USA 32.2%

Nauru

The Pacific Islands are home to the world's fattest populations. In the last 50 years, these small countries have been flooded with cheap, fatty, imported foods. In cultures like Nauru's that traditionally celebrate plumpness as a sign of wealth and fertility, obesity has risen dramatically.

Saudi Arabia

In the oil-rich Middle East, wealth and the hot climate encourage a sedentary lifestyle. Religious law makes it particularly difficult for Saudi women to exercise; commercial gyms and sports clubs for women have been banned, and women can only walk in public if accompanied by a male relative.

Health issues

Many serious diseases are more common in overweight and obese people. These include cardiovascular disease, high blood pressure, some cancers, and late-onset diabetes. The first case of diabetes in Nauru was registered in 1925, and the number of sufferers has risen with obesity. Worldwide, there are now 2.6 million patients. Similarly, in the Middle East, a third of all healthcare costs are linked to obesity.

TOP SIX DIABETIC COUNTRIES – % OF POPULATION THAT IS DIABETIC

NAURU 30.7%   UNITED ARAB EMIRATES 19.5%   SAUDI ARABIA 16.7%   BAHRAN 15.2%   KUWAIT 14.4%   OMAN 13.1%

Thrifty gene theory

Some scientists believe that people from Africa, Southeast Asia, and Polynesia are especially likely to become obese when they eat a Western diet. This is due to their genetic make-up; research suggests that people in these nations carry a "thrifty gene" that once helped them to store fat easily in case of famine. Even when the food supply is constant, their bodies continue to hold on to as much fat as possible.

BODY MASS INDEX

☐ Severely underweight	☐ Overweight
☐ Underweight	☐ Obese
☐ Healthy weight	☐ Clinically obese

Daily Diets

As more and more people move to towns and cities and living standards improve, global eating habits are changing rapidly. Food is more accessible and diverse than ever before, but, for many, fresh fruit, vegetables, and cereals are being replaced by highly processed, energy-dense foods. These foods are full of fat, sugar, and salt. This has led to an increase in diet-related diseases, and is a growing problem in developing countries.

UNITED STATES

SPAIN

MOROCCO

CHILE

VIETNAM

SUDAN

What's in the fridge?

A healthy diet means eating a variety of food groups in the right proportions. The food spilling out of the fridges above shows how much of each food group is eaten per day by an average person in a selection of countries. Across the world, people eat the main food groups in very different quantities, but the total amount of food they eat also varies greatly.

Sudan
The Sudanese diet mainly consists of rice, milk, eggs, fruit, and vegetables. In some areas, up to 40% of all food eaten is dairy. Access to the important nutrients found in meat and fish is limited.

Chile
Obesity rates in Latin America are soaring. Rapid modernization in Chile has led to a national diet packed with fast foods. Consumption of fruit, vegetables, and cereals has fallen.

Spain
The amount of fat consumed in Spain is similar to that in the USA, but a much greater proportion is made up of healthier vegetable oils. The average Spaniard eats only 7 g (0.2 oz) of animal fat per day.

Vietnam
The tradtional Vietnamese diet is high in rice, fruit, and vegetables, and low in meat. Some 25% of children under five are malnourished due to a lack of calcium and other nutrients.

Morocco
Cereal-based foods provide about 60% of daily calories in Morocco. Protein-rich meat, fish, and dairy are a much smaller part of the diet, leading to health problems, such as anaemia (red blood cell deficiency).

USA
The average American gets a third of their daily calories from fats and oils. Fatty meat and dairy products make up 42% of food consumed by weight. Two-thirds of US adults are classed as overweight.

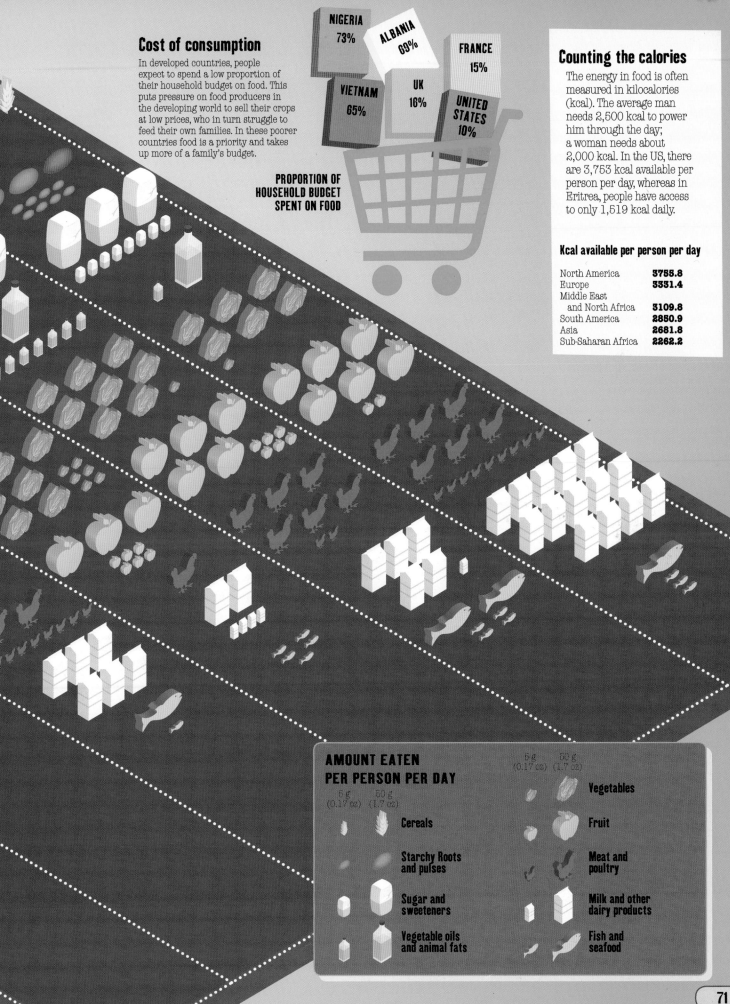

Cost of consumption

In developed countries, people expect to spend a low proportion of their household budget on food. This puts pressure on food producers in the developing world to sell their crops at low prices, who in turn struggle to feed their own families. In these poorer countries food is a priority and takes up more of a family's budget.

NIGERIA 73%
ALBANIA 69%
FRANCE 15%
VIETNAM 65%
UK 16%
UNITED STATES 10%

PROPORTION OF HOUSEHOLD BUDGET SPENT ON FOOD

Counting the calories

The energy in food is often measured in kilocalories (kcal). The average man needs 2,500 kcal to power him through the day; a woman needs about 2,000 kcal. In the US, there are 3,753 kcal available per person per day, whereas in Eritrea, people have access to only 1,519 kcal daily.

Kcal available per person per day

North America	3755.8
Europe	3331.4
Middle East and North Africa	3109.8
South America	2850.9
Asia	2681.8
Sub-Saharan Africa	2262.2

AMOUNT EATEN PER PERSON PER DAY

5 g (0.17 oz)   50 g (1.7 oz)

- Cereals
- Starchy Roots and pulses
- Sugar and sweeteners
- Vegetable oils and animal fats
- Vegetables
- Fruit
- Meat and poultry
- Milk and other dairy products
- Fish and seafood

Look who's Talking

From scary stories to stirring speeches, we use language to express emotions, impart knowledge, and share ideas. The world's 6,900 languages are also a vital part of cultural identity and diversity, yet half of all languages have fewer than 6,000 speakers. Ten disappear every year and 2,500 are threatened with extinction in the next century. Whole ways of life will fade, as poems, songs, and traditions are lost forever.

Top 25 languages

More than half of the world's population – 3.9 billion people – speak one of 25 major languages as their mother tongue. This word cloud shows each language sized proportionally to its number of native speakers. Chinese is by far the biggest, with nearly four times as many speakers as Spanish, the next most common.

TURKISH

RUSSIAN BENGALI

1.2 BILLION SPEAKERS

CHII

GERMAN
VIETNAMESE
MARATHI

ENGLISH

FRENCH LAHNDA

1. Chinese
With 1.2 billion speakers, Chinese is the world's most spoken language. It is a macrolanguage – one made up of many different regional forms, or dialects. The biggest of these is Mandarin Chinese with 845 million speakers. Chinese is a tonal language – the meaning of many words changes with their tone or pitch.

3. English
English is spoken as a first language in 112 countries, making it the most widely spread language and the foremost language for international communication. Around 329 million people speak English as their first language, but it is also the most learned foreign language, used by up to 350 million non-native speakers.

IN NUMBERS: HOW THE WORLD'S LANGUAGES COMPARE

Nearly extinct

More than 100 but fewer than 1 million speakers

7%	3%	87%	3%

Fewer than 100 speakers

More than 1 million speakers

Lost your tongue?
Only 300 languages have more than 1 million speakers. The remaining 6,600 are spoken by just 6% of the world's population. Around 470 are classed as nearly extinct, meaning only a few elderly speakers survive.

2. Spanish

Spanish is the world's second most spoken language, shared by 329 million people in 44 countries. Although Spanish developed in Europe, there are many more Spanish speakers in Latin America. Differences are minor, so Spanish speakers from any country can understand each other.

4. Arabic

A total of 221 million people in 57 countries across the Middle East and North Africa speak varieties of Arabic. They are often so different that speakers from different countries cannot understand each another. By 2050, Arabic is expected to be one of the top three languages, behind Chinese and Hindi.

SPANISH KOREAN ARABIC
NESE
MALAY

PORTUGUESE JAPANESE GUJARATI BHOJPURI
URDU

HINDI TAMIL ITALIAN TELUGU POLISH
JAVANESE

5. Hindi

Hindi is the first language of 182 million people and the most spoken of India's 445 living languages. Five other Indian languages make it into the top 25: Telugu, Marathi, Tamil, Gujarati, and Bhojpuri. The Indian film industry reflects the country's linguistic diversity – just 22% of films released are in Hindi.

Learning a second language

English, French, and German are the three most-studied foreign languages worldwide. Spanish comes fourth in Europe, but tops the chart in the USA. The most multilingual Europeans are the Luxembourgers: 99% speak at least one other language.

Mind your Manners!

Religion, superstition, and centuries of tradition have shaped each country's unique mixture of cultural norms — absorbed as we grow up, but often baffling to those from other cultures. While confused holidaymakers are happy to muddle through, there is a thriving market for etiquette coaches who help businesspeople to impress international colleagues and clients with their local know-how.

4 13 14

Numbers

Four is a very unlucky number in China, much like the number 13 is in other cultures. Chinese buildings don't have fourth floors. In Japan, the number 14 is avoided because it sounds like the word for death.

Chop-stuck

Eat out in China, Japan, Korea, or Vietnam, and you'll have to master the skill of eating with chopsticks. Not only that, but the etiquette of how to use them differs in each region. Just don't order the soup.

Straight up
Never stand chopsticks upright in a bowl of food. In Asia, this is a reminder of the incense sticks associated with death.

Parallel lines
Finished eating? Be careful to place your chopsticks side by side. Forming a V or X is a bad omen in Japan and Hong Kong.

Skewered
Stabbing food with your chopsticks may make life easier, but it is equivalent to licking food off a knife.

Chopstick shovel
Shovelling dripping food from bowl to mouth is acceptable everywhere except Korea, where fingers are used to eat rice.

Food faux pas

We're often told to eat everything up, but in some countries this would baffle or even insult your host. Make sure you know where to stuff and where to stop.

Eat it up
Make sure your eyes aren't bigger than your belly in Greece. Your host would rather remove surplus food than waste it.

Small portions
In Hong Kong, be sure to leave a little on your plate. Finishing everything suggests your host hasn't been generous enough.

Don't take no for an answer
Even a ravenous Chinese person will refuse food at first, for fear of appearing too greedy or eager to eat.

More, please!
Leaving food in Thailand signals that you are full. Force yourself to clear your plate and the host will bring even more.

Table manners

When it comes to eating, several things considered bad manners here are seen as courteous in China. But don't even think about flipping a fish over to eat the other side...

Noisy noodles
Slurping food signals that it is so delicious, you are eating it while it's hot. Slurping noisily cools the food as you go.

Flipping fish
Flipping a half-eaten fish is said to be bad luck, like turning a fisherman's boat. It's more polite to leave the bottom half.

Burping
Talking with your mouth full and finishing the meal with a loud burp will show how much you've enjoyed it.

Pass me the salt
Chinese hosts reach across the table to serve food. You can reach for the salt — if you stand up first.

Say it with flowers...

...but make sure you know what you're saying. Get the colour or number wrong and your beautiful bouquet might be seen as an omen of bad luck or even death to the unlucky recipient.

Marigolds
For Mexicans, marigolds are a symbol of grief, and represent the massacre of native Aztecs by the invading Spanish.

Yellow flowers
In Russia, giving a bunch of yellow flowers to a friend is a signal you want to end the relationship.

Red roses
A dozen red roses are the ultimate romantic gesture in some countries, but a favourite funeral bouquet in Latvia.

White flowers
In many Asian countries, white flowers symbolize tears and death, while an odd number of flowers brings bad luck.

Gifting gaffes

In many cultures, the most innocent-looking objects have hidden meanings. To avoid present-buying problems altogether, visit Iceland where it's considered rude to give your host a gift.

In the dog house
Cute puppy prints won't go down well in Malaysia and Indonesia, where many people see dogs as unclean.

Umbrella blunder
In China, giving an umbrella means you don't want to see someone again – the word for umbrella sounds like "split up".

Sniffy slip-up
In Korea and Mexico handkerchiefs are symbols of tearful goodbyes, and can signal the end of a friendship.

Your time's up
Giving a clock as a gift in China says you're counting the seconds until the recipient's death.

Silent signals

You're shopping in a foreign country, you don't speak the language, but you've spotted exactly want you want. How are you going to let the shopkeeper know without offending them?

Pointing
Pointing with one finger is effective, but considered very rude in many countries as it can indicate anger.

Thumbs up
In Indonesia, the best way to point is with a closed fist held sideways, thumb held towards the object.

Palms up
The Japanese and Chinese point with an open hand, extending all fingers towards the object – ready to receive it.

Pout with lips
Ecuadorians point by puckering or pursing their lips, so don't worry if you see an awful lot of people pouting.

Don't do it in public!

Do your bad habits include wiping your nose, chewing gum, and...licking stamps? Each of these must be kept behind closed doors in certain countries.

Stick to the right
Bad news for left-handers – touching people, food, and money with the left hand is considered unhygienic in India.

Burst that bubble
Chewing gum is illegal in Singapore. Smuggling it into the country earns you one year in jail and a £6,500 fine.

Royal respect
Thais hold their king in very high regard – even licking the back of a postage stamp is considered disrespectful.

Keep sniffing
Many Japanese think it's barbaric to blow your nose in public, and even worse to keep a used tissue in your pocket.

Tribal Peoples

About 150 million people live in tribal communities that are traditionally self-sufficient, relying on their local land to provide what they need. Their way of life is socially, culturally, and economically different from that of the industrialized world, and they have their own unique values, traditions, and methods of governing themselves. Some tribal peoples have lost their traditional organizations and no longer live off the land, but still identify with their culture. The world is beginning to realize how important it is to preserve their diverse knowledge and skills.

Indigenous inhabitants

Many tribal peoples are descended from their country's indigenous (or original) inhabitants. Today, they often live in mountains, forests, and deserts, far from the towns and cities that have been built on their ancestral land. As the world's demand for resources grows, even these remote areas are being invaded. These six tribes live on different continents, but their stories show some of the problems faced by indigenous peoples everywhere.

Tribal peoples make up **2%** of the world's population

Yanomami: Brazil and Venezuela

Since the 1980s, gold miners have invaded the Amazon forest bringing disease and pollution to tribes such as the Yanomami. They are one of the last tribal peoples to remain on their traditional lands, and currently number about 32,000 people. Hunting, gathering, and fishing provide 20% of their food, and the rest is grown in large gardens in forest clearings. In 2004, they formed an organization to establish education and healthcare, and to defend their rights.

Inuit: northern Canada, Alaska, Greenland, and eastern Russia

This is an *inunnguaq* – a distinctive human-shaped stone construction made by the Inuit people as a navigational aid. The Inuit have embraced many aspects of industrial society, but traditional hunting skills are still central to their way of life. Climate change threatens the 160,000 Inuit by disrupting the habitats of the seals, caribou, and other animals they hunt. Some Inuit are adapting by using their skills to guide tourists eager to go dog sledding or ice fishing.

Aborigines: Australia

Australia's indigenous people once led a nomadic lifestyle, hunting and gathering food. Today's 250,000 Aborigines are the poorest community in Australia, relying on paid labour and state support. Their legitimate claims to land face competition from mining and farming companies. The distinctive styles of Aboriginal artwork – such as this dot painting example – have become an important way for some groups to preserve their identity and unique skills.

Khanty: Siberia

By moving their reindeer herds to find grazing land, Siberia's 22,500 Khanty people survive in an environment too harsh for farming. No part of the reindeer is wasted: the Khanty eat reindeer meat, make utensils from their bones, and use the animal's hide to cover their tents (called "chum" tents). Oil drilling, mining, and military bases in these remote areas are destroying the Khanty way of life. Many have been forced off the land and settled in villages.

Saami: Sweden, Norway, and Finland

Northern Europe's 80,000 Saami have a strong political voice compared to other tribal peoples, and have protected their traditional way of life as reindeer herders. Now, climate change and modern forestry are threatening the lands they depend on, destroying the lichens that are the main winter food for reindeer. The Saami are also concerned about the exploitation of their colourful traditional clothes and culture by the tourist industry.

San: Namibia, South Africa, Botswana, and Angola

About 87,000 San live in and around southern Africa's Kalahari Desert. Most live in poverty, and few now follow their traditional hunter-gatherer lifestyle – they are often banned from entering the farms and game parks built on former hunting grounds. Some organizations are working to link the San's incredible tracking skills and use of local plants to commercial projects, which may benefit the San and stop their knowledge from dying out.

Beliefs and Believers

Most of the world's people identify with a religion. Their beliefs, customs, or ancestors link them to a particular religious community. Despite high numbers of followers, rates of participation in religious services vary enormously. For many in the Western world, religion is separated from everyday life and practised at weekends and holidays. In other areas of the world, religious traditions are central to everyday life.

Religions of the world

This diagram shows the number of followers of world religions. Most are single religions, but some are groupings of similar belief systems. Those shown here with symbols are the biggest single religions, and four of these – Hinduism, Christianity, Islam, and Buddhism – account for almost three-quarters of the world's population.

Almost **60 million** Hindus travelled to Allahabad, India, in 2001 for the 12-day Maha Kumbh Mela festival

394 MILLION

900 MILLION

2.1 BILLION

1.5 BILLION

Chinese traditional religion
This belief system draws heavily upon a variety of ancient Chinese mythologies, philosophies, and religious practices. There are hundreds of gods and goddesses, and many festivals to worship them.

Hinduism
With the longest history of any living religion, Hinduism is a collection of very diverse traditions and beliefs. Almost 80% of Hindus live in India and Nepal, where the vast population makes it the world's third largest religion.

Christianity
Christianity is the largest religion, followed by almost one-third of the world's population. The Christian cross is one of the most recognized symbols, found everywhere from jewellery to artwork.

Islam
Islam is the second largest religion in the world, and thought to be the fastest growing. The biggest Muslim populations are found in South and Central Asia, North Africa, and Eastern Europe.

Some **1 billion**
people do not follow any religion –
many of them are atheists, and
do not believe in the existence
of any god

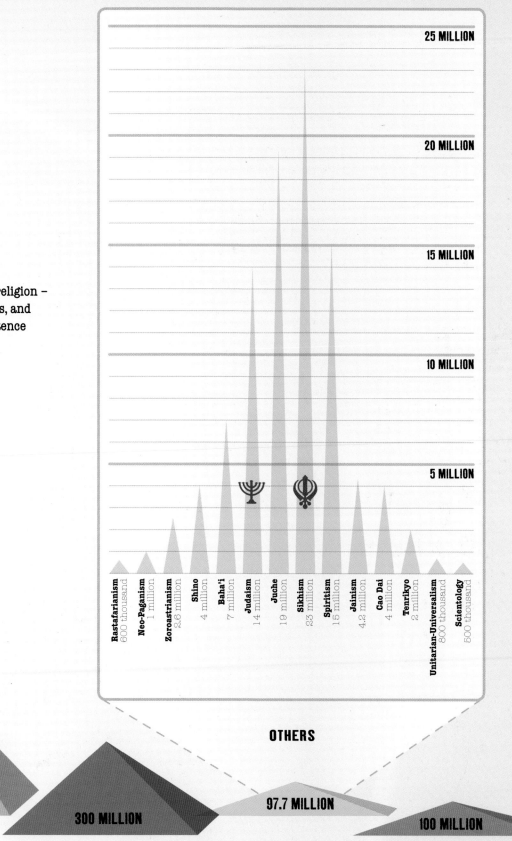

Rastafarianism 600 thousand	**Neo-Paganism** 1 million	**Zoroastrianism** 2.6 million	**Shino** 4 million	**Baha'i** 7 million	**Judaism** 14 million	**Juche** 19 million	**Sikhism** 23 million	**Spiritism** 15 million	**Jainism** 4.2 million	**Cao Dai** 4 million	**Tenrikyo** 2 million	**Unitarian-Universalism** 800 thousand	**Scientology** 500 thousand

OTHERS

376 MILLION

300 MILLION

97.7 MILLION

100 MILLION

Buddhism
This religion is not based on a personal god, but on the belief that spiritual development helps followers understand the nature of life. Originating in Asia 2,500 years ago, it has a growing number of followers in the West.

Indigenous
This group includes the diverse beliefs of tribal peoples around the world who often rely on songs, poems, and stories to pass on their religion. It incorporates thousands of different traditions, which shape diverse ways of life.

Others
Smaller religions tend to be concentrated in certain areas. About 80% of Sikhs live in one area of India, and Juche does not exist outside North Korea. Despite its small size, Judaism has influenced literature, science, and politics.

African traditional
Ancient African belief systems influence every aspect of day-to-day life. A sub-set of African religions has grown in the West, shaped by African migrants as they adjusted to new cultures.

Hinduism: 900 million believers

The roots of Hinduism go back thousands of years, but despite its long history, the religion has very little formal structure. Different traditions worship different gods and goddesses, such as Shiva and Kali, in a huge variety of ways, with pilgrimages and festivals throughout the year.

Judaism: 14 million believers

Originating during the Bronze Age, Judaism is the oldest of the three Abrahamic faiths. The different branches reflect different interpretations of the rules and duties God set out for Jews more than 3,500 years ago. Orthodox Judaism is more traditional, and Reform Judaism is the most recent.

Buddhism: 376 million believers

Mahayana Buddhism teaches that everyone can attain "enlightenment" – an understanding of the true meaning of life achieved by Gautama Buddha, the religion's founder. Theravada Buddhists believe that discipline is very important, and recommend becoming a monk to reach enlightenment.

Christianity: 2.1 billion believers

Since Christianity began with the birth of Jesus Christ, it has divided into many denominations, each with its own beliefs or practices. All Christians share the Bible as a holy text, and believe that salvation is offered through the life, teaching, death, and resurrection of Jesus.

The Big Six

The six biggest religions account for about 85% of the world's believers. Christianity, Judaism, and Islam share a common origin and values, and believe in just one God. They are often called the Abrahamic faiths, because their holy books feature many of the same stories, places, and people, including Abraham, an important figure in the history of each. Similarly, Hinduism, Buddhism, and Sikhism all began in the same region of the world and are closely related.

Every year, an estimated 300 million people travelling for pilgrimages and other faith-based activities spend

£11.3 billion

(\$18 billion)

Pilgrimages

Believers travel from all around the world to visit special places and holy sites connected to their religion.

Maha Kumbh Mela

The world's largest gathering takes place every 12 years on the banks of the River Ganges in India. During the festival, up to 60 million Hindu pilgrims bathe where three holy rivers meet.

The Western Wall of the Temple of Jerusalem

Judaism's holiest site, the Western Wall is all that remains of the Temple in Jerusalem, Israel, after it was destroyed in 70 CE. Pilgrims come every year to remember their people's struggles.

Shikoku

Every year, an estimated 100,000 Buddhists travel a 1,200-km (746-mile) circuit around 88 temples on the Japanese island of Shikoku. It takes some pilgrims two months to complete the tour.

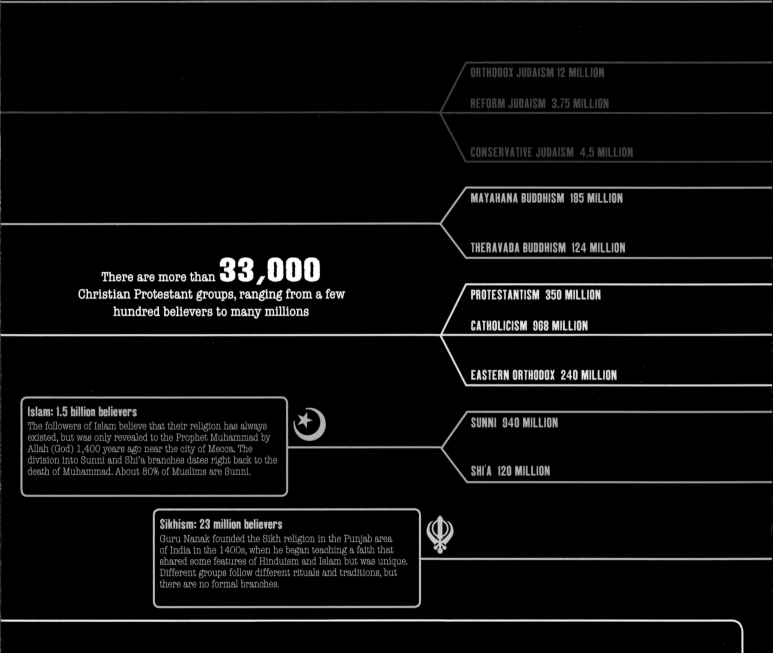

ORTHODOX JUDAISM 12 MILLION

REFORM JUDAISM 3.75 MILLION

CONSERVATIVE JUDAISM 4.5 MILLION

MAYAHANA BUDDHISM 185 MILLION

THERAVADA BUDDHISM 124 MILLION

There are more than **33,000** Christian Protestant groups, ranging from a few hundred believers to many millions

PROTESTANTISM 350 MILLION

CATHOLICISM 968 MILLION

EASTERN ORTHODOX 240 MILLION

Islam: 1.5 billion believers

The followers of Islam believe that their religion has always existed, but was only revealed to the Prophet Muhammad by Allah (God) 1,400 years ago near the city of Mecca. The division into Sunni and Shi'a branches dates right back to the death of Muhammad. About 80% of Muslims are Sunni.

SUNNI 940 MILLION

SHI'A 120 MILLION

Sikhism: 23 million believers

Guru Nanak founded the Sikh religion in the Punjab area of India in the 1400s, when he began teaching a faith that shared some features of Hinduism and Islam but was unique. Different groups follow different rituals and traditions, but there are no formal branches.

Santiago di Compostela
Catholics have travelled long distances to the city of Santiago di Compostela, Spain, since medieval times. The remains of St James are thought be buried in the city's cathedral.

Hajj
More than 2 million Muslims from around the world journey to Mecca, Islam's holiest place, to take part in the Hajj pilgrimage every year. Muslims are expected to do this at least once in their life.

Golden Temple
The holiest shrine in Sikhism is the Golden Temple in Punjab, India. It attracts Sikh visitors from all over the world to mark happy occasions such as marriage and the birth of children.

The Gender Gap

When women have equal access to education, healthcare, employment, and power, societies become richer, healthier, and more peaceful. The world is working towards equal rights, but there is still a long way to go. Of the 72 million children who do not attend primary school worldwide, 57% are female. Women and girls still make up 70% of the world's poor.

Trinidad and Tobago
Many Latin American and Caribbean countries have excellent scores in health and education, but lose points because few women join the workforce. Trinidad and Tobago has 60% of women in work and is the region's only country to make it into the top 20.

Iceland
Iceland tops the chart with a score of 0.8276. It has a female prime minister, and women make up one-third of the government. Other Nordic countries also score highly – Finland and Norway come second and third.

Mapping inequality
The Global Gender Gap Index scores countries on equality between men and women. It takes into account whether there are equal opportunities for work, political representation, and access to education and healthcare. The highest possible score is 1 (where men and women are completely equal) and the lowest is 0.

173

17

GLOBAL GENDER GAP INDEX

- 0.8000 and above
- 0.7000-0.7999
- 0.6500-0.6999
- 0.6000-0.6499
- 0.5000-0.5999
- Below 0.5000
- No data

Voting rights
In 1893, New Zealand became the first country to allow women to vote in national elections. Some countries have only followed suit very recently.

Date women were allowed the vote:
1979 **Micronesia**
1979 **Marshall Islands**
1980 **Iran**
1984 **Liechtenstein**
1986 **Central African Republic**
1990 **Samoa**
1994 **Kazakhstan**
1994 **South Africa**
2005 **Kuwait**
2010 **United Arab Emirates**

VOTE

Heads of state
The number of women in powerful political positions is growing. In 2009, Monaco became the last country to elect its first female member of government. Worldwide, women hold 18% of positions in national parliaments and there are currently 17 elected female heads of state or government.

Lesotho

Lesotho and South Africa are the only African countries in the top 20. Lesotho ranks number 10 in the world, boasting no gender gap in education and health. About 69% of women in Lesotho are in paid employment.

Yemen

Middle Eastern and North African countries perform well below the global average. Yemen has the lowest ranking of all 134 countries studied. Just 35% of adult women there can read and write, versus 73% of men.

Sri Lanka

Just two Asian countries – Sri Lanka and the Philippines – make the top 20. Sri Lanka has been led by a female head of state for 21 of the last 50 years, while the Philippines is one of just 12 countries worldwide with no gap in health and education.

Japan

Despite having above average access to healthcare and education, Japanese women are paid 33% less on average than their male counterparts in the workplace and represent just 9s% of government, putting Japan in 75th position.

Education

Closing the gender gap in education is a crucial step in fighting poverty and inequality. Educated girls are more likely to have better jobs and higher wages, fewer and healthier children, and safer childbirth.

FEMALE NOBEL PRIZE WINNERS 5%

MALE NOBEL PRIZE WINNERS 95%

Nobel Prize winners

Marie Curie became the first female Nobel Prize winner in 1903. Since the awards were established in 1901, 762 men and only 40 women have won the prestigious prizes in Science, Medicine, Peace, Literature, and Economics.

PERCENTAGE OF FEMALES ENROLLED IN PRIMARY EDUCATION

TOP 5 COUNTRIES
Canada 100%
Iran 100%
Japan 100%
Malaysia 100%
Uruguay 100%

BOTTOM 5 COUNTRIES
Liberia 39%
Central African Republic 38%
Guinea-Bissau 37%
Sudan 37%
Djibouti 34%

Happy Families

The traditional family structure of a married couple and their offspring is what many people think of when they imagine a typical family. But families are becoming more varied. The pace of change is quickest in Western Europe, where only one-third of households are made up of couples with children — compared to more than half of African and Asian households. In developed countries, people get married later or not at all, while divorce and second marriages are also on the rise. In the developing world, factors including migration for work mean that families are more likely to live apart.

Types of family

Nuclear and extended families are still the most common types worldwide, but there may soon be no typical family. Declining marriage and increasing divorce rates are giving rise to more single-parent families, and "patchwork" families of step-brothers and sisters.

Extended family

Families of three or more generations are still the norm in South Asia, where most young couples start married life with their parents. However, later marriage, migration for work, and demand for more living space mean that families in the developing world are becoming more dispersed every year.

Nuclear family

The nuclear family – two parents and their children – was once the standard model in richer countries. It is becoming less common as parents increasingly live apart, create new families with new partners, or involve other relatives in childcare, as more mothers go to work.

Single-parent family

The number of single-parent families is rising around the world, accounting for 10% or more households in some countries. Around a quarter of children in the UK and USA live with one parent. The USA has 10.4 million single-mother families and 2.5 million single-father families.

Legally wed

Globally, the most common legal age for marriage is 18 – seen as the end of childhood. There are wide differences between and within countries: in Lebanon, nine-year-old girls can get special consent to marry under religious law. Men often have to wait longer than women – Chinese women can marry at 20 as long as their husband-to-be is at least 22.

Average age at first marriage

The typical age at first marriage is rising steadily. Swedish newlyweds are oldest, at an average of 31.8 years for brides and 34 for grooms. Western European, North American, and Australian men are likely to marry someone less than two years younger, while men in Nigeria, Zambia, Colombia, and Iran prefer women at least four years younger.

In the UK, fathers spend **200%** more time interacting with their children than they did in the 1970s

Marriage rates

Marriage rates are falling across the developed world as people choose to live together for longer before they marry. Mongolians are most likely to get married, with 19 weddings per 1,000 people annually. Colombia has just 1.7 marriages per 1,000 people. One of the most violent countries in the world, its high murder rate means a shortage of available men.

Divorce rates

The tiny Southeast Asian island of Guam has the world's highest divorce rate, with 5.3 divorces per 1,000 people. It is a popular destination for visitors to get a quick divorce, but potential divorcees must visit the island for a week – a divorcemoon? Religion keeps divorce rates low in many Asian countries. Hindus believe that marriage is eternal and people cannot be divorced.

Solitary living

As people get married later and live longer, with women often outliving their spouses, the number of single occupancy households is on the rise. This is driving an increase in residential energy consumption. In Scandinavian countries, the energy consumption of everyone who lives alone could be cut by 60% if they moved to five-person households.

First-time mum

The age at which a woman starts to have babies affects the total number of children she might have in her life, so has a huge impact on the size and future growth of populations. In developed countries, more and more women are waiting until they are financially secure with established careers. The UK has the world's oldest first-time mums, with an average age of 30. In most European countries, 20–25% of pregnant women are now over 35. The age is also increasing in developing countries as women's access to education improves.

Full house

Most households in Africa and the Middle East (63% of total households), Latin America (53%), and Asia (51%) have five or more inhabitants. The majority are families with many children. Although households are much larger in developing countries, the size of dwellings is smaller: 78% of households in Asia have three rooms or less, with a big impact on living standards.

Childhood

Every child has the right to a safe and healthy childhood. Twenty years ago, world leaders signed the UN Convention on the Rights of the Child, agreeing that all children should be protected, respected, and educated. In countries like the USA and Japan most people take these rights for granted. But millions of children in sub-Saharan Africa and South Asia still lack the bare essentials.

1. Birth

For millions of children in developing countries, childhood begins with a struggle for survival. In Niger, almost 18 in every 100 children die before the age of five. In India, 2 million children a year die before their fifth birthday.

CHANCE OF LIVING BELOW THE POVERTY LINE

66%

42%

Game of life

Childhood experience is a lottery that depends on where you are born. This board shows the life chances of children in five very different countries by looking at some of life's most basic needs.

12.2%   12%   13%

98%   93%   97%

6. Poverty

Living below the poverty line means having less than the minimum needed for a decent life. In rich countries, the poverty line is considerably higher than in poor countries, as the ability to afford school trips and social activities is taken into account.

CHANCE OF BEING VACCINATED AGAINST MEASLES

Around the world, there are

246 million
child labourers,

171 million
of them doing jobs that expose them to dangerous chemicals or machinery

67%

47%

5. Health

One in seven children in the developing world have no access to essential healthcare, including vaccinations that prevent life-threatening diseases. In the US parents can be jailed or fined if they don't get their children vaccinated.

A costly affair

In wealthy countries, parents fork out thousands bringing their children up. The average amount spent over the course of one child's lifetime in both Japan and the US is thought to be roughly £160,000 ($250,000). In the US, parents spend an average of £180 ($286) on toys for each of their children every year.

89%

99%

99%

100%

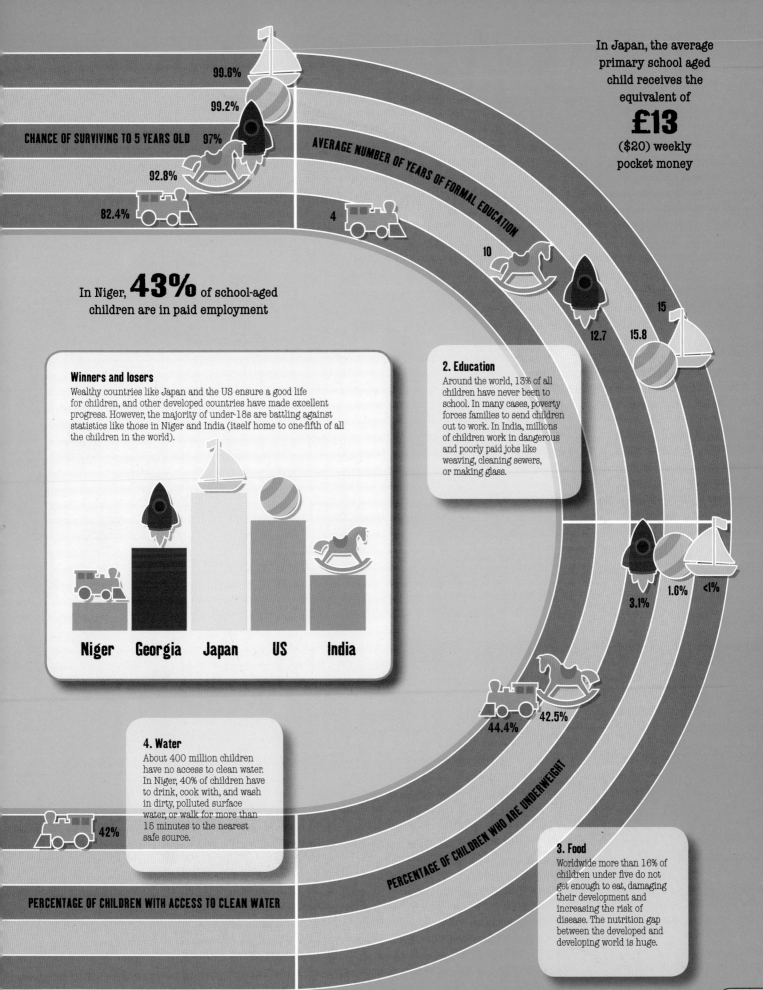

CHANCE OF SURVIVING TO 5 YEARS OLD

99.6%
99.2%
97%
92.8%
82.4%

AVERAGE NUMBER OF YEARS OF FORMAL EDUCATION

4
10
12.7
15.8
15

In Japan, the average primary school aged child receives the equivalent of **£13** ($20) weekly pocket money

In Niger, **43%** of school-aged children are in paid employment

Winners and losers
Wealthy countries like Japan and the US ensure a good life for children, and other developed countries have made excellent progress. However, the majority of under-18s are battling against statistics like those in Niger and India (itself home to one-fifth of all the children in the world).

Niger Georgia Japan US India

2. Education
Around the world, 13% of all children have never been to school. In many cases, poverty forces families to send children out to work. In India, millions of children work in dangerous and poorly paid jobs like weaving, cleaning sewers, or making glass.

3.1%
1.6%
<1%

42.5%
44.4%

PERCENTAGE OF CHILDREN WHO ARE UNDERWEIGHT

4. Water
About 400 million children have no access to clean water. In Niger, 40% of children have to drink, cook with, and wash in dirty, polluted surface water, or walk for more than 15 minutes to the nearest safe source.

42%

PERCENTAGE OF CHILDREN WITH ACCESS TO CLEAN WATER

3. Food
Worldwide more than 16% of children under five do not get enough to eat, damaging their development and increasing the risk of disease. The nutrition gap between the developed and developing world is huge.

School Days

Primary and secondary schools open their gates to one billion children every day. The world agrees that education is central to a child's development, bringing lifelong benefits for individuals, families, and communities. However, at least 72 million children cannot access education, often because their parents are simply too poor to afford it. For those who do get to school, the quality of education depends on where they live. The experience of children in the Netherlands is very different from that in Mali, one of the poorest countries in the world.

THE NETHERLANDS

A developed country in Europe

The Dutch education system prepares pupils for life in a modern economy, where 80% of the people live in towns and cities, and knowledge is more important than manual skills. In international tests, Dutch children score ninth best in the world and 99% of adults can read and write. Yet, they still face challenges, as 1.5 million Dutch adults cannot read and write well enough to apply for jobs.

Years of compulsory education

In the Netherlands, it is illegal to keep children out of school. All children younger than 18 must stay in education until they have earned a basic qualification.

= 13 years
(ages 5–17)

Average years of schooling

Around 95% of Dutch children move on to secondary school, and after that 60% move on to college or university.

= 16.6 years

Education expenditure

The Dutch government spends 11.5% of its total budget on education – 5,600 euros for each primary pupil. They are also one of the leading donors of education aid to poorer countries.

11.5%

PERCENTAGE OF TOTAL BUDGET SPENT ON EDUCATION

Teacher/pupil ratio

The average class ratio is 1 teacher to 17.2 students – 8.5 girls and 8.7 boys. Small classes allow teachers to give pupils close attention. Dutch primary teachers are trained for four years.

Classroom materials

Dutch schools are well equipped, with an average of one computer per seven children. In Mali, classrooms are very different. Some rural schools have just two seats per three pupils. Up to 10 pupils might share one textbook. Hi-tech teaching materials are virtually non-existent.

Enrolment ratio for primary education

98%

99% male   97% female

Who is missing out?

In both rich and poor countries, the children who miss out on education are most often those who are already disadvantaged through poverty or social status. In the Netherlands, the children of immigrants achieve less than native children, and the gap is getting bigger.

MALI

A developing country in Western Africa

About 90% of Mali's population lives on less than the equivalent of $2 per day. For the poorest, education is a low priority compared to the struggle to afford food. Nearly 70% of the population live in rural areas where the nearest school is a 6.6-km- (4.1-mile-) walk away. Mali has the world's lowest literacy rate, with just 26% of adults able to read and write.

Years of compulsory education

Basic primary education helps to tackle the causes of poverty, as educated adults are more likely to avoid exploitation, eat better diets, and have smaller families.

~~HHH~~ IIII = **9 years (ages 7–15)**

Average years of schooling

Many children who start school in Mali do not finish. Poverty forces around half of all Malian children aged 7 to 14 into paid labour.

~~HHH~~ II = **7 years**

Teacher/pupil ratio

A shortage of teachers hampers education in Mali, where fewer than half of primary teachers are trained. The average class ratio is 1 teacher to 54.4 students – 23.3 girls and 31.1 boys on average.

Radio lessons

In many developing countries, radio broadcasts are helping improve education in remote communities. The aid-funded Road to Reading project reaches more than 40,000 classrooms and 500,000 students in Mali.

14.8%

PERCENTAGE OF TOTAL BUDGET SPENT ON EDUCATION

Education expediture

Over the last 20 years, Mali's government has worked to improve education, increasing spending to 14.8% of the country's total budget. However, many pupils in rural areas attend poorly funded community schools, paid for by aid donations, parents, and community schemes.

Laptop initiative

The One Laptop Per Child initiative was set up to provide low-cost laptops to children in developing countries, and has been piloted in Mali. Such initiatives give children access to information taken for granted by pupils in the West.

Enrolment ratio for primary education

63%

67% male   **54% female**

Who is missing out?

Ten years ago, just 43% of Malian children enrolled in primary school. Rates are improving, but more than one-third of children aged 7 to 12 years never go to school. Of these, 60% are girls, who face greater pressure to help with domestic work.

Work

The typical jobs and pay in a country depends on a variety of factors, including education and training of the workforce, and the type of economy they live in. In less economically developed countries, up to two-thirds of people do "informal" jobs — small-scale, unofficial ways of making money — that are not regulated in any way or included in official statistics, but are hugely important to the economy. Informal sector workers tend to be poorly paid and vulnerable in financial crises.

ANNUAL HOURS AT WORK

- 1 **South Korea** 2,400 hours
- 2 **Australia** 1,850 hours
- 3 **United States** 1,815 hours
- 4 **Switzerland** 1,650 hours
- 5 **Germany** 1,400 hours
- 6 **Norway** 1,340 hours

The above list shows how many hours a person works per year. The average Korean clocks up 20 hours more work than the average Norwegian every week.

Global workforce

The world economy can be divided into three main sectors: agriculture, industry, and services. The number of people working in each sector is changing as the world develops. Higher incomes mean a greater demand for products, education, and healthcare, and this creates jobs in industry and services.

Agriculture 40.5%

In 28 developing countries, agriculture is still the largest sector of the economy. In eight sub-Saharan countries, at least two-thirds of the workers are employed in farming, forestry, and fishing. The figure is much lower in developed countries, with just 5% of people working in this sector.

Industry 20.5%

Jobs in this sector include construction, processing, and manufacturing, producing everything from cars and chemicals to electricity. About 46% of China's workforce is employed in this sector.

Services 39%

People working in this sector provide services to the public and to businesses, including transport, entertainment, restaurants, media, tourism, banking, IT, healthcare, and law. It also includes academics, government workers, and the arts. More than 80% of the workforce in many developed countries is employed in services.

PROPORTION OF PEOPLE WORKING IN EACH AREA

Size of workforces

Their huge populations give China and India the biggest workforces in the world. An increasing number of Western businesses "outsource" jobs to these countries, where wages are lower. In 2008, Indian workers did $12.2 billion of IT work for overseas companies.

CHINA	INDIA	USA	INDONESIA	BRAZIL	RUSSIA
807.7 MILLION	523.5 MILLION	155.2 MILLION	112 MILLION	100.9 MILLION	75.7 MILLION

Farmer

The world is producing more crops than ever before, but as countries invest in new technologies, fewer people are needed to farm the land. Twenty-first century farmers need to know as much about business as they do about crops.

What do you want to be?

Media influence means that almost half of British teenagers aspire to be a celebrity above all else. While a new reality TV star seems to be created every week, the odds of becoming famous are much lower than those of ending up in most other jobs.

Basketball

US citizens have a 1 in 676,635 chance of becoming one of the country's 450 professional – and well-paid – basketball players.

Doctor

About 10% of US teenagers would like to work in medicine. There are 8.8 million physicians in the world, so 1 in every 770 people is a doctor.

Fisherman

China has 12.2 million fishermen, meaning that a Chinese citizen has odds of 1 in 109 of working in fishing.

Astronaut

Don't mind long commutes? You have a 1 in 58.6 million chance of getting a job that's out of this world.

Construction worker

Demand for energy-efficient buildings and sustainable materials has created a "green sector" with new opportunities for those working in industry. The global market for green building materials is expected to reach $600 billion in the next five years.

Teacher

Service-sector jobs like teaching often demand more educated workers than other sectors, and are not easily replaced by machines. Even so, the role of teachers is changing as new technologies enter the classroom.

Only about **50–75%** of working-age people in developed countries actually work. The proportion is often higher in poorer countries, as more people have to sell their labour to survive.

180 HOURS MUMBAI

9 HOURS NEW YORK

iPod index

The ease of affording popular items can be used to compare wages around the world. Working for nine hours on New York's average wage would buy you an iPod Nano, but the average earner in Mumbai would need to work 20 nine-hour days to afford the same product.

The Teenage Day

The world's 1.2 billion teenagers are trendsetters, influencing their peers, parents, and culture as a whole. The average US high school student (aged 15–17) spends two-thirds of their time sleeping, at school, or doing homework. The rest of the day is theirs to spend as they like, and with more than £127 billion ($200 billion) in disposable income, the way they spend it influences not only their own lives, but also the entire US economy.

8 HRS 6 MINS

Sleep

Teenagers need an average of 9 hrs 15 mins of sleep every night, but the teen's stubborn body clock makes it hard to fall asleep before 11 pm. Early school start-times mean that they miss out on 1 hr 9 mins of sleep every night, and 15% of US teenagers have fallen asleep at school. To help teens get more time in bed, more than 80 school districts in the US and UK have shifted school hours.

Education (school, homework)

Teenagers spend the largest chunk of their waking time at school and in education-related activities. It's a good thing, then, that 78% of US students feel a sense of belonging when they're at school. However, 1 in 7 report feeling awkward or out of place there. At home, teenage girls spend 19 minutes longer on homework than boys do, and boys are less likely to do homework at all.

Sport and leisure

Teenage boys devote 1 hr 12 mins more to leisure activities than girls do, and are most likely to spend part of this time playing sports. Boys also spend more time watching TV, and double the time using computers, but they give less time to shopping than girls. The sexes are equal, though, when it comes to socializing, with an average of 41 minutes per day dedicated to spending time with friends or family.

Teen TV viewing around the world

The average US teen lives in a home with three televisions and two home movie players. It's not surprising then that American teens watch more TV than ever, but they are far from being the world's biggest couch potatoes; teenagers in South Africa hold that title, spending more than 5 hours in front of the TV screen every day.

Taiwan: 2 hrs 47 mins
Australia: 3 hrs 8 mins
United States: 3 hrs 20 mins
Italy: 3 hrs 24 mins
Poland: 3 hrs 47 mins
Lebanon: 3 hrs 48 mins
Ireland: 4 hrs 21 mins
Indonesia: 4 hrs 35 mins
Venezuela: 4 hrs 54 mins
South Africa: 5 hrs 2 mins

72% of teenagers around the world mainly listen to music via an MP3 player or computer; the typical US teen buys just **2** CDs a year

77% of American teenagers have their own mobile phone, using it to send or receive an average of **191** calls and **2,899** texts every month – that's **96** texts every day

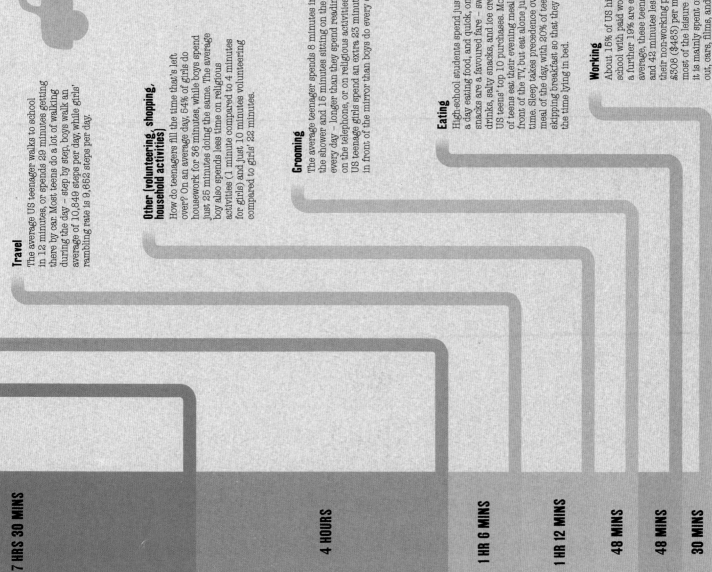

Travel

The average US teenager walks to school in 12 minutes, or spends 29 minutes getting there by car. Most teens do a lot of walking during the day – step by step, boys walk an average of 10,849 steps per day while girls' rambling rate is 9,652 steps per day.

Other (volunteering, shopping, household activities)

How do teenagers fill the time that's left over? On an average day, 54% of girls do housework for 36 minutes, while boys spend just 25 minutes doing the same. The average boy also spends less time on religious activities (1 minute compared to 4 minutes for girls) and just 10 minutes volunteering compared to girls' 22 minutes.

Grooming

The average teenager spends 8 minutes in the shower and 15 minutes sitting on the loo every day – longer than they spend reading, on the telephone, or on religious activities. US teenage girls spend an extra 23 minutes in front of the mirror than boys do every day.

Eating

High-school students spend just 48 minutes a day eating food, and quick, on-the-move snacks are a favoured fare – sweets, fizzy drinks, salty snacks, and ice cream are among US teens' top 10 purchases. More than a third of teens eat their evening meal on their laps in front of the TV, but eat alone just 15% of the time. Sleep takes precedence over their first meal of the day, with 20% of teenagers skipping breakfast so that they can spend the time lying in bed.

Working

About 15% of US high school students balance school with paid work during the week, and a further 19% are employed at weekends. On average, these teens get 36 minutes less sleep and 42 minutes less leisure time every day than their non-working peers. Their income, averaging $308 ($483) per month, helps them to make the most of the leisure time they do have, though – it is mainly spent on clothes, followed by eating out, cars, films, and mobile phones.

7 HRS 30 MINS

4 HOURS

1 HR 6 MINS

1 HR 12 MINS

48 MINS

48 MINS

30 MINS

Celebrations

No matter where you are in the world, everyone likes to party. In the past, festivals were linked to the best times for planting and harvesting crops. Many of these ancient events are still marked in weird and wonderful ways around the world, and have been joined by a host of newer celebrations. Read on for a selection of celebrations from around the world.

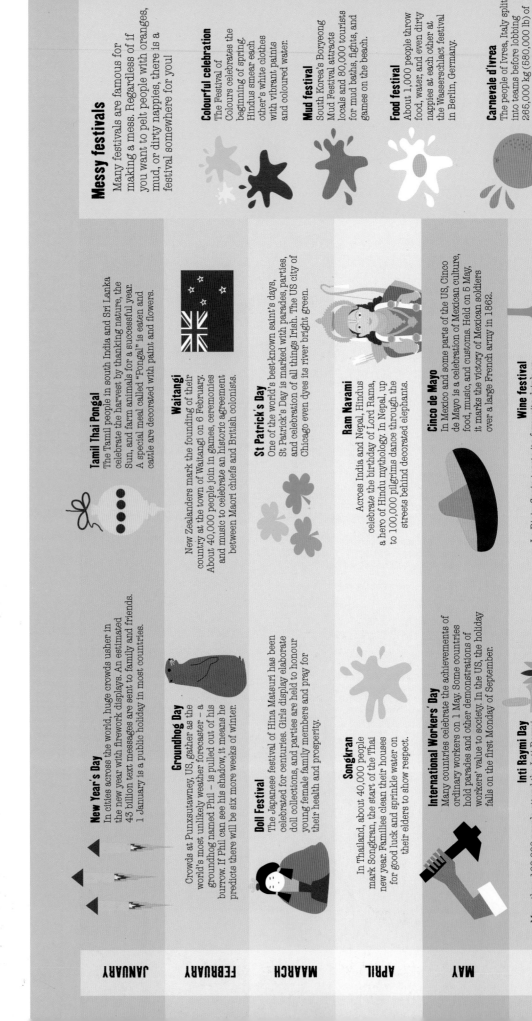

Messy festivals

Many festivals are famous for making a mess. Regardless of if you want to pelt people with oranges, mud, or dirty nappies, there is a festival somewhere for you!

Colourful celebration
The Festival of Colours celebrates the beginning of spring. Hindus smear each other's white clothes with vibrant paints and coloured water.

Mud festival
South Korea's Boryeong Mud Festival attracts locals and 80,000 tourists for mud baths, fights, and games on the beach.

Food festival
About 1,000 people throw food, water, and even dirty nappies at each other at the Wasserschlact festival in Berlin, Germany.

Carnevale d'Ivrea
The people of Ivrea, Italy split into teams before lobbing 265,000 kg (580,000 lb) of oranges at each other during the town's carnival.

JANUARY

New Year's Day
In cities across the world, huge crowds usher in the new year with firework displays. An estimated 43 billion text messages are sent to family and friends. 1 January is a public holiday in most countries.

FEBRUARY

Groundhog Day
Crowds at Punxsutawney, US, gather as the world's most unlikely weather forecaster – a groundhog named Phil – is pulled out of his burrow. If Phil can see his shadow, it means he predicts there will be six more weeks of winter.

Tamil Thai Pongal
The Tamil people in south India and Sri Lanka celebrate the harvest by thanking nature, the Sun, and farm animals for a successful year. A special meal called "Pongal" is eaten and cattle are decorated with paint and flowers.

Waitangi
New Zealanders mark the founding of their country at the town of Waitangi on 6 February. About 40,000 people join in games, ceremonies and music to celebrate an historic agreement between Maori chiefs and British colonists.

MARCH

Doll Festival
The Japanese festival of Hina Matsuri has been celebrated for centuries. Girls display elaborate doll collections, and parties are held to honour young female family members and pray for their health and prosperity.

St Patrick's Day
One of the world's best-known saint's days, St. Patrick's Day is marked with parades, parties, and celebration of all things Irish. The US city of Chicago even dyes its river bright green.

APRIL

Songkran
In Thailand, about 40,000 people mark Songkran, the start of the Thai new year. Families clean their houses for good luck and sprinkle water on their elders to show respect.

Ram Navami
Across India and Nepal, Hindus celebrate the birthday of Lord Rama, a hero of Hindu mythology. In Nepal, up to 100,000 pilgrims dance through the streets behind decorated elephants.

MAY

International Workers' Day
Many countries celebrate the achievements of ordinary workers on 1 May. Some countries hold parades and other demonstrations of workers' value to society. In the US, the holiday falls on the first Monday of September.

Cinco de Mayo
In Mexico and some parts of the US, Cinco de Mayo is a celebration of Mexican culture, food, music, and customs. Held on 5 May, it marks the victory of Mexican soldiers over a large French army in 1862.

JUNE

Inti Raymi Day
More than 100,000 people attend the Inti Raymi Festival in Cuzco, Peru. The week-long "Festival of the Sun" survives from Inca times, and marks the winter solstice and the beginning of a new year.

Wine festival
La Rioja, Spain toasts its favourite drink on 29 June. After a special mass, 10,000 festival-goers spray 50,000 litres (13,000 gallons) of wine at each other from water pistols.

Movable festivals

Some of the most important religious festivals do not take place on a fixed date. They are often guided by ancient calendars based on seasonal changes.

Easter
The life of Jesus is celebrated at Easter, during spring. Christians go to mass and children eat chocolate eggs.

Vesak
During the first full Moon in May, the vivid decorations and candle-lit processions of Vesak honour the life of Buddha.

Passover
This feast marks the liberation of the Jews from slavery in Egypt, and begins in the middle of the first month of the Hebrew calendar.

Diwali
The "Festival of Lights" is a new year festival in the Hindu calendar, celebrating the victory of good over evil.

Eid-Al-Adha
Muslims celebrate Eid-Al-Adha in the last month of the lunar Islamic calendar, at the end of the annual Hajj pilgrimage.

JULY

Independence Day
Many countries mark the anniversary of the date on which they became independent nations. In the US, 4 July is celebrated with picnics, parades, concerts, and fireworks, with the American flag flown everywhere.

Bastille Day
All across France, the storming of the Bastille prison on 14 July 1789 – the event that started the French Revolution – is honoured with dancing, champagne, fireworks, and fun.

AUGUST

Awa Odori
More than a million tourists descend on the town of Tokushima, Japan, to enjoy costumed performers dancing through the streets. It began more than 400 years ago, when citizens danced in celebration of the town's new castle.

Death of San Martín
The military leader General José de San Martín is a national hero in Argentina, where he defeated royalist forces to liberate the country. The anniversary of his death on 17 August is marked by a national holiday.

SEPTEMBER

French Community Day
On 27 September, Belgium's 3.5 million French-speaking citizens celebrate their culture with folk singing, classical concerts, and exhibitions. They are one of three official groups of Belgian citizens, each with its own government.

Heritage Day
In South Africa, 24 September is a national holiday to celebrate the country's rich cultural heritage. Events are held showcasing the creative arts, dance, languages, and food, as well as the country's landscape.

OCTOBER

International Day of Non-violence
In 2007, the United Nations made Mahatma Gandhi's birthday of 2 October the "International Day of Non-violence", recognizing his influence on peaceful protest around the world.

Dia de la Raza, or Columbus Day
Across the Americas, the "Day of the Race", or Columbus Day, marks the arrival of Christopher Columbus in the Americas, a significant event in the history of Europe and the civilizations of the American continent.

NOVEMBER

Day of the Dead
Mexico's happy, colourful festival remembers loved ones who have died. Ancient Aztec traditions are mixed with Christian All Saints' Day customs, as families decorate elaborate altars and visit cemeteries to tend their relatives' graves.

Turkey time
Thanksgiving was first celebrated in the US to mark the harvest of 1621. These days, families in the US come together to eat more than 45 million turkeys to remember the occasion. Thanksgiving is celebrated in Canada in October.

DECEMBER

Christmas Day
Christmas is both a Christian festival marking the birth of Jesus Christ, and a secular family celebration. It has many non-religious traditions, from decorated trees to Santa Claus and yule logs.

Incwala
Swaziland's king eats pumpkin and other food on the "Festival of the First Fruits". Over three weeks, the nation comes together for dances and other rituals to renew the King's strength and bring blessings for the harvest, and the new year.

Chinese festivals

Unlike the Western calendar, the Chinese calendar is based on the phases of the Moon. A year does not have a set number of months, so festivals do not take place on the same date every year.

Chinese New Year
The Chinese Spring Festival marks the start of the first month in the Chinese calendar. Red and gold paper decorations are thought to bring happiness, wealth, and long life, and people buy special presents, food, and clothing.

Moon festival
The Mid-Autumn Festival is celebrated in the eighth month of the Chinese year, falling around September or October in the Western calendar. Traditionally a harvest festival, families gather to watch the bright full Moon and eat round decorated cakes.

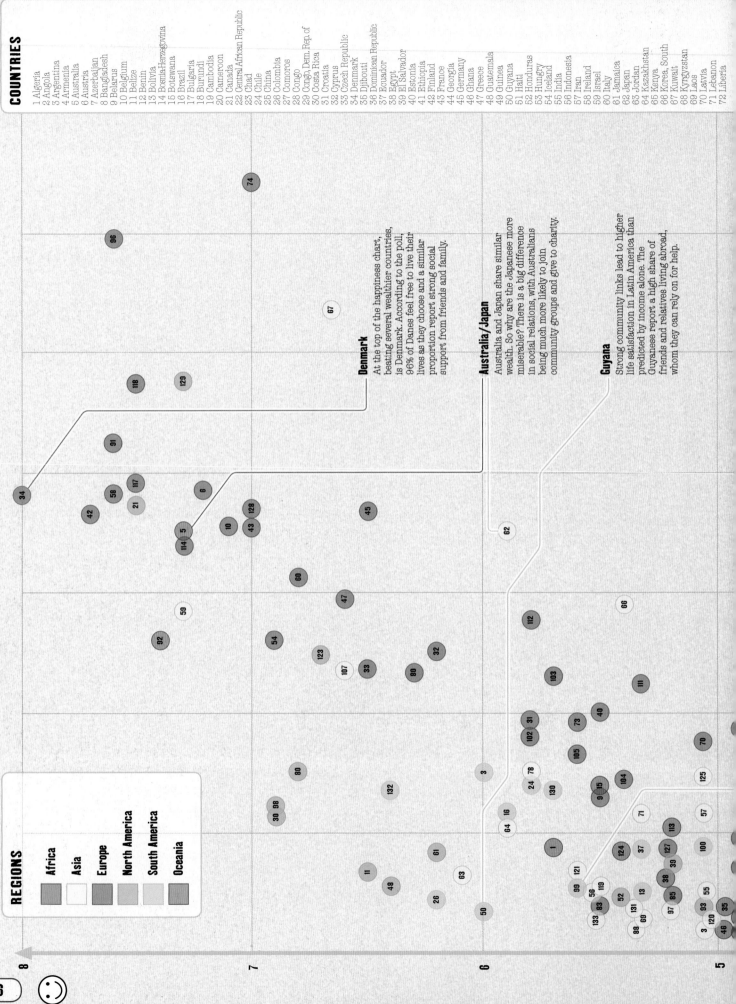

COUNTRIES

1 Algeria
2 Angola
3 Argentina
4 Armenia
5 Australia
6 Austria
7 Azerbaijan
8 Bangladesh
9 Belarus
10 Belgium
11 Belize
12 Benin
13 Bolivia
14 Bosnia-Herzegovina
15 Botswana
16 Brazil
17 Bulgaria
18 Burundi
19 Cambodia
20 Cameroon
21 Canada
22 Central African Republic
23 Chad
24 Chile
25 China
26 Colombia
27 Comoros
28 Congo
29 Congo, Dem. Rep. of
30 Costa Rica
31 Croatia
32 Cyprus
33 Czech Republic
34 Denmark
35 Djibouti
36 Dominican Republic
37 Ecuador
38 Egypt
39 El Salvador
40 Estonia
41 Ethiopia
42 Finland
43 France
44 Georgia
45 Germany
46 Ghana
47 Greece
48 Guatemala
49 Guinea
50 Guyana
51 Haiti
52 Honduras
53 Hungary
54 Iceland
55 India
56 Indonesia
57 Iran
58 Ireland
59 Israel
60 Italy
61 Jamaica
62 Japan
63 Jordan
64 Kazakhstan
65 Kenya
66 Korea, South
67 Kuwait
68 Kyrgyzstan
69 Laos
70 Latvia
71 Lebanon
72 Liberia

REGIONS

Africa
Asia
Europe
North America
South America
Oceania

Denmark

At the top of the happiness chart, beating several wealthier countries, is Denmark. According to the poll, 96% of Danes feel free to live their lives as they choose and a similar proportion report strong social support from friends and family.

Australia/Japan

Australia and Japan share similar wealth. So why are the Japanese more miserable? There is a big difference in social relations, with Australians being much more likely to join community groups and give to charity.

Guyana

Strong community links lead to higher life satisfaction in Latin America than predicted by income alone. The Guyanese report a high share of friends and relatives living abroad, whom they can rely on for help.

8

7

6

5

96

Who's Happiest?

Surveying life satisfaction reveals what you might expect: happiness rises with income. People in North America, Western Europe, Japan, Australia, and New Zealand are rich and happy with their lives. Those living in poorer countries are dissatisfied. But money doesn't explain everything. The control people have over their lives, trust in government, and the support of friends and family all influence well-being.

Life satisfaction chart

Polling organization Gallup asked people from 135 countries to score how they felt about their lives, from 0 ("the worst possible life") to 10 ("the best possible life"). No country scored less than 2. Gross national income per capita shows how much money a country makes per person. Plotting a country's life satisfaction score against its per capita income shows that happiness and wealth are linked, but also throws up some surprising exceptions.

Armenia/Paraguay

Despite similar incomes, people in Paraguay are much happier than those in Eastern European countries. They report greater satisfaction with their health and social life, spending just under 9 hours a day socializing, compared to just 38 minutes in Armenia.

Bulgaria

Bulgarians are significantly less happy than their income might suggest. A lack of confidence in others is to blame – 98% of Bulgarians believe their government is corrupt, and a similar percentage believes local businesses are corrupt.

Togo

Most sub-Saharan African countries appear on the bottom left of the chart. In Togo, approximately 40% of people live on less than $1.25 a day. Among the poorest countries, small rises in income generally lead to large increases in life satisfaction as more of life's basic needs can be met.

73 Lithuania
74 Luxembourg
75 Macedonia
76 Madagascar
77 Malawi
78 Malaysia
79 Mali
80 Malta
81 Mauritania
82 Mexico
83 Moldova
84 Mongolia
85 Montenegro
86 Morocco
87 Mozambique
88 Myanmar (Burma)
89 Namibia
90 Nepal
91 Netherlands
92 New Zealand
93 Nicaragua
94 Niger
95 Nigeria
96 Norway
97 Pakistan
98 Panama
99 Paraguay
100 Peru
101 Philippines
102 Poland
103 Portugal
104 Romania
105 Russia
106 Rwanda
107 Saudi Arabia
108 Senegal
109 Serbia
110 Sierra Leone
111 Slovakia
112 Slovenia
113 South Africa
114 Spain
115 Sri Lanka
116 Sudan
117 Sweden
118 Switzerland
119 Syria
120 Tajikistan
121 Thailand
122 Togo
123 Trinidad and Tobago
124 Tunisia
125 Turkey
126 Uganda
127 Ukraine
128 United Kingdom
129 United States
130 Uruguay
131 Uzbekistan
132 Venezuela
133 Vietnam
134 Yemen
135 Zambia

GROSS NATIONAL INCOME PER CAPITA

$10,000 $20,000 $30,000 $40,000 $50,000 $60,000 $70,000

POOR

RICH

US SPENDING ON PETS

$17.4bn
$2.2bn
$3.4bn
$10.2bn
$12.2bn

- Food
- Veterinary care
- Medicine
- Grooming/boarding
- Live animal purchases

Pricey pooches

Every year US pet owners spend a whopping £28 billion ($45 billion) on feeding, healing, grooming, and accessorizing their companions. That's double what Americans spend on toys and greater than the GDP of more than half of the world's countries.

Half of US pet owners think of their pets as members of the family

Pets in the USA

An estimated 63% of US households own at least one pet. The images on the right show the most popular US pets and their population numbers. Keeping fish is a very popular hobby, and fish owners tend to have more than one fish. Although there are fewer dogs in total, two in every five US households own a dog and there are more pet dogs than under-16-year-olds.

REPTILES
13.6 MILLION

BIRDS
15 MILLION

SALTWATER FISH
11.2 MILLION

FRESHWATER FISH
171.7 MILLION

CATS
93.6 MILLION

DOGS
77.5 million

SMALL MAMMALS
15.9 MILLION

HORSES
13.3 MILLION

Top cat and dog owning countries

The USA is the world's top pet-loving nation but other countries are nipping at their heels. Almost half of Russian families keep a cat or dog. Pets were once banned in China but it now boasts a booming market – despite dog featuring on some restaurant menus.

1. USA
2. BRAZIL
3. CHINA
4. MEXICO
5. JAPAN
6. RUSSIA
7. FRANCE
8. PHILIPPINES
9. THAILAND
10. SOUTH AFRICA

1. USA
2. CHINA
3. RUSSIA
4. BRAZIL
5. JAPAN
6. FRANCE
7. UK
8. GERMANY
9. UKRAINE
10. ITALY

People and their Pets

Pets are more popular now than at any time in history. The pet care industry is worth billions, and it's not just the animals that benefit. Scientists have found that owning a pet can reduce stress, lower blood pressure, and cut the risk of a heart attack by nearly a third. But keeping pets comes at a cost. The amount American pet owners spend on their pets in a year is twice NASA's annual budget.

DOGS

CATS

Dog and cat litters

Cats and dogs breed very quickly, so unneutered stray animals are a huge worldwide problem. Every year up to 7 million former pets end up in US animal shelters, where more than half are put down.

CATS

18 kittens a year on average

180 kittens in a lifetime

DOGS

12 puppies a year on average

120 puppies in a lifetime

Pampered pets

What do you buy for the pet that has everything? If your cat can't face another fake mouse and your dog doesn't dig chew toys, look no further than these weird and wonderful pet accessories.

Luxury hotel stay
Pet packages at top hotels include a welcome treat, ice cream, pet massage, and dog-walking services.

Diamond dog collar
The world's most expensive collar features 1,600 diamonds, platinum, white gold, and crocodile leather.

Doggy treadmill
Nearly 40% of dogs in the US are overweight, fattening the market for pet exercise equipment.

Designer clothes
Doggy dinner jackets and crystal-studded Kimonos hit the catwalk at Pet Fashion Week in New York.

In 2008, an American dog called Trouble inherited

£7.6 million
($12 million) from her billionaire owner

In loving memory

Even the most pampered pet is unlikely to outlive its owner. A typical pet cat lives for 12–18 years, while the average dog will live to age 11. Luckily, the pet care industry has come up with some creative ways to immortalize our furry friends. See below for some of the more inventive options.

Deep freeze
For £3,600, you can freeze your dead pet in liquid nitrogen, ready to be defrosted when a cure is found. More than 60 US pets are in "cryostasis".

A diamond is forever
Turn man's best friend into a girl's best friend by converting a pet's ashes into a diamond. The process takes six months and costs up to £11,000.

Get stuffed
Some taxidermists will stuff and mount pets in a playful pose, for display in your home. Alternatively, a Nevada business turns pets into cushions for just £50.

Copy cats
The super-rich don't buy memorials to dead pets – they order identical copies. The technology is very new and the procedure costs up to £465,000.

Mummification
For about £2,500 to £79,500, one American company will mummify your pet and seal it inside a bronze container to keep forever.

In a spin
Pet fur can be spun into yarn for just £7 per 100 g (3.5 oz). Owners can then knit anything from a shaggy-dog sweater to a rabbit-hair handbag.

THE World IN ONE Day

PEOPLE

What's happening to the planet's 6.8 billion inhabitants right now? What a difference a day can make...

The population of India increases by **50,378** – enough to fill **121** Boeing 747 **jets**

380,028 babies are **born**
(that's 264 per minute)

There are about **100 million** people called **Chang** (or Zhang), the world's most common surname

9.8 million people are in prison

Apples	Bananas	Tomatoes	Oranges
eaten:	eaten:	eaten:	eaten:
1 billion	**1.5 billion**	**2.5 million**	**800 million**

22 billion toilets are **flushed** each day – enough for **66%** of the world's total population to take a **bath**, (though they wouldn't want to use the same water!)

There are **339** million **obese people** in the world, but more than **3** times as many people are **not** getting **enough food**

0.1 languages die out, experts think half of the **world's languages** will **die out** by 2100

11,847 people get **married** in the US

In the US, **pet dogs poo** a total of **7,500 tonnes**, the same weight as **1,500 elephants**

2,425 mobile phones are lost in the UK by accidentally flushing them down the **toilet, 160** more are chewed by pet dogs

30,000 people pelt each other with tomatoes in the world's biggest **food fight** at La Tomatina in **Valencia, Spain**

For four days every year, **500,000** people **dance** in the streets of Rio de Jainero, Brazil for the **Rio carnival**

1 million people go to the world's largest **music festival** at Summerfest in **Milwaukee**, USA

18,368,904 people have a **birthday** (and the average age of the whole world is **28.4** years old)

8,814,000 doctors are at work across the world, which means there are **771** people for every doctor

110 million people go **bowling**

820,000 golf balls are sold, and **7 million** people enjoy a **game** of golf

77 million primary-school children **don't** have a place to **go to school** – that's more than the population of Turkey

1,073 people die from **accidental falls**

5,480 people die in **road accidents**

155,539 people die in total

411 people die from **global warming**-related issues

Power

The way a country is governed can determine whether its inhabitants are free to live their lives as they choose. International organizations that allow countries to work together can improve conditions and provide opportunities for people. Some rich, powerful countries affect the lives of people all over the world, while multinational companies bring economic stability to their huge global workforces and influence the lives of people all over the world who buy their goods and services.

Countries and Flags

Today, there are more countries in the world than ever before. A country is a place that has its own government, a permanent population, and is widely recognized by other countries. Most governments recognize at least 193 countries – those shown in the main chart. All but one of these, the Vatican City, are members of the United Nations. Each country has its own national flag, used as a symbol of the nation.

REGIONS
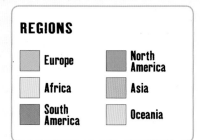
- Europe
- Africa
- South America
- North America
- Asia
- Oceania

ALBANIA — Tirana 3.19
DENMARK — Copenhagen 5.52
ANDORRA — Andorra la Vella 0.08
ESTONIA — Tallinn 1.34
AUSTRIA — Vienna 8.37
FINLAND — Helsinki 5.33

Country	Capital	Pop.	Country	Capital	Pop.	Country	Capital	Pop.
BELARUS	Minsk	9.66	ITALY	Rome	60.2	POLAND	Warsaw	38.1
FRANCE	Paris	62.6	MALTA	Valletta	0.41	SLOVAKIA	Bratislava	5.41
BELGIUM	Brussels	10.7	LATVIA	Riga	2.25	PORTUGAL	Lisbon	10.6
GERMANY	Berlin	81.9	MOLDOVA	Chisinau	4.13	SLOVENIA	Ljubljana	2.04
BOSNIA AND HERZEGOVINA	Sarajevo	3.84	LIECHTENSTEIN	Vaduz	0.03	ROMANIA	Bucharest	21.4
GREECE	Athens	11.2	MONACO	Monaco	0.03	SPAIN	Madrid	46.9
BULGARIA	Sofia	7.59	LITHUANIA	Vilnius	3.33	RUSSIA	Moscow	141
HUNGARY	Budapest	10.0	MONTENEGRO	Podgorica	0.62	SWEDEN	Stockholm	9.28
CROATIA	Zagreb	4.43	LUXEMBOURG	Luxembourg	0.49	SAN MARINO	San Marino	0.03
ICELAND	Reykjavík	0.32	NETHERLANDS	Amsterdam	16.5	SWITZERLAND	Berne	7.75
CZECH REPUBLIC	Prague	10.5	MACEDONIA	Skopje	2.04	SERBIA	Belgrade	7.32
IRELAND	Dublin	4.52	NORWAY	Oslo	4.82	UKRAINE	Kiev	46.24

Country	Capital	Pop.	Country	Capital	Pop.	Country	Capital	Pop.
ALGERIA	Algiers	35.3	COMOROS	Moroni	0.67	GUINEA	Conakry	10.0
BURUNDI	Bujumbura	8.30	EQUATORIAL GUINEA	Malabo	0.67	GUINEA-BISSAU	Bissau	1.61
ANGOLA	Luanda	17.0	CONGO	Brazzaville	3.68	ERITREA	Asmara	5.07
CAMEROON	Yaoundé	18.8	CÔTE D'IVOIRE	Yamoussoukro	21.3	ETHIOPIA	Addis Ababa	82.8
BENIN	Porto-Novo	8.93	CAPE VERDE	Praia	0.50	KENYA	Nairobi	39.0
BOTSWANA	Gaborone	1.99	DEM. REP. CONGO	Kinshasa	68.6	GABON	Libreville	1.47
CENTRAL AFRICAN REP.	Bangui	4.51	DJIBOUTI	Djibouti	0.86	LESOTHO	Maseru	2.13
BURKINA FASO	Ouagadougou	15.7	GAMBIA	Banjul	1.60	LIBERIA	Monrovia	3.95
CHAD	N'Djamena	10.3	EGYPT	Cairo	78.6	GHANA	Accra	23.8
UNITED KINGDOM	London	61.8	VATICAN CITY	Vatican City	>0.0001	LIBYA	Tripoli	6.28

Country	Capital	Pop.	Country	Capital	Pop.	Country	Capital	Pop.
ARGENTINA	Buenos Aires	40.2	PARAGUAY	Asunción	6.34	BELIZE	Belmopan	0.32
BOLIVIA	La Paz	9.86	SURINAME	Paramaribo	0.50	COSTA RICA	San José	4.50
CHILE	Santiago	16.9	ANTIGUA & BARBUDA	Saint John's	0.08	DOMINICA	Roseau	0.07
ECUADOR	Quito	13.6	BAHAMAS	Nassau	0.34			
BRAZIL	Brasilia	191	VENEZUELA	Caracas	28.3	CUBA	Havana	11.2
COLOMBIA	Bogotá	45.0	BARBADOS	Bridgetown	0.28	DOMINICAN REPUBLIC	Santo Domingo	10.0
GUYANA	Georgetown	0.77	CANADA	Ottawa	33.7			
PERU	Lima	29.1						
URUGUAY	Montevideo	3.36						

East Timor, a former Indonesisan colony that won its independence in 2002, is one of the world's newest countries

MOZAMBIQUE —— Name

—— National flag

Maputo —— Capital city

21.9 —— Country's population in millions

TURKEY
Ankara
74.8

MICRONESIA
Palikir
0.11

BRUNEI
Bandar Seri
Begawan 0.38

IRAN
Tehran
73.2

LEBANON
Beirut
3.87

PHILIPPINES
Manila
92.2

TURKMENISTAN
Ashgabat
5.11

NAURU
(no capital)
0.01

CAMBODIA
Phnom Penh
14.8

IRAQ
Baghdad
30.0

MALAYSIA
Kuala Lumpur
28.2

QATAR
Doha
1.40

UNITED ARAB EMIRATES
Abu Dhabi
5.06

NEW ZEALAND
Wellington
4.31

CHINA
Bejing
1,331

ISRAEL
Jerusalem
7.63

MALDIVES
Malé
0.31

SAUDI ARABIA
Riyadh
28.6

UZBEKISTAN
Tashkent
27.5

PALAU
Melekeok
0.02

MADAGASCAR
Antananarivo
19.4

MOZAMBIQUE
Maputo
21.9

AFGHANISTAN
Kabul
28.3

ARMENIA
Yerevan
3.09

BAHRAIN
Manama
1.21

CYPRUS
Nicosia
1.07

JAPAN
Tokyo
127

MONGOLIA
Ulaanbaatar
2.70

SINGAPORE
Singapore
5.11

VIETNAM
Hanoi
87.2

PAPUA NEW GUINEA
Port Moresby
6.61

MALAWI
Lilongwe
14.2

NAMIBIA
Windhoek
2.17

SENEGAL
Dakar
12.5

AZERBAIJAN
Baku
8.78

BANGLADESH
Dhaka
162

EAST TIMOR
Dili
1.08

JORDAN
Amman
5.91

MYANMAR (BURMA)
Naypyidaw
50.0

SOUTH KOREA
Seoul
48.7

YEMEN
Sana'a
22.8

SAMOA
Apia
0.19

MALI
Bamako
12.72

NIGER
Niamey
14.73

SEYCHELLES
Victoria
0.08

SUDAN
Khartoum
39.44

BHUTAN
Thimphu
0.68

GEORGIA
Tbilisi
4.61

KAZAKHSTAN
Astana
15.8

NEPAL
Kathmandu
27.5

SRI LANKA
Colombo
20.5

AUSTRALIA
Canberra
21.8

SOLOMON ISLANDS
Honiara
0.51

MAURITANIA
Nouakchott
3.29

NIGERIA
Abuja
152

SIERRA LEONE
Freetown
5.69

SWAZILAND
Mbabane
1.18

TUNISIA
Tunis
10.4

INDIA
New Delhi
1,171

KUWAIT
Kuwait City
2.98

NORTH KOREA
Pyongyang
22.6

SYRIA
Damascus
21.9

FIJI
Suva
0.84

TONGA
Nuku'alofa
0.10

MAURITIUS
Port Louis
1.27

RWANDA
Kigali
9.87

SOMALIA
Mogadishu
9.13

TANZANIA
Dodoma
43.7

UGANDA
Kampala
30.7

INDONESIA
Jakarta
243

KYRGYZSTAN
Bishkek
5.30

OMAN
Muscat
3.10

TAJIKISTAN
Dushanbe
7.45

KIRIBATI
South Tarawa
0.09

TUVALU
Funafuti
0.001

MOROCCO
Rabat
31.4

SAO TOME & PRINCIPE
São Tomé
0.16

SOUTH AFRICA
Pretoria
50.6

TOGO
Lomé
6.61

ZAMBIA
Lusaka
12.5

ZIMBABWE
Harare
12.5

LAOS
Vientiane
6.32

PAKISTAN
Islamabad
180

THAILAND
Bangkok
67.7

MARSHALL ISLANDS
Majuro
0.05

VANUATU
Port Vila
0.23

EL SALVADOR
San Salvador
7.33

GUATEMALA
Guatemala City
14.0

HONDURAS
Tegucigalpa
7.46

MEXICO
Mexico City
109

PANAMA
Panama City
3.45

SAINT LUCIA
Castries
0.17

TRINIDAD AND TOBAGO
Port of Spain
1.33

GRENADA
Saint George's
0.10

HAITI
Port-au-Prince
9.24

JAMAICA
Kingston
2.70

NICARAGUA
Managua
5.66

SAINT KITTS AND NEVIS
Basseterre
0.05

ST VINCENT & GRENADINES
Kingstown
0.11

UNITED STATES
Washington D.C.
306

TAIWAN
Taipei
23.0

KOSOVO
Pristina
2.22

Disputed countries

Sometimes an area may declare independence from an established state, but not be universally accepted as a new country. Neither Taiwan, which broke away from China, nor Kosovo, which used to be part of Serbia, are recognized by the UN.

All Change

The number of countries around the world has grown substantially in recent decades. The total has reached about 193, mainly as a result of former colonies seeking independence and the emergence of new territories after war. Each new country requires clearly defined borders, but these are not always permanently fixed. Politics, conflict, and climate change can alter them, causing some countries to grow larger, others to become smaller, and some to disappear altogether.

Breaking up

War and political changes can cause countries to break up. The USSR was a superpower that collapsed in 1991, leading 15 new countries, including Russia, Ukraine, and Belarus, to come into existence. Yugoslavia was a country in eastern Europe that split into five states after years of ethnic tensions and fighting.

Joining together

When countries become divided after war, people who once shared the same nationality are separated. In South and North Vietnam, East and West Germany, and North and South Yemen, the borders were rigidly controlled until changes to the political landscape brought them back together again.

YUGOSLAVIA

SLOVENIA

CROATIA

BOSNIA & HERZEGOVINA

SERBIA & MONTENEGRO

MACEDONIA

Collapse of Yugoslavia

Yugoslavia was once a large country, but in the early 1990s it became the scene of bloody battles and ethnic tensions. It split into five states: Slovenia, Croatia, Bosnia and Herzegovina, Serbia and Montenegro, and Macedonia. Later on, Montenegro and the territory of Kosovo split from Serbia, but Kosovo is still seeking international recognition as a sovereign state.

SERBIA

MONTENEGRO

KOSOVO

GERMANY

No borders

Within the European Union, 25 countries have signed up to the Schengen Agreement. This has created an area without border checks, so people can pass from one country to another without passports or visas.

Famous borders

China, which shares its land borders with 14 other nations, also boasts the Great Wall of China, a towering wall border that was built in the 5th century BCE. It stretches for 8,852 km (5,500 miles).

Natural change

Global warming has led to changes to country boundaries. It is causing the Alpine glaciers between Switzerland and Italy to melt, so much so that the countries were forced to meet in 2009 to redraw their borders.

Gaining land and disputed territory

There are many places in the world where ownership is not clear. Japan and Russia argue over the Kuril Islands that lie between them, Kashmir is claimed by Pakistan and India, and there are campaigns to free Tibet from Chinese rule. The most hotly disputed land, however, lies in the Middle East.

Israel

In 1948, territory from the Arab country Palestine was given to Israel to form an independent Jewish state. Tensions between Israel and the Arab populations both inside Israel's borders and in neighbouring countries have led to its borders being redrawn many times. Control of the West Bank, Gaza Strip, and Golan Heights is still a major issue.

GOLAN HEIGHTS

WEST BANK

GAZA STRIP

ISRAEL

SINAI PENINSULA

Golan and Sinai

After the Six-Day War in 1967, Israel made huge territorial gains by capturing the West Bank and the Gaza Strip from Palestine, the Golan Heights from Syria, and the Sinai Peninsula from Egypt. Israel has since given the Sinai Peninsula back to Egypt, but has been negotiating with its neighbours over the rest in return for peace and security.

West Bank and Gaza Strip

Israel still holds considerable influence over both the Gaza Strip and the West Bank, though it partially withdrew from the Gaza Strip in 2006. The Palestine Liberation Organization (PLO) and Israel are negotiating a peace deal that may eventually see Israel fully withdraw from both territories.

East and West Germany

Berlin

EAST GERMANY

WEST GERMANY

After World War II, Germany was split into two separate countries, East and West Germany. Its old capital city, Berlin, was also divided by a high wall border from 1961. The communist government in East Germany restricted movement between the two, and people risked death if they attempted to cross into the West. In 1989, the East German government fell, leading both East and West Germans to pull down the Berlin Wall and reunite Germany.

ISRAEL AND ITS NEIGHBOURS

- Israel in 1948
- Gained in 1967 and returned to Egypt in 1982
- Gained in 1967 and still disputed

There were **90** independent countries in **1950**

Biggest and Smallest

Although size isn't everything, Russia is by far the world's largest country by land mass. The Vatican City, a mere speck on the globe by comparison, would fit into it a staggering 38,859,640 times. However, some of the smallest countries have a profile much larger than their tiny stature. Monaco is extremely wealthy, with high living standards and celebrity residents, while the Vatican City is the centre of the Catholic Church and attracts thousands of visitors a year.

 Monaco occupies just 5 sq km (2 sq miles) of the Cote D'Azur in southern France. A constitutional monarchy, it is a luxury resort and playground for the rich.

 More than 32,000 people enjoy the benefits of life in Monaco. Living standards are high and unemployment is low.

Tourism and banking are big businesses. Monaco has many casinos and hosts a Grand Prix.

The country boasts an underground railway, helicopter service, bus routes, and two ports.

 A group of nine low-lying islands in the South Pacific, Tuvalu covers 26 sq km (10 sq miles). Rising sea levels caused by climate change could see it wiped out.

 The 11,000 islanders live a simple life. Access to drinking water is a big issue as there are no rivers or streams.

Tuna-fishing licences, postage stamps, and foreign aid are the main sources of revenue.

 The capital, Funafuti, has an airport, but islanders get around by bicycle and motorbike.

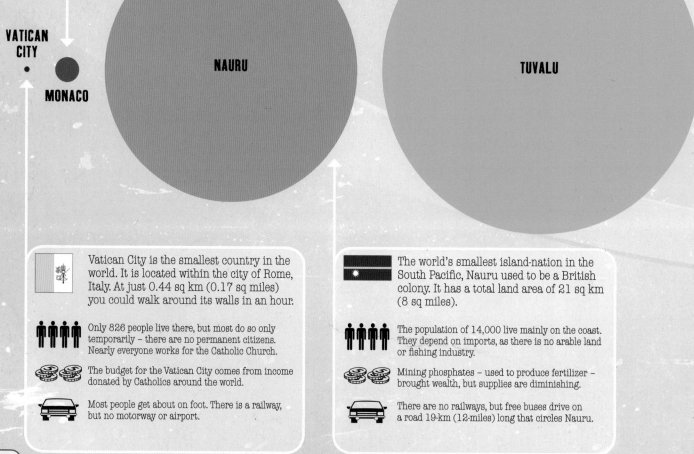

VATICAN CITY

MONACO

NAURU

TUVALU

 Vatican City is the smallest country in the world. It is located within the city of Rome, Italy. At just 0.44 sq km (0.17 sq miles) you could walk around its walls in an hour.

Only 826 people live there, but most do so only temporarily – there are no permanent citizens. Nearly everyone works for the Catholic Church.

The budget for the Vatican City comes from income donated by Catholics around the world.

Most people get about on foot. There is a railway, but no motorway or airport.

The world's smallest island-nation in the South Pacific, Nauru used to be a British colony. It has a total land area of 21 sq km (8 sq miles).

The population of 14,000 live mainly on the coast. They depend on imports, as there is no arable land or fishing industry.

Mining phosphates – used to produce fertilizer – brought wealth, but supplies are diminishing.

There are no railways, but free buses drive on a road 19-km (12-miles) long that circles Nauru.

With only **134 members**, the tiny force of the Swiss Guards protects the Pope and acts as the military of the Vatican

Almost double the size of the next largest country, Russia covers one-eighth of Earth's land surface and spans 11 time zones.

Boasting more than 142 million people, Russia has one of the world's most diverse societies, with 160 ethnic groups living there.

As of 2009, Russia is the largest exporter of natural gas and the world's largest oil producer.

With 154,000 km (95,690 miles) of rail, Russians previously preferred trains to cars, though this is slowly changing.

Ever increasing circles

The green circles are sized in proportion to each country's geographic area. Russia's circle would be far too big to fit on the page. It would be 280,299 times the size of San Marino's circle.

Completely surrounded by Italy, San Marino is the world's oldest sovereign state. One-tenth the size of New York City, it is only 60 sq km (23 sq miles).

Living standards are high for the 30,324 living there. Inhabitants enjoy close links with Italy and low unemployment.

Tourism, postage stamps, coins, wine, and ceramics are major sources of income.

A superhighway runs through San Marino, stretching for 220 km (137 miles).

SAN MARINO

Founded in **301 CE**, San Marino is the world's oldest republic

If Russia's circle was to scale, it would be so big that the actual Vatican City could fit inside it **52.8 times**

RUSSIA

Theocracies

Literally meaning the "rule of God", theocracy is one of the oldest forms of government. In Iran and the Maldives, government officials believe they are guided by God, and their legal systems are based on Islamic religious law.

Military governments

This type of government is often the result of a military coup, when the armed forces claim power through force and dictate policy. A military government will either rule openly, as in Mauritania and Myanmar (Burma), or through a civilian front.

Communist governments

Only one party – the Communist Party – is allowed to exist under communist rule, and it controls all aspects of life and government. Its core belief is that wealth should be spread equally. The number of communist countries has declined in recent years.

Transitional governments

When a government collapses due to war or the sudden death of a leader, it leaves a vacuum. An emergency government is sometimes put in place to help maintain security and stability when time is needed to set up elections or decide who will rule next.

THEOCRACIES

MILITARY GOVERNMENTS

COMMUNIST GOVERNMENTS

TRANSITIONAL GOVERNMENTS

Myanmar (Burma)

Myanmar is ruled by a military junta who have absolute power; dissenting voices and opposition are suppressed. The National League for Democracy Party won a landslide victory of votes in 1990, but the military will not allow them to govern.

Eritrea

Following independence from Ethiopia in 1993, a provisional government in Eritrea was established, composed entirely of the People's Front for Democracy and Justice. General elections have yet to be held.

Political
Systems

In the modern world there are two main types of political system: Western-style democracy and single-party rule, which is mostly found in the developing world. In Western-style democracy great emphasis is placed on individual freedom, and governments are answerable to the people who elect them. Single-party rulers and dictators are all-powerful and strive to preserve their established order. However, this style of government is fragile, and these countries are increasingly veering towards democracy.

Country categorization

Each figure shown here represents a UN-recognized country that adheres to a particular political system. Theocracies are the rarest form of government, while democracy dominates the world's stage. Democracy appears in many forms: established, transitional, and those with constitutional monarchies.

Vatican City

The Vatican City is one of only a few theocracies – the head of the Catholic Church, the Pope, is head of state and holds supreme power. While the Vatican City participates within the UN under the name "Holy See", it is different from other countries as it does not serve its citizens. It is purely an administrative base for the Church, with a population made up of church officials.

Democracy

Established throughout Europe, North America, and Oceania, democracy today is becoming more widely adopted, with 62% of the world's countries now being electoral democracies. Within a democracy, the elected body must represent the views of the majority, and "one person, one vote" is a fundamental principle.

Absolute monarchies

Monarchs who are head of state and government are called absolute monarchs. Usually a king or queen, they often stay in power for decades, until they die or choose to abdicate. Saudi Arabia and Bhutan are well-established absolute monarchies.

One-party republics

Sometimes called a one-party state, these are countries where only one political party is allowed to run and people with opposing views cannot be elected. It is often associated with Communism, but is also present in former colonies where one party dominated following independence.

Transitional democracies

Countries in Latin America and parts of the developing world, formerly controlled by single parties or military dictatorships, are gradually becoming democracies but are not yet fully established. Well-established democracies, like the USA, generally support a country's transition to democracy.

Established democracies

The majority of countries in the world are democratic, based on the belief that every citizen over a certain age is entitled to vote and participate in politics. Democracy thrives in those countries that willingly permit free speech and dissent, as in most Western countries.

ABSOLUTE MONARCHIES

ONE-PARTY REPUBLICS

TRANSITIONAL DEMOCRACIES

ESTABLISHED DEMOCRACIES

Saudi Arabia

One of the wealthiest nations in the Middle East, Saudi Arabia was named after its ruling Al Saud family, which has been in power since the 18th century. Political parties and opposition to the system are banned.

Belarus

Since 1994, Belarus has been ruled by President Alexander Lukashenko. He suppresses all opposition and is regarded as "Europe's last dictator".

Paraguay

The death of Paraguay's dictator, Alfredo Stroessner, in 2006 was followed by an historic election win for the Patriotic Alliance for Change, led by Fernando Lugo in 2008. The country is only just emerging as a democracy.

Constitutional monarchies within democracies

Many countries that were once ruled by autocratic kings and queens went on to establish democracies. Nations such as Spain and the United Kingdom regard their monarch as a symbolic head, but real power lies in the hands of the people. These countries are shaded purple within the two democracy categories.

United States of America

The USA is a federal country, which means that political power is shared between the national government, based in Washington, D.C., and the individual governments of each state. The American political system is based on the Constitution, drafted in 1787. The central word cloud, shown here within the outline of the USA, gives the most-occuring and significant words from this key document, describing the fundamental principles of American democracy and governance.

Constitution

The USA has a written constitution, which is the highest law in the land. The Consitution is a set of rules that state the basic rights and duties of its citizens, and stipulates how the government works, and how the President is elected.

States

The USA is split into 50 provinces, called states. Each has a great deal of authority, with its own executive, laws, and courts. The head of the executive is called the Governor. States largely manage their own taxation, criminal justice, education, and health systems.

★ ALABAMA   ★ MONTANA
★ ALASKA   ★ NEBRASKA
  ARIZONA   ★ NEVADA
★ ARKANSAS   NEW HAMPSHIRE
  CALIFORNIA   ★ NEW JERSEY
★ COLORADO   NEW MEXICO
  CONNECTICUT   ★ NEW YORK
★ DELAWARE   ★ NORTH CAROLINA
  FLORIDA   ★ NORTH DAKOTA
★ GEORGIA   OHIO
  HAWAII   ★ OKLAHOMA
★ IDAHO   ★ OREGON
  ILLINOIS   ★ PENNSYLVANIA
★ INDIANA   RHODE ISLAND
  IOWA   ★ SOUTH CAROLINA
  KANSAS   SOUTH DAKOTA
  KENTUCKY   ★ TENNESSEE
★ LOUISIANA   TEXAS
  MAINE   ★ UTAH
★ MARYLAND   VERMONT
  MASSACHUSETTS   ★ VIRGINIA
★ MICHIGAN   WASHINGTON
  MINNESOTA   ★ WEST VIRGINIA
★ MISSISSIPPI   WISCONSIN
  MISSOURI   ★ WYOMING

President

The President heads the executive branch and is responsible for running the entire machinery of government. He or she is elected for four years, limited to two terms of office. As military commander-in-chief he or she has considerable power and influence around the world.

Government structure

Power in the US is spread over three "branches": the executive (under the President), the legislature (or Congress), and the judiciary (headed by the Supreme Court). This ensures that no single institution has too much power.

Legislative branch
(The Congress is made up of the Senate and House of Representatives)

Executive branch
(The president and vice president are elected for four-year terms)

Judicial branch
(The Supreme Court interprets the Constitution)

Law

The Supreme Court is the highest court in the United States. Its nine judges, who are appointed by the President, deal with interpreting the Constitution. Below them are several Courts of Appeal and District Courts. Together, these three levels of court represent the federal judicial system.

Amendment

It is difficult to change, or amend, the Constitution. There have only been 27 amendments in its history. The first 10 changes are called the Bill of Rights; a set of basic rules that protect the liberties of the individual.

1 **Right** of free speech, religion, and press

2 **Right** to keep and bear arms

3 **Conditions** of quarters for soldiers

4 **Search and seizure** to be regulated

5 **Provisions** concerning prosecutions

6 **Right** to a speedy trial and witnesses

7 **Right** to a trial by jury

8 **Protection** from excessive bail, and from cruel punishment

9 **Rule** of construction of the Constitution

10 **Right** of the states under Constitution

Congress

The law-making branch of the US Government is Congress, which is made up of two houses: the House of Representatives, in which each state is represented by a number of electees proportional to its population, and the Senate, which is made up of two senators from each state. Both houses have equal powers and work through committees that play a major role in steering though bills, which may become laws.

Votes

Every American citizen over the age of 18 has the right to vote. Whilst members of Congress are elected directly by the people, the President is chosen by an Electoral College, as stipulated in the Constitution: voters in each state vote for delegates who, in turn, form an Electoral College. The Electoral College then chooses the President. Most delegates support a candidate from either the Republican or Democratic Party.

China

The People's Republic of China is one of the most powerful countries in the world. China's government is dominated by the Communist Party, which controls all aspects of official activity. In the past, China's economy was run centrally by the government, with most industries government-owned and international trade discouraged. In the last 30 years, however, the economy has become more driven by private ownership, and it is expanding at a rapid rate.

The red flag

For 2,000 years, China was ruled by emperors, but in the 1800s power was lost to Western nations. In 1949, after a long civil war, a communist ruling government was formed. The large yellow star on China's flag represents the Communist Party of China (CPC). The smaller stars are said to represent the unity of the Chinese people, while the colour red symbolizes revolution.

How China is governed

The Chinese people vote in direct elections at a local level. Local assemblies then choose delegates for regional and provincial assemblies. The number of candidates who may stand is limited, and only parties approved by the CPC are permitted. The chief assembly is the National People's Congress (NPC), which meets each year in Beijng. The Congress is dominated by CPC members and officials.

Communist Party of China
The CPC has about 74 million members. It does not govern China directly, but it effectively controls government appointments and sets the agenda for the NPC.

Politburo (Political Bureau)
The Politburo is the most important committee of the CPC. It makes important policy decisions and many of its members also hold posts in the the NPC and the State Council.

Leadership

The Chinese head of state is the President, appointed by the NPC to serve a maximum of two 5-year terms. The President nominates a Premier to the chair of the State Council, and this must also be approved by the NPC. In practice, the Politburo influences both appointments. The head of the Politburo – called the General Secretary – is the country's real leader and will typically take the job of President.

Military affairs commission
This 11-person committee is responsible for China's military policy. Its chairman, elected by the NPC, is commander-in-chief of the armed forces.

National People's Congress
The NPC is the chief body of government in China. It currently has 2,987 members, of whom 888 belong to non-CPC parties. It works closely with the CPC.

State Council
This is the cabinet of the Chinese goverment, with about 50 members. It meets monthly and manages the state budget. Many of its members are also important officials of the CPC.

People's Liberation Army
China has the biggest armed forces in the world. They number about 3 million, including both conscripts and full-time soldiers.

Courts of law
Laws passed by the NPC are implemented by law courts. The highest court is the Supreme People's Court, based in Beijing.

Provinces and cities
The State Council appoints officials to oversee regional and city government. Below them are local-level governments and party organizations.

Media and censorship

China has a huge and rapidly growing press and broadcasting media. Until about 20 years ago, almost all media outlets were state-owned, but independent outlets have since developed. Many news organizations are still censored by the CPC, and access to certain websites is prevented.

Work and wealth

China is developing its industrial power at an astonishing rate. This has created environmental and social problems, as people from rural communities pour into cities to seek work in the factories. There is a growing middle class in the cities, but poverty is still widespread throughout the country.

About **1 in 5** people in the world live in China – the population in 2009 numbered about

1,338,600,000

INDUSTRY 49%

AGRICULTURE 11%

SERVICES 40%

CONTRIBUTION OF SECTORS TO CHINA'S GDP

What makes the money?

China has the world's biggest workforce, and 40% of people work on the land. However, it is industry that creates the biggest share of China's wealth. Factories, mines, and mills, using cheap labour, produce coal, iron, steel, concrete, textiles, toys, electronics, and cars. Much of the output is exported, but China is aiming to increase its home market for consumer goods. The growing services sector contributes the next greatest proportion of China's wealth.

How many children?

With the population exploding in numbers, the government in 1979 decided that each couple should be allowed to bear just one child. The policy was not applied in many rural areas and regions, and today affects about one-third of China's couples nationwide.

The wider world

China invests billions of dollars in foreign countries, especially in Africa and the Middle East, where its interests include energy, oil, gold, non-precious metals, diamonds, timber, and car production. China is also the largest overseas holder of bonds issued by the US government.

China's minority groups number **114 million** people. Around the world, only 10 independent nations have larger populations.

Many peoples

The government recognizes 56 "nationalities", differentiated by ethnic origin, language, religion, or culture. The Han is by far the largest group. There have been political disputes between the Han government and many of China's minorities, including the Tibetans in the southwest of the country, and the Uighurs in the far west.

Han Chinese 91.5%

The Han Chinese is the largest ethnic group in the world and dominates every aspect of life in China. They speak several varieties and dialects of the Chinese language and live in the most densely populated regions of China.

Other nationalities 8.5%

China's 55 other nationalities, which include the Zhuang, Uighurs, Mongolians, Tibetans, Miao, and Dai, make up a small percentage of the population compared to the Han. However, altogether they occupy more than half of China's land area.

North Atlantic Treaty Organization

Set up in 1994, NATO is the world's most powerful regional defence alliance. Member countries from North America and Europe work together to protect each other's safety.

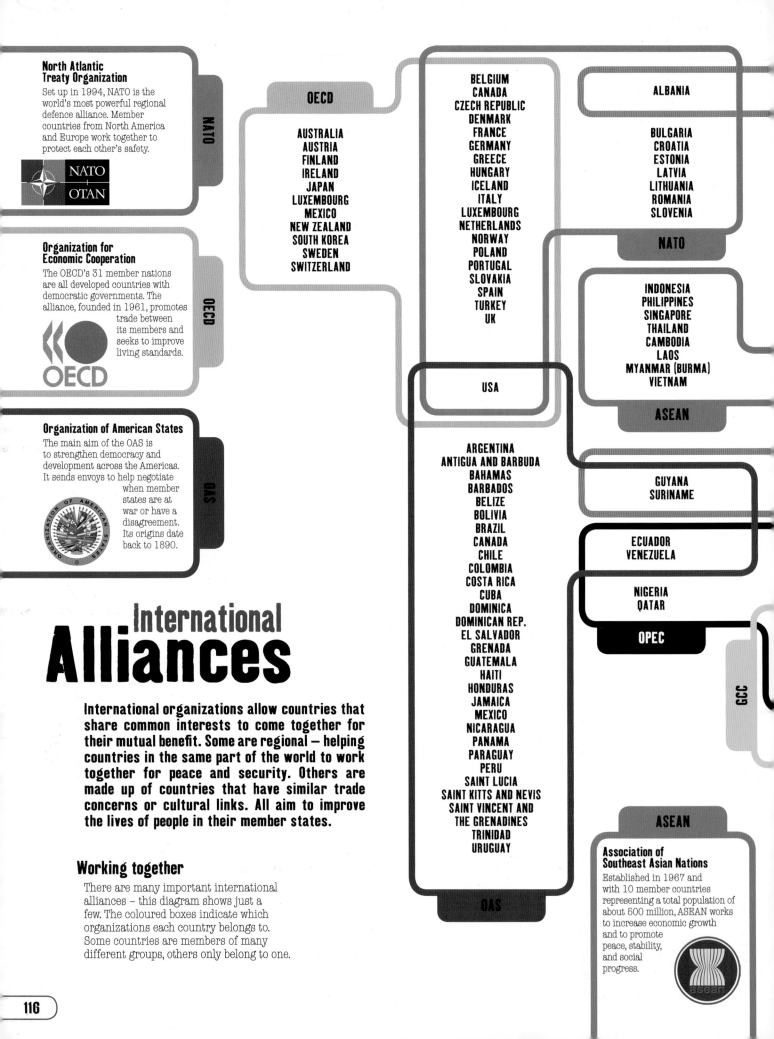

NATO

Organization for Economic Cooperation

The OECD's 31 member nations are all developed countries with democratic governments. The alliance, founded in 1961, promotes trade between its members and seeks to improve living standards.

OECD

OECD

Organization of American States

The main aim of the OAS is to strengthen democracy and development across the Americas. It sends envoys to help negotiate when member states are at war or have a disagreement. Its origins date back to 1890.

OAS

International Alliances

International organizations allow countries that share common interests to come together for their mutual benefit. Some are regional – helping countries in the same part of the world to work together for peace and security. Others are made up of countries that have similar trade concerns or cultural links. All aim to improve the lives of people in their member states.

Working together

There are many important international alliances – this diagram shows just a few. The coloured boxes indicate which organizations each country belongs to. Some countries are members of many different groups, others only belong to one.

OECD

AUSTRALIA
AUSTRIA
FINLAND
IRELAND
JAPAN
LUXEMBOURG
MEXICO
NEW ZEALAND
SOUTH KOREA
SWEDEN
SWITZERLAND

BELGIUM
CANADA
CZECH REPUBLIC
DENMARK
FRANCE
GERMANY
GREECE
HUNGARY
ICELAND
ITALY
LUXEMBOURG
NETHERLANDS
NORWAY
POLAND
PORTUGAL
SLOVAKIA
SPAIN
TURKEY
UK

ALBANIA

BULGARIA
CROATIA
ESTONIA
LATVIA
LITHUANIA
ROMANIA
SLOVENIA

NATO

USA

INDONESIA
PHILIPPINES
SINGAPORE
THAILAND
CAMBODIA
LAOS
MYANMAR (BURMA)
VIETNAM

ASEAN

ARGENTINA
ANTIGUA AND BARBUDA
BAHAMAS
BARBADOS
BELIZE
BOLIVIA
BRAZIL
CANADA
CHILE
COLOMBIA
COSTA RICA
CUBA
DOMINICA
DOMINICAN REP.
EL SALVADOR
GRENADA
GUATEMALA
HAITI
HONDURAS
JAMAICA
MEXICO
NICARAGUA
PANAMA
PARAGUAY
PERU
SAINT LUCIA
SAINT KITTS AND NEVIS
SAINT VINCENT AND THE GRENADINES
TRINIDAD
URUGUAY

GUYANA
SURINAME

ECUADOR
VENEZUELA

NIGERIA
QATAR

OPEC

GCC

OAS

ASEAN

Association of Southeast Asian Nations

Established in 1967 and with 10 member countries representing a total population of about 500 million, ASEAN works to increase economic growth and to promote peace, stability, and social progress.

OIC

AFGHANISTAN
ALBANIA
AZERBAIJAN
BAHRAIN
BANGLADESH
BENIN
BURKINA FASO
CAMEROON
GUINEA
GUYANA
INDONESIA
KAZAKHSTAN
KYRGYZSTAN
MALDIVES
PAKISTAN
SURINAME
SYRIA
TAJIKISTAN
TURKEY
TURKMENISTAN
UZBEKISTAN

BRUNEI
MALAYSIA

IRAN

ALGERIA
IRAQ

KUWAIT
QATAR
SAUDI ARABIA
UNITED ARAB EMIRATES

BAHRAIN
OMAN

JORDAN
LEBANON
MOROCCO
PALESTINE
YEMEN

COMOROS
DJIBOUTI
EGYPT
THE SUDAN

MAURITANIA
SOMALIA

AFRICAN UNION

ALGERIA
ANGOLA
BOTSWANA
BURKINA FASO
CAMEROON
CAPE VERDE
CENTRAL AFRICAN REP.
CONGO
EQUATORIAL GUINEA
GHANA
KENYA
LESOTHO
LIBERIA
NAMIBIA
WESTERN SAHARA
SÃO TOMÉ AND PRÍNCIPE
SOUTH AFRICA
SWAZILAND
TANZANIA

BENIN
CHAD
COTE D'IVOIRE
GABON
GAMBIA
GUINEA-BISSAU
MALI
MOZAMBIQUE
NIGER
NIGERIA
SENEGAL
SIERRA LEONE
TOGO
TUNISIA
UGANDA

LIBYA

ANGOLA

TUNISIA

SYRIA

LAS

BURUNDI
DEM. REP. CONGO
ETHIOPIA
MALAWI
MAURITIUS
RWANDA
SEYCHELLES
ZAMBIA
ZIMBABWE

Organization of the Islamic Conference

Established in 1969, the OIC has 57 member countries spread over four continents. They aim to protect the interests of the Muslim world and promote Islamic values.

OIC

African Union

The AU was formed in 2002 and has 52 members. Its key aims are to promote unity, eradicate poverty, and reduce conflict across Africa. The AU has sent peacekeeping missions to African nations in conflict.

AU

The United Nations is **192** the biggest international alliance with member countries

League of Arab States

Also known as the Arab League, this organization brings together Arabic-speaking nations. Since its foundation in 1945, it has played an important role in settling conflicts. Its headquarters are in Cairo.

LAS

Organization of Petroleum Exporting Countries

The world's main oil-producing nations set up OPEC in 1960. Today, 12 member states work to ensure there is a constant supply of oil at a stable price.

OPEC

Gulf Cooperation Council

Six states bordering the Persian Gulf united to form the GCC in 1981. The alliance guards against threats from neighbouring states and aims to strengthen links between members.

GCC

WTO (World Trade Organization)

Most of the countries listed here – as well as many others – are members of this influential alliance. The WTO regulates 97% of the world's trade, bringing together member states to agree trading rules and helping to negotiate international disputes over trade.

European Union

The European Union (EU) is a political and economic community made up of 27 member states. Set up after World War II by six original states, it aimed to bring peace and raise living standards for its members. Since then, the EU has become a major world power, and grown to more than 500 million inhabitants. It operates as a kind of super-government, presenting a united front for its member states on matters of concern such as agriculture, trade, and defence.

European Commission

The budget and the day-to-day running of the EU is managed by the Commission. One member is appointed from each state, and they meet regularly to propose new laws to the Council and Parliament. Once these laws are passed, the Commission manages their implementation.

EU Parliament

The EU mainly governs through its Parliament, Commission, and Council. The Parliament votes on how much money the EU should spend, and, with the Council, decides which suggestions from the Commission should be made into new laws. The Parliament's 751 members are elected every five years by EU citizens. The number of seats per state is decided on population size – as the most populous country, Germany has the most seats.

SPAIN

UK

ITALY

FRANCE

GERMANY

EU MEMBERS

This diagram shows how many seats each state has in the Parliament and when they joined the EU.

1 seat	1973	1986	2004
1957	1981	1995	2007

EU POLICIES

Aid donations

Currently the world's biggest aid donor, EU aid to developing countries will reach £4.5 billion ($7.2 billion) by 2012. The EU is aiming to halve extreme poverty, improve education, and halt the spread of AIDS around the world by 2015.

Fisheries

The EU fishing industry is the third largest in the world, and is regulated by the EU fisheries policy. This aims to protect the fish stocks from overfishing, but also to ensure a fair standard of living for those working in the fishing industry.

Free movement

Every EU citizen is allowed to live and work in any EU member state. The trade of goods and services are also completely free in the union, a move that has increased trade between member states and helped to make it the world's biggest trading group.

Council of the European Union

This is where the EU's big decisions are made by the ministers of each member state. Every six months, a different member state hosts the Council's sessions and sets the agenda.

How to be a member

Before a country can join the Union, it must prove that it has a secure democratic government, respect for human rights, a stable economy, and be capable of implementing EU laws. Croatia, Macedonia, and Turkey are currently being considered for membership.

Non-members

Not all European countries are, or wish to be, EU members. Non-EU members include Iceland, Liechtenstein, Norway, and Switzerland. Some dislike the idea of giving too much power to the EU, whilst others feel that EU policies would damage their economy.

POLAND

ROMANIA

NETHERLANDS

BELGIUM

CZECH REPUBLIC

GREECE

HUNGARY

PORTUGAL

SWEDEN

AUSTRIA

BULGARIA

FINLAND

DENMARK

SLOVAKIA

IRELAND

SLOVENIA

CYPRUS

LUXEMBOURG

LITHUANIA

MALTA

LATVIA

ESTONIA

16 countries use the euro, the official currency of the European Union

Total income
£108.8 billion
($175.8 billion)

Total expenditure
£104.6 billion
($169 billion)

EUROPEAN UNION

Amount paid in
£17 billion
($27.3.9 billion)

Amount received
£10 billion
($16.2 billion)

GERMANY

Amount paid in
£1.8 billion
($3 billion)

Amount received
£7.6 billion
($12.3 billion)

GREECE

Money matters

Every member state pays part of its wealth into a central fund, and receives something back. Those that are more prosperous, such as Germany, pay in more than they get back, whereas others like Greece take more than they put in. This money is used for building projects such as roads, schools, and hospitals.

United Nations

The United Nations (UN) is the world's largest international organization and nearly every country is a member. The UN and its many agencies work to improve welfare around the globe. The organization has two main bodies – the General Assembly and the Security Council. The UN's administrative service, known as the Secretariat, is headed by the Secretary-General, who also speaks as head of the UN.

General Assembly
The General Assembly is the main governing body of the UN, comprising all 192 Member States. Each state has one vote, regardless of its size. The Assembly's main function is to discuss the world's difficult problems and to make recommendations on them.

The **flags** of all
192 Member States, arranged alphabetically, fly in front of the UN Headquarters in New York, USA, and the UN European Headquarters in Geneva, Switzerland

International Monetary Fund (IMF)
The IMF offers loans to poorer countries and tries to stabilize the world economy. By working with its members from 186 governments, it aims to promote economic growth, better living standards, international trade, and higher employment.

Specialized agencies
The UN works with many organizations to combat world problems, such as poverty, disease, and environmental issues. Featured here are 15 of the specialized organizations that are linked to the UN via special agreements.

United Nations Educational, Scientific and Cultural Organization (UNESCO)
UNESCO aims to improve education throughout the world by building schools and training teachers, especially in poorer areas. It promotes international cooperation and stresses mutual respect and shared knowledge.

World Meteorological Organization (WMO)
Everyone can be affected by changes in the Earth's atmosphere, weather, climate, oceans, and water resources. The WMO plays a powerful role in helping to protect humanity from natural disasters by sharing data, technology, training, and research.

International Labour Organization (ILO)
The ILO pushes for better working conditions, and equal opportunities, and promotes human rights around the world.

Food and Agricultural Organization (FAO)
The FAO was set up to address the problem of hunger around the globe. It advises countries on growing crops, fishing, forestry, modernizing production, and good nutrition.

International Fund for Agriculture Development (IFAD)
Like many UN agencies, IFAD seeks to eliminate poverty in poorer countries. It works not only to improve food production, but also helps people in rural areas access technology and financial services.

World Intellectual Property Organization (WIPO)
WIPO helps protect work with patents, copyright, and trademarks. It ensures that writers, designers, artists, and inventors benefit from their creative ideas.

The UN was founded with **51** Member States, and the 192nd Member State was Montenegro, which joined in 2006

International Civil Aviation Organization (ICAO)
Safety in the air has improved as a result of the ICAO's focus on standards for pilots, the condition of planes, and the orderly growth of the aviation industry. It is also concerned about the pollution that aircraft can cause to the air.

World Health Organization (WHO)
The WHO aims to improve health in poorer countries. In the 1960s, its actions made the deadly smallpox disease extinct. It is now concerned with the effects of climate change, HIV/AIDS, and malaria.

World Bank
This UN agency offers financial assistance and investment to developing countries. Its aim is to eliminate poverty and help countries sustain themselves so they will be less dependent on foreign aid.

United Nations Industrial Development Organization (UNIDO)
The promotion of industry in underdeveloped countries is handled by UNIDO. It shares knowledge and expertise, provides technical support, and sets up projects to help poorer people earn a living.

Universal Postal Union (UPU)
This non-political organization works within the UN to offer advice and develop technical services for post worldwide. It works closely with other agencies, such as environment groups, to improve global mail distribution.

International Telecommunication Union (ITU)
The ITU deals with information and technology issues. It tries to coordinate satellite use, build better infrastructure in poorer countries, and improve communications across the globe.

World Tourism Organization (WTO)
Developing countries are encouraged to improve access for tourists and reap the benefits. The WTO helps to minimize the environmental and social impacts with a Code of Ethics for Tourists.

International Maritime Organization (IMO)
World experts meet under the IMO to help prevent shipping disasters, improve ship design, and discuss the prevention of pollution by the maritime industry. Its motto is "Safe, Secure, and Efficient Shipping on Clean Oceans".

The budget for the UN's main operations, paid by member countries, is

$2.5 billion
a year

Security Council
The Security Council deals with peacekeeping around the world. It aims to settle disputes without force, but can send in peacekeeping troops to prevent more violence. The Council has 15 members – 10 are elected by the General Assembly and five (France, China, UK, USA, and the Russian Federation) are permanent.

Some 40,000 people work in the Secretariat.

UN Day is celebrated on 24 October.

Peacekeeping troops are called The Blue Helmets.

The UN has its own post office and postage stamps.

There are 17 current peacekeeping missions.

Since 1948, there have been 63 UN peacekeeping missions.

The UN was established in 1945, just after World War II.

$1.00 · International Day of Non-Violence · UN 2009

International Day of Peace
World Peace Day, observed on 21 September, is a global event established by the UN to promote peace across the world.

Tension in Turkey

Turkey is home to the Kurds – a large ethnic group who have no country of their own. Since 1984, the radical Kurdistan Workers' Party (PKK) have launched a violent campaign against the Turkish government for an ethnic homeland in the southeast. Turkey is now seeking a peaceful solution.

2

In World War I, civilians made up fewer than **5%** of all casualties, but they account for **75%** now

1

3

Unrest in the Middle East

The ongoing conflict between Israel and Palestine is one of most complicated in the world. Both sides believe the other side is occupying land that rightly belongs to them. Palestinian groups have used suicide bombings against Israel, and Israel has responded with rocket attacks and blockades. Many civilians are caught up in the violence.

WARS AND CONFLICTS

Open warfare

These tanks show where battles between two states are happening, with a death toll of at least 1,000 soliders in a year.

Civil war

Civil wars can last for decades and devastate millions of lives, with civilians suffering most.

Terrorist attacks

A single violent attack carried out by an individual or group is called a terrorist attack.

Turmoil in Sudan

Sudan has been torn apart by decades of civil war, mainly over the control of oil reserves in the south of the country. All of the factions, government or guerrilla, have committed atrocities. The death toll is unknown but is believed to be in the millions, with about 4 million people forced to flee their homes.

Hostilities in the Congo

Fighting over rich mineral resources in the Democratic Republic of Congo has pitted government forces against rebels. Neighbouring countries have taken sides, with Angola, Namibia, and Zimbabwe supporting the government and Uganda and Rwanda helping the rebels. Despite a peace deal, parts of the country are still volatile.

War and Terrorism

The world is a much safer place today than it was in the 20th century. Open warfare between two or more nations is rare, but war has not gone away. Conflicts within countries – known as civil wars – are more common these days, with parts of Africa in particular torn apart by this kind of strife. Border disputes and tension between different ethnic or religious groups cause misery to millions, and terrorist attacks, a new type of warfare, are increasing.

Fighting around the world

This map shows current conflicts, and a selection of the most significant civil wars and terrorist attacks. There are many smaller conflicts, particularly in Africa and South America, that are not shown.

Trouble in Georgia

After months of border clashes between Georgia and the breakaway region of South Ossetia, Georgia launched a major military offensive in late 2008. Russia intervened on the side of South Ossetia. Although a ceasefire was soon called, tension in the region remains high.

4

5

6

War in Afghanistan

Following the 11 September 2001 terrorist attacks in New York City, a military coalition led by the US toppled Afghanistan's Taliban regime for sheltering Osama bin Ladin, the mastermind behind the atrocity. A new government was elected, but the war has dragged on due to Taliban resistance.

Philippines fighting

The south Philippines has a long history of conflict. Followers of Islam, called Moros, have been fighting for an independent nation. Peace negotiations began in 2008, though skirmishes and terrorist attacks continue. More than 2 million civilians have been displaced.

7

War in Iraq

US-led forces invaded Iraq in 2003, in the belief that the country was hiding "weapons of mass destruction". The invasion of Iraq led to an occupation and the execution of President Saddam Hussein, but the fighting has not stopped, and attacks by suicide bombers and rebels are weekly occurrences in the country.

8

Somali conflict

Years of fighting between rival groups has led to a humanitarian crisis in Somalia. One-third of the population is dependant on food aid and thousands have been displaced. Warlords have forced many children to become soldiers.

Terrorist attacks

1. New York City, US
On 11 September 2001, Islamic extremists launched attacks on the World Trade Centre. It led to the USA declaring a "War on Terror".

2. London, UK
In July 2005, 56 people were killed when four bombs exploded on London's transport system, set off by Islamic suicide bombers.

3. Madrid, Spain
Commuter trains were bombed in Madrid, in protest against Spanish troops serving in the US-led invasion of Iraq. The total killed reached 191.

4. Beslan, Russia
Militants took over a school in Russia and held teachers and children hostage in 2004. More than 300 died before the standoff ended.

5. Moscow, Russia
Rebels took 700 theatre-goers hostage in 2002. The rebels were eventually killed, but more than 100 hostages also died.

6. Sharm el-Sheik, Egypt
Egypt suffered the worst terrorist attack in its history when 64 people died in three bomb attacks in Sharm el-Sheik, a holiday resort.

7. Mumbai, India
A series of attacks launched in 2008 in India's financial hub of Mumbai saw more than 170 killed in shootings and grenade attacks.

8. Bali, Indonesia
In October 2002, terrorists bombed the tourist district of Bali. Killing 202 people, it was the worst attack in Indonesian history.

Lockheed Martin

This aerospace manufacturer, based in the US, is the world's largest defence contractor. It supplies a whole index of countries with spy planes and fighter jets, including the F-16 Falcon.

THE US HAS 732 F-16 FALCONS IN ACTIVE DUTY

F-16 FALCON

PRICE TAG: $18.8 MILLION EACH

Explosive Budgets

War, unfortunately, plays a major part in our world history, both past and in the making. The increase in threat from terrorism following the attack on the World Trade Centre and the war in Iraq, has seen military spending soar, particularly in the United States. They invest more on defence than the next 45 highest spending countries combined, while strong economic growth in nations such as China and India has enabled those countries to dramatically increase the size of their military. The total amount spent on defence for each person in the world is today estimated to be $217 per year.

Spending per person

Countries in the Middle East, such as Oman and Kuwait, have increased their wealth due to oil. With this, their military spending has also grown. But topping the charts of spending on defence per person in the country is Israel.

ISRAEL	USA	OMAN	SINGAPORE	KUWAIT	SAUDI ARABIA	NORWAY	GREECE	UK	FRANCE
$2,300	$1,950	$1,650	$1,625	$1,600	$1,500	$1,250	$1,125	$1,075	$1,050

In 2008, the total world spending on defence reached **$1.46 trillion**

Total spending

The biggest spender by far in this well-funded moneypot is the United States. With a budget of $607 billion, it accounts for almost 50% of world military spending.

USA $607 billion

SOUTH KOREA	$24.2 BILLION
INDIA	$30 BILLION
SAUDI ARABIA	$38.2 BILLION
ITALY	$40.6 BILLION
JAPAN	$46.3 BILLION
GERMANY	$46.8 BILLION
RUSSIA	$58.6 BILLION
UK	$65.3 BILLION
FRANCE	$65.7 BILLION
CHINA	$84.9 BILLION

GLOCK-19 PISTOL
$400 EACH

Hand-held guns
It is estimated that there are more than 650 million guns circulating the globe, claiming a devastating 1,000 lives a day.

ARSENAL-SHIPKA SUBMACHINE GUN
PRICE TAG: $300 EACH

Aircraft carriers
The average cost of an aircraft carrier is an impressive $4 billion. More than 20 of these warships roam the oceans, from 10 different countries.

PRICE TAG: $4 BILLION EACH

US aircraft carriers are named after presidents

AIRCRAFT CARRIER

NORTH KOREA 2
PAKISTAN 60
INDIA 65
ISRAEL 80
UK 160
CHINA 186
FRANCE 300

106,000
Worldwide, there are approximately tanks in existence

STEYER AUG-A1 ASSAULT RIFLE
PRICE TAG: $2,245 EACH

JAVELIN ANTI-TANK MISSILE PRICE TAG: $125,000 EACH

TANK
PRICE TAG: UP TO $4 MILLION EACH

KALASHNIKOV AK-47 ASSAULT RIFLE
PRICE TAG: $140 EACH

Ammunition
Many countries have a domestic arms industry to make cartridges, landmines, and grenades for their army. However, illegal trade in small arms is a widespread problem.

AN ESTIMATED 2,702 NUCLEAR WARHEADS
USA

The nuclear family
The number of countries with nuclear warheads is slowly growing. The amount that each country is thought to have is shown here, with an estimated 8,392 nuclear warheads worldwide.

AN ESTIMATED 4,834 NUCLEAR WARHEADS
RUSSIA

A 1-MEGATON BOMB LEVELS EVERYTHING WITHIN A 3.2 KM (2 MILE) RADIUS

HAND GRENADE
PRICE TAG: UP TO $25 EACH

Refugees

Those forced to leave their country of origin due to war, violence, or persecution are known as refugees. They are different from migrants, who leave their homes in search of a better life. Most refugees flee to neighbouring countries, though some seek sanctuary further afield.

9,146,000

Where do they come from?

In 2008, more than one-third of the world's 15.2 million refugees came from just five countries: Afghanistan, Iraq, Colombia, Sudan, and Somalia. These countries have seen intense conflict in recent years. In countries divided by war, people may get caught up in the fighting or persecuted due to their race or religion.

COUNTRIES OF ORIGIN

- Other
- Afghanistan
- Iraq
- Somalia
- The Sudan
- Colombia

2,800,000

REST OF THE WORLD 465,200

32,700   43,900

Asylum seekers

When a person seeks refuge in a foreign country, they must prove that their life was at risk before they are recognized as a refugee and allowed to stay. While the host country decides, the person is known as an asylum seeker. Asylum seekers have limited rights and are often held in specially built detention centres.

SOUTH AFRICA	USA	FRANCE	SUDAN	CANADA
207,000	49,600	35,400	35,000	34,800

Host countries

Sometimes it can be difficult to tell whether a person is genuinely in danger or has come to a new country to find work. It can take host countries months to decide whether or not someone will be allowed to stay. Asylum seekers whose claims are rejected are usually deported (sent home).

Far from Home

Every year armed conflict, natural disasters, and the threat of persecution force millions of people to leave their homes and seek protection elsewhere. Some are homeless within their own countries, while others seek refuge abroad. Most countries take in refugees, but the process of being recognized as a refugee can be strict and not everyone is allowed to stay. Those whose cases have not been decided yet are called asylum seekers.

Causes

In 2008, the number of people around the world who were uprooted from their homes stood at 42 million. There are many reasons why people flee their homes, but most do so because they no longer feel safe.

 In some parts of the world, people who speak out against their government are threatened with violence.

Some people's homes are destroyed by natural disasters, such as earthquakes or hurricanes.

War is one of the main reasons why people flee their homes.

Communities may be uprooted when the effects of climate change make their land uninhabitable.

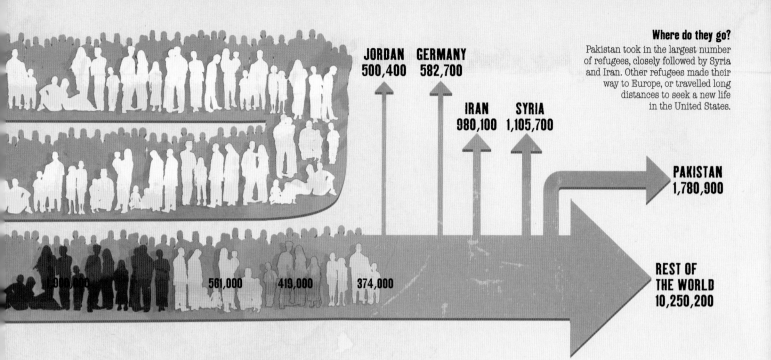

Where do they go?

Pakistan took in the largest number of refugees, closely followed by Syria and Iran. Other refugees made their way to Europe, or travelled long distances to seek a new life in the United States.

JORDAN
500,400

GERMANY
582,700

IRAN
980,100

SYRIA
1,105,700

PAKISTAN
1,780,900

REST OF THE WORLD
10,250,200

561,000   419,000   374,000

51,900   62,700

118,500

465,000

COUNTRIES OF ORIGIN

- Other
- South Africa
- Eritrea
- Somalia
- Iraq
- Dem. Rep. Congo

Where do they come from?

At the end of 2008 the number of undecided asylum cases was 827,000. Many of these cases involved people who had turned to neighbouring countries for asylum. Every day, 400 Zimbabweans cross the Limpopo River, which forms the border with South Africa, to escape political instability and poverty.

Internally Displaced Persons

Those who are forced to flee their homes but remain within their country of origin are known as Internally Displaced Persons (IDPs). At the end of 2008, there were 26 million such people living in vast temporary camps, often suffering extreme hardship.

IDP populations

Countries with ongoing internal conflict have the largest IDP populations, with many located in Africa. Countries with growing IDP numbers include Afghanistan, Pakistan, Sri Lanka, and Yemen.

REST OF THE WORLD
17,196,000

COLOMBIA
3,000,000

IRAQ
2,600,000

DEM. REP. CONGO
1,500,000

SOMALIA
1,300,000

KENYA
404,000

IDP POPULATIONS

Human Rights

The Universal Declaration of Human Rights was adopted by the United Nations in 1948. it set out the rights and freedoms that every human being is entitled to, such as a right to education, free speech, and self-expression. Despite international support of the declaration, abuses of the rights it contains still take place around the world. There are agencies that try to monitor human rights violations, but many abuses take place in secret, sometimes with powerful governments behind them.

Massacre of journalists

On 23 November 2009, a convoy carrying candidates for a mayoral election in the Philippine province of Maguindanao was brutally massacred. Of the 57 people killed, 34 were journalists – the worst single attack on journalists ever recorded. The Philippines is one of the most dangerous countries for journalists, second only to Iraq.

Discrimination in education

Roma people in Europe have often faced discrimination at work and school. Discrimination in education is unlawful, but Roma children receive inferior schooling in the Czech Republic. Almost one-third of Roma children are placed in schools designed for children with mild mental disabilities, or in segregated schools that provide second-rate education.

Extraordinary rendition

The alleged practice of extraordinary rendition involves the abduction and transportation of suspected terrorists to places such as Jordan, Egypt, and Guantanamo in Cuba, where they are interrogated and imprisoned on behalf of the UK and US governments. About 3,000 people are alleged to have been treated in this way.

Silenced in Myanmar (Burma)

Since the military seized power in Myanmar in 1988, the pro-democracy campaigner Aung San Suu Kyi has criticized its grip on the country. She was elected Prime Minister in 1990, but instead the military placed her under house arrest, where she has been for 14 of the last 20 years, often in solitary confinement. There are currently 2,000 political prisoners in the country.

Girls in Equatorial Guinea

In Equatorial Guinea, thousands of girls as young as eight are forced to work up to 18 hours a day as domestic workers. The majority are not paid, and are frequently beaten by their employers, refused education, and receive no help when they are sick.

Religious expression in France

France has traditionally kept religion and everyday life separate. In 2004, the wearing of religious symbols in schools was banned. This has led to tensions over the right of the individual to express themselves and observe the traditions of a religious faith. The issue is particularly heated around the question of whether Muslim schoolgirls should wear a hijab (headscarf).

CHILD LABOUR
(percentage of children aged 5–14 engaged in work)

- No data
- Less than 10%
- 10–29%
- 30% or more

Child labour

There are an estimated 158 million children aged between five and 14 working worldwide. This map shows that many exploited children live in developing countries, such as the 75 million children working in India. Child labour accounts for 22% of the workforce in Asia, and 32% in Africa.

FREEDOM OF RELIGION

BY COUNTRY

- High or very high — 32%
- Low — 48%
- Moderate — 20%

BY WORLD POPULATION

- High or very high — 70%
- Low — 15%
- Moderate — 15%

Freedom of religion

Though it has decreased in recent decades, religious prejudice remains a serious problem around the world. Some countries discriminate against any religion that does not correspond to their official faith. About 70% of the global population live in countries that experience high levels of religious intolerance.

Press freedom

The freedom of the press to express ideas and report truthfully plays a key role in society. It contributes to greater accountability and good governance, yet press freedom is in decline in almost every part of the world. Only 17% of the world's citizens currently enjoy a totally free press.

PRESS FREEDOM

BY COUNTRY

- Free — 36%
- Partly free — 31%
- Not free — 33%

BY WORLD POPULATION

- Free — 17%
- Partly free — 41%
- Not free — 42%

Crime

Large urban populations and abundant consumer goods are all linked with high crime rates – if there are more things to steal, more things will be stolen. These are common features of life in Europe, where robbery, violent crime, and drug trafficking have increased by about 4% in the last decade. The willingness of victims to report crimes also influences statistics: it is estimated that 30–60% of crimes in European countries are never recorded.

Reporting crimes

The figures shown on this map reflect the number of crimes that were reported to the police, rather than the number of crimes that were committed. Across Europe, 28% of robberies are not reported to the police because victims feel the police can't or won't do anything.

Crime hotspots

The most common crimes vary widely between countries. UK households are the most burgled in Europe, and the UK also has the highest number of assaults. Lithuania is the murder capital of Europe, with one homicide per 12,500 people. You are most likely to get robbed in Spain but to have your car stolen in Switzerland, where there is one car theft per 130 people every year.

CRIME HOTSPOTS
(Rankings are based on the number of crimes reported per 100,000 people over a two-year period, 2005-2006)

- Murder
- Assault
- Robbery
- Car theft
- Burglary
- Fraud
- Drug offences
- Kidnapping

NORTHERN IRELAND 1,407
1,543
8
868
SCOTLAND
1,406
ENGLAND & WALES
1,207
184
DENMARK 1,318
NORWAY 623
SWEDEN 736
566
569
ESTONIA 7
LATVIA 6
LITHUANIA 8
SWITZERLAND 771
MONACO 1,808
6
GERMANY 1,203
AUSTRIA 1,198
ITALY 477
TURKEY 14
PORTUGAL 198
SPAIN 1,079

The global trade in illegal drugs is worth an estimated **£250 billion** ($400 billion) a year

Crime rate in Europe

More Swedish victims report crimes to the police than in any other European country. A huge proportion of these are property crimes, such as burglary, robbery, and car theft. Interestingly, fear of crime in Europe does not reflect actual crime rates. The populations of Poland and Greece feel least safe on the streets after dark, while Finns, facing Europe's third highest crime rates, are the least fearful.

TOTAL RECORDED NUMBER OF CRIMES PER 100,000 PEOPLE
Top ten European countries

FINLAND 9,825

SWEDEN 13,493

AUSTRIA 7,079

GERMANY 7,628

NETHERLANDS 7,439

NORTHERN IRELAND 7,144

ENGLAND & WALES 10,399

SCOTLAND 8,200

80% of crime victims surveyed in Finland, Denmark, and Austria were pleased with the response of their police force

Organized crime

Criminal gangs make a business operation out of their illegal activity, organizing themselves centrally to make even bigger profits from activities like drug trafficking and fraud. Easier travel between countries in the European Union means this "organized crime" is thriving in Europe.

Police personnel

Police officers are the frontline in protecting the public against crime. More than 1% of Kuwait's population works for the police and crime rates are low. But more police doesn't always mean less crime. Despite its large police force, Mexico has some of the world's highest murder and kidnapping rates.

NUMBER OF POLICE OFFICERS PER 100,000 PEOPLE

KUWAIT 1,116

CYPRUS 618

ITALY 558

MEXICO 491

US 326

AUSTRALIA 304

UK 257

S. AFRICA 224

JAPAN 182

MOROCCO 141

Punishment

When someone commits a crime, most countries have strict laws outlining how they should be punished. Justice differs around the world – some countries focus on rehabilitating offenders, while others have zero-tolerance policies for even the slightest of crimes. In some countries, criminals pay with their lives for their misdemeanours.

Under lock and key

Imprisonment is one of the most common forms of punishment for serious crimes. The number of people in prison around the world – either serving their sentence or awaiting trial – currently stands at 9.8 million. Just three countries account for nearly half of all the world's prisoners – the USA has 2.29 million prisoners, China has 1.57 million, and Russia 890,000.

USA 23%

RUSSIA 9%

REST OF THE WORLD 52%

CHINA 16%

For every 100,000 people in the world, **145** are serving time in prison

Laying down the law

Punishments are determined by the laws of the land. In some countries, an elected parliament makes the laws. In others, the law is dictated by the ruling group. Some countries also observe religious law, which uses a code of ethics that followers believe has been laid down by god.

In China, there are

850,000

people in "administrative detention" (held without trial for security reasons). Including them would bring the world prisoner number to 10.6 million.

Prisoners in the USA

The US has the world's highest prison population. The cost of holding their 2.29 million inmates clocks in at about £44 billion ($68 billion) a year. More than 70% of inmates in US prisons are non-white, compared to only 20% in the population at large.

Death penalty

There are 56 countries that use the death penalty for murder and other violent crimes. China has the most death sentences, with more than 1,700 executions estimated to have taken place in 2009. Iraq, Pakistan, and Algeria each average 200 annually. The US stands out as the only Western democracy that uses the death penalty.

Paying the price

Commit the same crime in different countries and the punishment varies dramatically. Theft, for example, can result in a public caning in Singapore. In the UK, you might get community service. According to Sharia (Islamic) law, a thief can have a hand cut off.

The longest prison sentence ever was handed down in Alabama to murderer Dudley Wayne Kyzer in 1981. He was sentenced to

10,000 years
in prison.

Prison population rate

The number of prisoners per 100,000 people shows the different levels of imprisonment around the world. The US tops the list with 756 prisoners for every 100,000 people, whilst India has only 33. Prison rates are growing in many parts of the world, especially in developing countries.

AUSTRALIA 129

ENGLAND 153

MOROCCO 167

RUSSIA 629

USA 756

NUMBER OF PRISONERS PER 100,000 PEOPLE

Surveillance

Once the domain of secret agents, surveillance – the monitoring of people's activities – now affects nearly everyone. Our use of the internet, mobile phones, and smart cards has increased dramatically in recent years. Along with the increasing number of CCTV cameras, almost every move we make is monitored. Officials say surveillance is a crucial tool in combating terrorism and controlling crime, but there are growing concerns about invasions of privacy and restrictions on personal freedom.

Google-eyed

Google's recent "Earth" and "Street View" projects have caused some controversy. These ambitious undertakings have mapped countries from the air, and photographed towns and cities at street level, with the information then freely available to view online. Some people have complained about having images of their private property posted online without their permission.

Tangled in the net

Every time you use the Internet, it is possible for your browsing to be seen by a third party. Emails can be intercepted on any of the servers they are stored on before they reach their final destination. Photographs posted online can be seen by anyone online unless you are extremely careful. Social networking sites and search engines gather data about their users' interests, and sell it on to companies, who use it to target their advertising.

NUMBER OF CCTV CAMERAS

Camera action

Closed Circuit Television (CCTV) cameras are put in many public places primarily to record criminal activity, but in doing this they essentially monitor us all. It is estimated that the UK has nearly 5 million cameras, making it the most watched society in the world. The UK spent 78% of its crime prevention budget in the 1990s on CCTV cameras, but studies have shown that only one crime is solved for every 1,000 cameras.

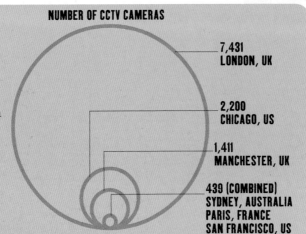

7,431
LONDON, UK

2,200
CHICAGO, US

1,411
MANCHESTER, UK

439 (COMBINED)
SYDNEY, AUSTRALIA
PARIS, FRANCE
SAN FRANCISCO, US

Smart cards

Many bank, travel, and identity cards are "smart" – this means they record when and where the card is used. In the wrong hands, the data collected can be used to build up a picture of the user's life, such as preferred products or journeys made. This kind of technology will become more common in the future. The majority of the one billion bank cards in circulation are in the developed world, but the developing world is catching up.

US: 5 CARDS PER PERSON

BANK CARDS PER PERSON

BRAZIL: 2.5 PEOPLE PER CARD

RUSSIA: 5.9 PEOPLE PER CARD

INDIA: 64.6 PEOPLE PER CARD

CHINA: 33 PEOPLE PER CARD

96% of travel on London's transport system is paid for by smart card

Biometric scanning

Physical traits, such as facial features and fingerprints, can be used to confirm your identity. Biometric scanners check your details against a database, but there are fears that data could be gathered and used without an individual's consent. Some airports have already installed full-body "naked" scanners that allow airport security staff to see under your clothes, which many feel is a massive invasion of privacy.

MAST ONE

MAST TWO

MOBILE PHONE TRIANGULATION

MAST THREE

LOCATION OF PHONE

Phone tracking

Each mobile phone can be used to work out the position of its user, meaning that it is possible to track more than three billion people who have one. Mobile phone triangulation measures the distance the mobile signal travels from the phone to the three nearest phone masts. The phone (and its user) will be in the area where the signals overlap (triangulate).

Big Business

Multinational companies have operations in multiple countries; they tend to have a strong presence in their home nation, but have expanded across the globe, often to take advantage of cheaper labour. Investment from multinationals leads to jobs and training for people in the host country, but the power and influence multinationals have over foreign governments, as well as the low wages they sometimes pay, make them the target of intense criticism.

Powerhouses

The number of multinational companies in the world exceeds 60,000. With their subsidiaries spread across the globe, the top 500 account for almost a quarter of world trade and earn vast profits, rivalling the GDPs of entire countries. The top 10 companies by revenue are shown here. The most successful company, US retail giant Wal-Mart, earned a whopping $401 billion in 2008 – more than the GDP of Sweden.

1. **WAL-**
2. **EXXON**
3. **ROYAL DU**
4. **BRITISH P**
5. **TOYOTA MOTORS**
7. **iNG GROUP**
9. **GENERAL MOTORS**

Biggest employers

Multinationals employ more than 200 million people worldwide. Wal-Mart, whose vast empire comprises a chain of retail stores, is the largest employer with 2.1 million people on its books. Four of the top 10 employers are businesses run by the Chinese state.

Biggest employers
(with country of origin)

1 **Wal-mart Stores (US)** 2,055,000
2 **State Grid (China)** 1,486,000
3 **China National Petroleum** 1,117,345
4 **US Postal Service** 785,929
5 **Sinopec (China)** 634,011
6 **Hon Hai Precision Industries (Taiwan)** 650,000
7 **Carrefour (France)** 490,042
8 **Deutsche Poste** 475,100
9 **Agricultural Bank of China** 447,519
10 **Gazprom (Russia)** 436,096

1 in 8

Americans have worked in a McDonalds restaurant at some point in their lives

Global reach of select multinationals

Some multinationals have expanded their businesses to foreign countries more than others. The transnationality index helps us to measure this by looking at the number of assets, employment figures, and sales for each company outside its home country. Wal-Mart may be top of the list of multinationals for revenue, but its transnationality percentage is just 41%. By comparison, Vodafone has a global reach of 85%.

WAL-MART (US) 41%	EXXON MOBIL (US) 68%	ROYAL DUTCH SHELL (UK AND NETHERLANDS) 70%	BRITISH PETROLEUM (UK) 80%

The most profitable sectors

Certain industries perform consistently better than others when it comes to profitability. Oil and gas, which provide energy for transport, heating, and industrial production, generate huge revenues for companies such as Royal Dutch Shell and British Petroleum. Other essential services, such as medicine, hospitality, and information technology (IT), are also high earners.

MINING AND CRUDE OIL PRODUCTION 19.8%

PHARMACEUTICALS 17.7%

BEVERAGES 11.9%

HOUSEHOLD AND PERSONAL PRODUCTS 11.8%

COMMUNICATIONS EQUIPMENT 11.6%

MOST PROFITABLE INDUSTRIES BY REVENUE

MART
MOBIL
CH SHELL
TROLEUM
6. **CHEVRON**
8. **TOTAL**
10. **CONOCOPHILLIPS**

Developing countries
(amount invested, 2008, figures given in millions)
1 **Hong Kong** $1,184
2 **Brazil** $328.4
3 **China** $327
4 **Russia** $334
5 **Mexico** $266.7
6 **Singapore** $249.7
7 **Turkey** $145.5
8 **South Korea** $119.6
9 **Chile** $105.6
10 **South Africa** $93.5

Foreign investment
Multinational businesses take advantage of new technology to relocate to developing countries where costs are lower. The 10 countries listed here receive 70% of the foreign investment that is made by multinationals in developing countries.

Multi-branding

The name of a successful company in one country does not necessarily translate well in another. Wal-Mart's discount department stores are emblazoned with more than 60 different names around the world.

Hello, my name is

WAL-MART, also known as: ASDA, BEST PRICE, BOMPREÇO, SEIYU, TODO DIA, WALMEX, WOOLCO...

If all the sandwiches Subway make in a year were placed end to end, they would wrap around Earth **6 times**

TOYOTA (JAPAN) 45%	COCA-COLA (US) 78%	NESTLE (SWITZERLAND) 83%	VODAFONE (UK) 85%	SONY (JAPAN) 59%	TOTAL (FRANCE) 74%

Making Money

Money enables us to pay for goods and services. When something is sold at a higher price than it cost to buy or make, the difference between the two is profit. Businesses try to make a profit to pay their workers and meet their costs. Money deposited in bank accounts is used by banks to provide credit (loans). The banks make a profit by charging fees for their services and interest on money borrowed from them.

All the money in the world
Cash is just one part of all the money in the world. There is also money held in bank accounts and money tied up in assets (property) and investments (things bought in the hope that they will become more valuable).

Cash in circulation
The total value of all the banknotes and coins in circulation around the world is a hefty $4 trillion.

Bank accounts
The money held in bank accounts worldwide amounts to $45 trillion – 11 times more than all the cash in circulation.

Assets
All the land, buildings, company shares, and other assets comes have an estimated value of an astonishing $290 trillion.

Global currencies

Nearly three-quarters of all the cash in circulation belongs to just four currencies. These are the European euro, US dollar, Japanese yen, and Chinese yuan – the currencies of the world's biggest economies. The US dollar is one of the longest running currencies, dating from 1792. Only the British pound sterling is older, dating back to 1694.

Every year the United States Mint makes around
14–20 billion
new coins

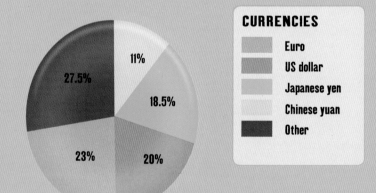

11%

27.5%

18.5%

23%

20%

CURRENCIES
- Euro
- US dollar
- Japanese yen
- Chinese yuan
- Other

How banking works

When people deposit money in banks, the banks use it to make more money by loaning most of it to other people and to businesses and charging interest (a regular fee).

CUSTOMER MAKES A DEPOSIT

BANK 1

BANK 1 KEEPS 10% AND LOANS THE REST TO BANK 2

BANK 2

BANK 2 KEEPS 10% AND LOANS THE REST TO BANK 3

BANK 2 PAYS BANK 1 INTEREST ON THE LOAN

BANK 3 PAYS BANK 2 INTEREST ON THE LOAN

Life expectancies of dollar bills

Banknotes and coins wear out and have to be replaced. Notes with smaller values are used more often than larger ones and so have to be replaced more frequently. Banknotes wear out faster than coins. A dollar bill lasts about 22 months, compared to a dollar coin's life expectancy of at least 30 years.

Safe money

Security features, including watermarks and metal thread, make banknotes harder to forge. Some countries have even introduced banknotes made of plastic instead of paper.

1.8 YEARS $1

2 YEARS $20

4.6 YEARS $50

HOW LONG A US BANKNOTE REMAINS IN CIRCULATION

JAPAN 765.2
SWITZERLAND 1,040.1
CHINA 1,054
FRANCE 2,435.4
ITALY 2,451.8
IMF 3,005.3
GERMANY 3407.6
UNITED STATES 8,133.5

THE BIGGEST GOLD RESERVES (TONNES)

Who's got the gold?

Governments and central (national) banks keep gold as part of a nation's wealth. Some large international financial organizations, such as the International Monetary Fund (IMF), have gold reserves, too. Approximately 28,000 tonnes – about 19% of all the gold that has ever been mined – is held in this way. The USA's gold reserve is the biggest of any country.

All the gold

If all 120,000–140,000 tonnes of gold ever mined was melted down it would fill fewer than three Olympic-sized swimming pools. Together, it would be worth about $1.8 trillion.

One tonne of gold is worth around **$35 million**

BANK 3 KEEPS 10% AND LOANS THE REST TO OTHER BANKS

BANK 3

BANK 3 PAYS BANK 2 INTEREST ON THE LOAN

Hyperinflation

Inflation is the increase in the cost of goods and services in a country from year to year. It is a normal part of a country's economy. However, if prices rise too quickly, a unit of currency is able to buy fewer and fewer things and the value of the currency goes down. This is called hyperinflation. Throughout the 2000s Zimbabwe suffered from record hyperinflation. At its peak, prices were doubling every 24 hours and the Zimbabwean dollar became worthless.

Wealth of Nations

The wealth of a nation can be measured in several ways. The most common is to calculate the total value of all the goods and services that a country produces in a year. This is called the Gross Domestic Product (GDP) and is usually measured using the world's most common currency – the US dollar.

USA: $14.4 trillion

Topping the world rankings is the USA. Much of its great wealth – around 68% – is generated by services such as banking, though the USA is also the world's biggest manufacturer and has plenty of natural resources.

Japan: $4.9 trillion

Japan may be a tiny country with few natural resources, but it makes second place due to its advanced manufacturing sector and successful policies on industry in the wake of World War II.

China: $4.3 trillion

China is the world's fastest growing economy. By 2050, it is expected to leapfrog Japan and the US to become the world's largest. It has booming manufacturing businesses and is the largest exporter of goods.

Germany: $3.7 trillion.

Once called the "sick man of Europe", Germany now has Europe's biggest economy and is the world's second largest exporter. Employment rates are steady, and manufacturing and engineering are strong.

The EU has a total GDP of

$18.4 trillion

World's largest economies

The dollar sign shown here represents world GDP – the total wealth generated in the world in one year. It has been broken up proportionately to reveal which countries generate the most of the world's wealth. The top six account for more than half the world's GDP.

UNITED STATES

JAPAN

CHINA

GERMANY

FRANCE

France: $2.9 trillion

Agriculture plays a large role in France, and the country is among the world's foremost wine producers. Its leading industries produce metals, machinery, and chemicals.

UK: $2.7 trillion

The UK is an important financial centre, making a significant portion of its income from international banking. It also benefits from large coal, natural gas, and oil reserves.

LUXEMBOURG
$113,044

NORWAY
$94,387

THE REST OF THE WORLD

Total world GDP is about
$60 trillion

Rest of the world: $27 trillion

All the other countries in the world account for the remaining 46% of world GDP. In many developing countries, GDP stays flat from year to year. But in some countries the picture is changing, Brazil, India, and Mexico have all seen their economies boom in recent years.

GDP per capita

When the size of a country's population is considered, a new picture of wealth emerges. Dividing GDP by the number of people in a country shows how much wealth is being generated per person, and produces a very different list of top countries. GDP per capita doesn't represent how much the average person earns, but it can be used to compare rough standards of living.

Income groups

The World Bank groups countries into income brackets according to their GDP per capita. High-income countries are sometimes referred to as developed nations, and those in the other three bands as developing nations. This map shows how countries in the same bracket tend to be grouped together geographically, with many high-income countries in the Northern Hemisphere, and the world's poorest located in sub-Saharan Africa.

INCOME KEY

High income $11,906 or more

Middle income $3,856–$11,905

Low income $976–$3,855

Very low income $975 or less

QATAR $93,204

SWITZERLAND $68,433

DENMARK $62,097

Haves and have nots

The world's riches are shared out very unequally. Of all the household wealth – the money and assets owned by individuals – a massive 40% is owned by just 1% of the world's people. At the other end of the scale, half the world's population share just 1% of household wealth between them. The wealthy few live mostly in the industrialized nations of Europe, North America, and Asia.

The average American has $144,000 in assets, whereas in India the average is just $1,100 per person

WEALTH DISTRIBUTION

$ 1% of world wealth

👤 1% of world population

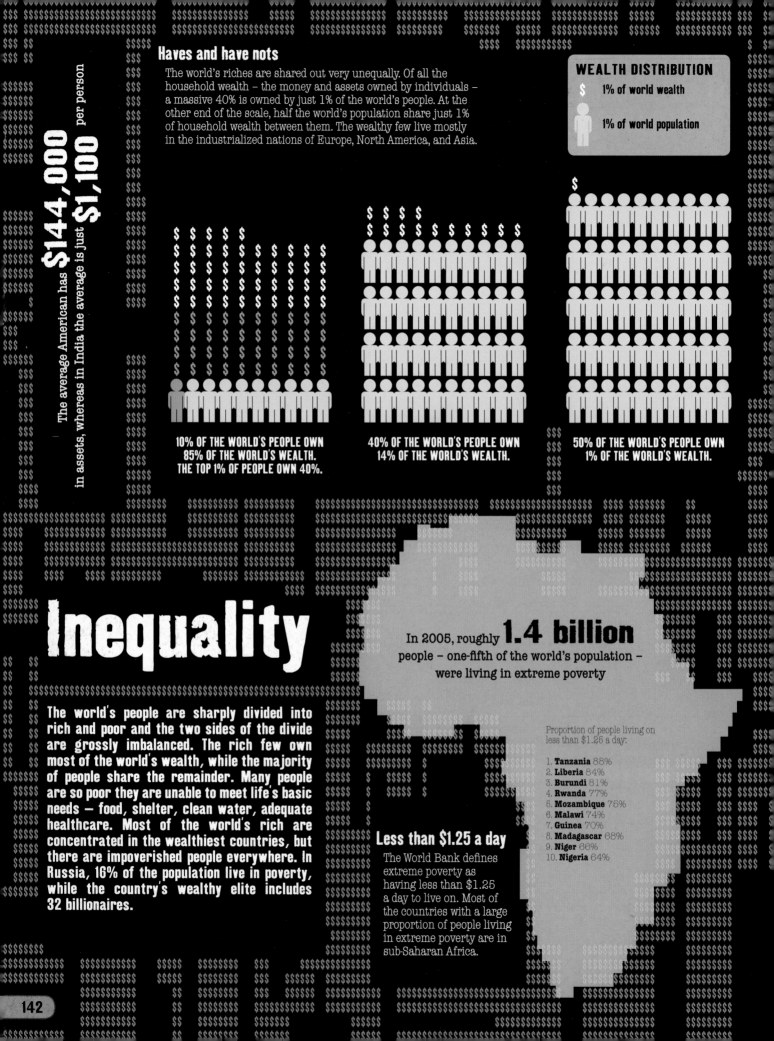

10% OF THE WORLD'S PEOPLE OWN 85% OF THE WORLD'S WEALTH. THE TOP 1% OF PEOPLE OWN 40%.

40% OF THE WORLD'S PEOPLE OWN 14% OF THE WORLD'S WEALTH.

50% OF THE WORLD'S PEOPLE OWN 1% OF THE WORLD'S WEALTH.

Inequality

The world's people are sharply divided into rich and poor and the two sides of the divide are grossly imbalanced. The rich few own most of the world's wealth, while the majority of people share the remainder. Many people are so poor they are unable to meet life's basic needs — food, shelter, clean water, adequate healthcare. Most of the world's rich are concentrated in the wealthiest countries, but there are impoverished people everywhere. In Russia, 16% of the population live in poverty, while the country's wealthy elite includes 32 billionaires.

In 2005, roughly 1.4 billion people – one-fifth of the world's population – were living in extreme poverty

Proportion of people living on less than $1.25 a day:

1. **Tanzania** 88%
2. **Liberia** 84%
3. **Burundi** 81%
4. **Rwanda** 77%
5. **Mozambique** 75%
6. **Malawi** 74%
7. **Guinea** 70%
8. **Madagascar** 68%
9. **Niger** 66%
10. **Nigeria** 64%

Less than $1.25 a day

The World Bank defines extreme poverty as having less than $1.25 a day to live on. Most of the countries with a large proportion of people living in extreme poverty are in sub-Saharan Africa.

Who wants to be a billionaire?

Forget being a millionaire – today's wealthiest people are measured by their billions. There are currently an estimated 793 dollar billionaires in the world. Nearly half of them come from the US. Together, the fortunes of the world's billionaires amounts to about $2.4 trillion.

World's richest people

Some individuals are so rich that their personal fortunes rival the wealth of entire nations. Bill Gates – the world's richest man for 14 of the last 15 years – made his billions founding the computer giant Microsoft. His wealth is greater than the GDP of roughly half of the world's countries.

COUNTRY
- USA
- Other countries
- Germany
- China and Hong Kong
- Russia
- UK
- India
- Japan
- Canada

1 Carlos Slim Helú, Mexico: $53.5 billion
This telecommunications tycoon controls 90% of Mexico's landlines. Beat Gates to the top spot in 2010.

2 Bill Gates, USA: $53 billion
Founded Microsoft in 1975. Like many of the world's richest people, he now dedicates himself to charity work.

3 Warren Buffett, USA: $47 billion
Made his fortune investing in companies. Known as the "sage of Omaha" for his successful track record.

4 Mukesh Ambani, India: $29 billion
Owns a 48% stake in Reliance Industries, a multibillion-dollar oil company founded by his father in 1966.

5 Lakshmi Mittal, UK: $28.7 billion
Indian-born, UK-based steel magnate who built his business up from scratch, buying steel plants all over the world.

Wealth within countries

How rich or poor a country is as a whole is not the end of the story. Within countries, wealth is often spread out unequally. In the poorest countries, wealth tends to be concentrated in the hands of the few, though many richer countries also have a wide wealth gap. These diagrams show how a country's income is spread out.

POPULATION BANDS

POOREST 20%	SECOND 20%	THIRD 20%	FOURTH 20%	RICHEST 20%

% OF INCOME

1.4 3.0 5.4 11.5%   78.7%

Namibia
Namibia has one of the most uneven distributions of wealth in the world. The richest 20% of the population enjoy a high standard of living, with access to more than 70% of the country's assets. The remaining 80% of people share just 30% of the wealth. Nearly one-third of Namibia's 1.8 million people live on $1 a day or less.

POPULATION BANDS

POOREST 20%	SECOND 20%	THIRD 20%	FOURTH 20%	RICHEST 20%

% OF INCOME

10.6% 14.2% 17.6% 22%   35.7%

Japan
In Japan, there is a narrower gap between the rich and the poor. The country has one of the world's most even distributions of wealth, but even so the richest 20% of people there still possess more than a third of the country's wealth, leaving the poorest with just under 11%.

Balancing the Books

Two big issues seriously affect a country's chance of beating poverty. One is the amount of aid they get, the other is the amount of debt they owe. International aid helps developing countries to build up their economies so they will prosper independently in the future. However, many countries receiving aid have to pay huge amounts of interest to rich nations on money they have borrowed, which can outweigh the amount of aid received. Some people have called for the debts of the poorest nations to be cancelled.

A helping hand
Many rich countries give financial help to the world's poorer nations. Aid is given freely and does not have to be paid back. Humanitarian aid is used to respond to emergencies, such as natural disasters, whereas development aid is money intended to help countries out of poverty in the long term. More than 90% of development aid comes from the 22 members of OECD (Organization for Economic Cooperation and Development). The countries that give the most in relation to their population size are all European.

NORWAY $600
LUXEMBOURG $570
DENMARK $388
SWEDEN $371
NETHERLANDS $313
SWITZERLAND $237

DEVELOPMENT AID ($ DONATED PER CAPITA, 2005)

Indebted countries
A country's debt burden can be measured by the debt to export ratio – this shows how much of what the country earns from their exports must be spent on debt repayments or interest charges. Many heavily indebted countries are those that have suffered long-term political unrest. Brazil, the most indebted nation, is an emerging economy – a developing country that is growing rapidly. It has greatly reduced its debt burden in recent years.

COLOMBIA 35.3%
URUGUAY 38.2%
TURKEY 38.2%
LATVIA 39.1%

DEBT SERVICE AS A PERCENTAGE OF EXPORT EARNINGS

Latvia's external debt is **$42 billion**

SOLOMON ISLANDS 60%

LIBERIA 54%

BURUNDI 48%

AID AS A PERCENTAGE OF INCOME

MICRONESIA 41%

AFGHANISTAN 36%

PALESTINIAN TERRITORIES 35%

Dependent on aid

Official Development Assistance (ODA) consists of loans, grants, and technical aid given to developing countries to help them grow. Some countries depend very heavily on this. When measured as a percentage of total income, the Solomon Islands and Liberia – countries that have been torn apart by civil unrest – are the most reliant on international aid. Aid makes up more than half of both countries' total income.

The US donated **$27.6 billion** of development aid in 2005 – $93 per US citizen

BRAZIL 44.7%

KAZAKHSTAN 42.2%

BURUNDI 41.5%

IRAQ $8.7 BILLION

NIGERIA $6.5 BILLION

Top recipients

Development aid is given to countries according to who needs it most. Sometimes attention is focused on restructuring war zones – Iraq was the top recipient in 2007, and Afghanistan received the third highest aid package. Nigeria, the second highest, is the most populous country in Africa, and, despite its rich oil reserves, one of the poorest. China, as a large developing nation, receives development aid, but due to its rapid industrial growth and desire to be seen as a major world power, it is also a top donor.

AMOUNT OF DEVELOPMENT AID RECEIVED IN 2007

CAMEROON $1.8 BILLION

INDONESIA $2.2 BILLION

CHINA $2.4 BILLION

AFGHANISTAN $2.7 BILLION

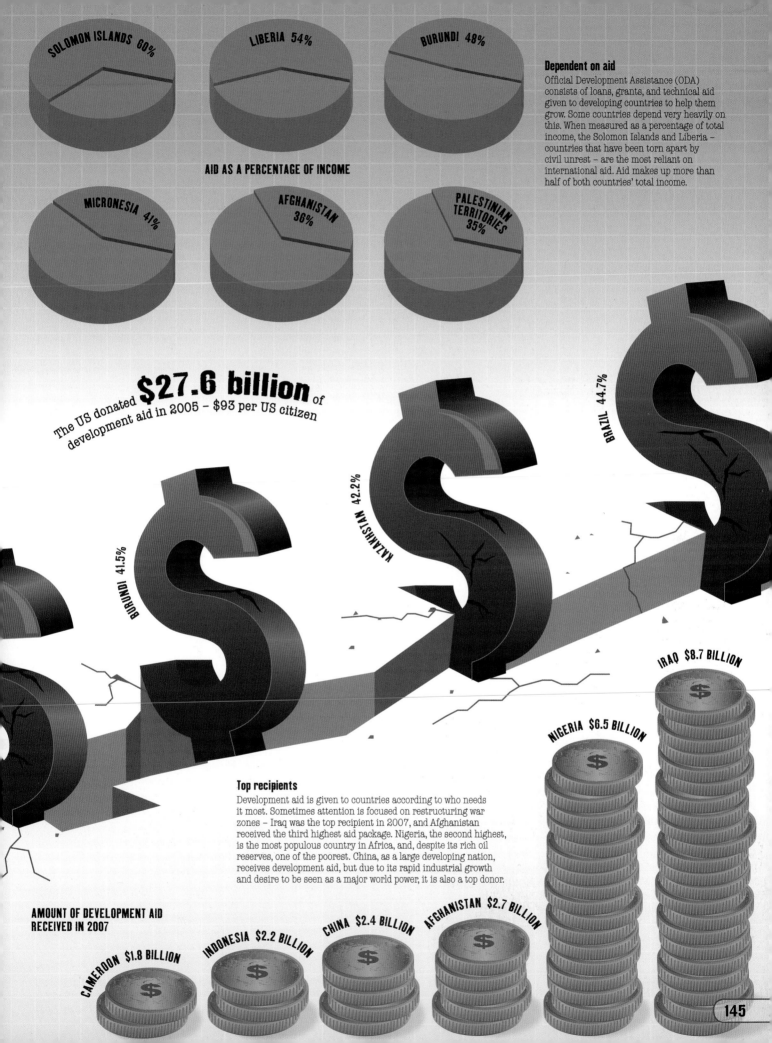

THE World IN ONE Day

POWER

Governments, money, big business, international affairs – these are the things that make the world go around.

The **United Nations** (UN) is currently involved in **17 peacekeeping** operations around the world, involving **121,169** UN representatives

In 2008, **7** people were **executed** and **24** sentenced to **death** per day around the world

2,880 court cases are filed in the US every day

There are about **11.9 million illegal** immigrants in the US

There are **6,500** people employed by the United States' **Secret Service**

The Federal Reserve Bank in New York transfers **£1.1 trillion** ($1.8 trillion) between itself and other **banks** around the world

Giant **stone discs** are still recognized as legal currency in **Yap**, Micronesia

There are **182 official currencies** in circulation

23,000 people work in **The Pentagon**, the headquarters of the US Department of Defense – they make **200,000** telephone calls and receive about **40,000** pieces of mail

Iraq receives **£15 million** ($23.5 million) in **development aid**

75,750 ambulances could be bought with the **£5.4 billion** ($8.7 billion) spent on **healthcare** by governments worldwide

There are **75 million military troops** ready for action worldwide

£2.4 billion ($3.8 billion) is spent on the world's **militaries**

The UN spends **£47 million** ($74 million) on **children** – a tiny fraction of the world's military budget

There are **31,000 McDonald's** restaurants employing **1.5 million** people, a population that's bigger than **51 countries** of the world

Chefs in the **White House** are able to serve **140** guests in one sitting

According to UNICEF, **25,000 children** die each day due to **poverty**

The average **Londoner** is caught on CCTV cameras **300 times** – the city has about **7,500 cameras**

Governments spend about **£4.2 billion** ($6.8 billion) on **education**

There are **5 communist states** in the world – **China, Cuba, Laos, Vietnam, and North Korea**

Only **2 flags** show **guns**: Guatemala's flag shows rifles, but Mozambique's flag is the only one to show a modern weapon – an **AK-47**

There is only **1** non-rectangular **flag** in the world – **Nepal's** consists of two triangles

Industry

The products of industry are all around us — from the goods we buy to the services we rely on. Taking the Earth's resources and turning them into manufactured products allows countries to make money. But the way we're using the Earth's resources is having an effect on the planet's health. Our consumer society uses a vast amount of energy, and with fossil fuels running out in the near future, we'll need to turn to different energy sources to power our way of life.

World Market

The buying and selling of products and services between countries is called international trade. Things bought from other countries are called imports, and those sold are called exports. Trading between countries enables them to sell what they produce and buy the things they need but cannot make themselves.

Top imports

Below are the top 10 imports in 2008. Industrial produce makes up the majority of the list, with coal and oil at the top, but farm produce also features prominently. The prices for these rise and fall according to supply and demand: prices rise when demand rises, or when supply falls.

COAL: 3.1 BILLION TONNES

CRUDE OIL: 2.2 BILLION TONNES

SALT: 163 MILLION TONNES

ELECTRICAL ENERGY: 482 MILLION MEGAWATT HOURS

WHEAT: 157 MILLION TONNES

IRON ORES: 814 MILLION TONNES

IRON PRODUCTS: 153 MILLION TONNES

CEMENT: 264 MILLION TONNES

CORN: 243 MILLION TONNES

SOYA BEANS: 72 MILLION TONNES

Balancing the scales

One of the most important figures in a country's finances is its balance of trade, which is the difference between the value of its exports and the cost of its imports. The US has a trade deficit as it pays more for imports than it earns from exports. Ideally, a country will aim to have a trade surplus like China, which sells more than it buys, meaning that the country is not overly dependent on its trading partners.

2008 BALANCE OF TRADE (ALL FIGURES IN BILLIONS)

CHINA

US

EXPORTS
$1,429

IMPORTS
$1,132

BALANCE:
$297
SURPLUS

EXPORTS
$1,291

BALANCE:
−$826
DEFICIT

IMPORTS
$2,117

Raw materials and finished goods

Many countries in the developing world do not have the facilities to turn their raw materials into finished goods. Nigeria produces a large amount of oil, but cannot turn it into the petrol it needs. Its total petrol imports are made using 22 billion litres (5.8 billion gallons) of oil – almost a fifth of what it exports.

NIGERIA EXPORTS 115 BILLION LITRES (30 BILLION GALLONS) OF CRUDE OIL PER YEAR

NIGERIA IMPORTS 11 BILLION LITRES (2.9 BILLION GALLONS) OF PETROL PER YEAR

Trading fair

Fair Trade is a global movement with the aim of ensuring higher payments for food producers in developing nations, by ensuring that they get a decent minimum price for their produce, as well as money to invest in improving their communities. Bananas, coffee, and cocoa are all popular Fair Trade products.

FAIRTRADE

Tariffs

Customers like to pay as little as possible, but cheap imported goods can stifle home businesses. In some cases, special taxes called tariffs are placed on foreign products. In the example here, despite starting off cheaper, the 50% tariff makes the foreign shoes more expensive. This raises money for the government, but also protects the country's own industry. On the downside, it gives the consumer less choice.

HOME SHOES:	NO TARIFF ADDED	FINAL PRICE:
BASE PRICE £20 ($31)		£20 ($31)
FOREIGN SHOES:	50% TARIFF ADDED	FINAL PRICE:
BASE PRICE £18 ($28)	+£9 ($14)	£27 ($42)

Japanomics

Japan is one of the world's leading economies, with a high standard of living and high life expectancy for its people. The word "economy" refers to a country's wealth and resources, and all the goods and services it produces and consumes. Japan has few natural resources so it relies on exports to pay for the raw materials, food, and fuel it must import.

Using land

Japan is a chain of hundreds of mountainous volcanic islands. About 68% of its rugged landscape is blanketed with forests. Cities are located on the earthquake-prone coastal plains.

Power of the Yen

Japan is one of the world's biggest economies. Its GDP (gross domestic product, the value of all the goods and services produced by a country) of $4.9 trillion is second only to that of the United States. The Japanese currency is the yen (¥).

Ups and downs

During the decades after World War II, Japan's economy boomed. Its GDP grew by an average of 10% in the 1960s, and continued to grow rapidly until the end of the 1980s. But by the end of the 1990s the boom was over. Economic crises, huge levels of public debt, and the burden of an ageing population meant that the economy got smaller at the beginning of the 21st century.

Wealth creation

Japan's wealth is based largely on services, such as banking, insurance, and tourism, which account for nearly three-quarters of GDP. Vehicle manufacture and other industries create about one-quarter of the share, while farming contributes only a tiny fraction.

AGRICULTURE 1.6%

INDUSTRY
25.3%

SERVICES
73.1%

BREAKDOWN OF
JAPAN'S GDP

60% OF FOOD IS IMPORTED

Filling the ricebowl
Only 12% of Japan's land is suitable for growing crops. Rice is the chief food crop, but wheat, maize, sugar beet, and tea are also grown. Very large amounts of food need to be imported to meet the country's needs.

11,563,629
cars were manufactured in Japan in 2008

People at work
Japan's workforce numbers about 66.5 million, many of whom are highly skilled. The country's fixed gender roles have meant that until recently most women did not go out to work. This is now changing – 40% of workers are female – but the number of women in senior positions remains low.

Exports
Cars, semiconductors (components used to make electronic circuits), iron, and steel are the country's biggest exports. In total, its exports amounted to $746.5 billion in 2008.

Imports
Japan imports goods worth a total of $708.3 billion. It is the world's second biggest importer of natural gas and the third biggest importer of oil. Other major imports include foodstuffs and textiles.

Ro-bot-ics!
Japan leads the world in robotics. In 2005, there were 370,000 robots in Japan's factories – more than 40% of the world's total. That means there were roughly 30 programmed automatic helpers for every 1,000 Japanese factory workers.

Cost of consumption
Like other developed nations, Japan has a heavy ecological footprint. The amount of carbon dioxide emitted per person in 2007 was 9.7 tonnes, putting Japan 35th in the world. But the country is one of the largest consumers of fish and tropical timber. Its economic activity leads to the depletion of these resources in other parts of the world.

Fishing fleets
The Japanese eat more fish than any other nation. They are the biggest importers of fish and their own fleet takes almost 15% of the global catch. However, the size of their catch has fallen in recent years, due to restrictions brought in to prevent overfishing.

Oil

Without oil, much of the world's transport would come to a standstill. North America has a huge number of vehicles and used eight times the amount of oil as Africa in 2008.

Coal

The most common use for coal is to generate electricity – as much as 93% of the USA's coal is used in this way. Burning coal is one of the most polluting ways to generate electricity.

Gas

Many homes need gas for cooking and heating, and it is also used widely to power industry. The Middle East has the largest gas reserves, but uses less than one-third of what Europe uses.

Renewables

Renewable energy sources still represent only a small fraction of the world's total energy production. Denmark is leading the way, with wind power generating 20% of its electricity.

Nuclear

Nuclear power stations use uranium to generate electricity. Nuclear power is cleaner than fossil fuels, but concerns over dealing with radioactive waste have led to a reduction in nuclear power.

Energy use

Industry is the world's biggest user of energy. Heavy industries like steel-making and mining use the most. By comparison, each individual home consumes very little energy, but there are millions upon millions of homes. Added together, they use nearly as much energy as industry.

34%
26%
21%
13%
6%

2.5%
5.1%
5.5%
7.8%
31.9%
19.7%
27.5%

Different sources

The energy we use comes from a variety of sources, but the source we rely on more than any other today is oil. It supplies more than a third of all global energy. Above is a breakdown of the five main energy sources, while the pie chart to the left identifies where the energy is used.

Energy Resources

The modern world requires an enormous supply of energy. People demand a constant and reliable supply for heating, lighting, cooking, transport, communications — almost every daily activity. Energy consumption in the developed world dwarfs that of poorer nations, but as countries become more prosperous, their needs will increase. And as the world's energy needs grow, the sources we depend on most are running out.

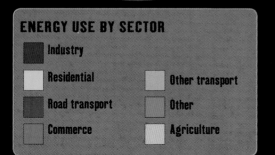

ENERGY USE BY SECTOR

- Industry
- Residential
- Road transport
- Commerce
- Other transport
- Other
- Agriculture

AFRICA 0.77

WORLD
AVERAGE 1.82

GERMANY 4.03

USA 7.75
PER CAPITA ENERGY CONSUMPTION
(tonnes oil equivalent)

UNITED ARAB EMIRATES 11.83

World energy usage

If all the energy used in the world was divided up between everyone equally, each person would use as much energy in a year as there is in 1.8 tonnes of oil. However, consumption is very uneven around the world. People in developed countries use a lot more than this.

Increase in energy consumption

As economies grow and people become wealthier, more cars and electrical equipment are bought. Manufacturing expands to meet the rising demand, and, as a result, energy consumption increases. In 2010, the world consumed 508 quadrillion BTU (British thermal units) of energy. By 2030, this is set to increase by about a third.

2010

E — F

(QUADRILLION BTU)

2030

E — F

(QUADRILLION BTU)

How long will supplies last?

Most of the energy sources we depend on now will run out one day. Oil is expected to be the first to go, probably in about 40 years. Renewable energy, such as solar and wind energy, is the only source that will not run out.

COAL 120 YEARS

URANIUM 80 YEARS

NATURAL GAS 60 YEARS

OIL 40 YEARS

Fuel wood

About 2.4 billion people – just over one-third of the world's population – depend on wood for heating and cooking. In most of the world, the use of fuelwood is in decline, but it is increasingly used in Africa.

The world's nuclear power stations use 65,000 tonnes of uranium every year

Fossil Fuels

Fossil fuels are substances that formed from dead plants or animals as a result of natural processes. Coal, oil, and natural gas are fossil fuels, and are burned to release energy. This energy – in the form of heat – is used for warmth, light, powering machines, and making electricity. When fossil fuels burn, they emit gases that contribute to global warming.

In one year, a coal-fired power station supplying
140,000 homes
with electricity burns
1.5 million tonnes of coal

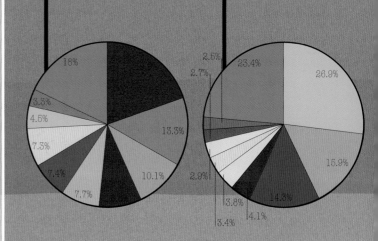

How gas and oil are formed

Most of the oil and gas that we use today formed from trillions of microscopic plants and animals. These tiny organisms lived in the sea hundreds of millions of years ago, before the age of the dinosaurs.

1. Buried remains

When the tiny organisms died, their bodies sank to the seabed. Their remains were then covered by sand and fine silt. Over millions of years, they were buried deeper and deeper below the seabed as more sand and silt piled up above them.

2. Heat and pressure

The deep layers of sediments that built up on the seabed slowly changed to rock. Below them, heat and pressure changed the organic remains into oil and gas. If the oil and gas could not escape through the rock above them, they became trapped.

3. Fields of fuel

The oil and gas are still trapped underground today, forming the oilfields and gasfields that fuel our energy-hungry way of life. These valuable fuels are reached by drilling down through the rock until the oil and gas rush up through the hollow drill pipe.

Oil reserves

The amount of oil still under the ground is estimated to be 213 trillion litres (1,342.2 billion barrels). A barrel of oil contains 159 litres (42 US gallons). Saudi Arabia has the biggest share.

Gas reserves

Gas reserves amount to 177 trillion cubic metres (6,254 trillion cubic feet). Nearly half of this is located in the Middle East, and more than a quarter is beneath Russia's territory.

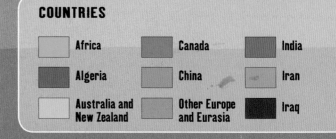

COUNTRIES

- Africa
- Algeria
- Australia and New Zealand
- Canada
- China
- Other Europe and Eurasia
- India
- Iran
- Iraq

Coal consumption

The Asia Pacific region, and China in particular, is by far the world's biggest coal user. China burns more than twice as much coal as the USA and more than four times as much as all 27 countries of the European Union combined.

61.5%   **18.4%**   **15.8%**   **3.3%**   **0.7%**   **0.3%**

Asia Pacific   North America   Europe   Africa   Central and South America   Middle East

PROPORTION OF WORLD COAL CONSUMPTION

How coal is formed

Coal was created in a similar way to gas and oil, forming on land from plants and trees that lived hundreds of millions of years ago in vast swampy forests.

Coal reserves

The worldwide coal reserves amount to 843 billion tonnes. The USA holds the largest share, at just over a quarter. The types and quality of the coal vary from place to place.

4.1%
5.9%
6.7%
9.2%
13.7%
13.6%
18.6%
28.3%

1. Decaying plants

Giant ferns, primitive trees, mosses, and many other strange plants covered most of the land with a thick green carpet. When these plants died, they fell to the forest floor and formed layers of decaying vegetation that were soon covered with soil.

2. Squash and squeeze

The heavy soil on top of the plants squashed them, squeezing out the moisture and slowly changing them into coal. As the levels of land and sea changed over millions of years, some of the land with coal forming beneath it disappeared under water.

3. Harder and blacker

A soft brown coal called lignite is formed first. After more time, the coal becomes harder and blacker, finally forming coal called anthracite. To reach the coal today, the land lying above it is stripped away, or shafts are dug down to mine it.

Kuwait   Russia   Venezuela

Libya   Saudi Arabia   Rest of the world

Nigeria   United Arab Emirates

Qatar   USA

Renewable Energy

Renewable energy is produced from natural sources that will never run out. These sources include the Sun, wind, water, plants, animal waste, and the heat found below the Earth's surface. Renewable sources currently generate 13% of energy used globally, for heating, electricity, and powering industry. With fossil fuels running out, renewable power will be even more important in the future.

Power for the people

Much of the energy generated by renewables is used to produce electricity. Today, renewables contribute 18% to the amount of electricity produced worldwide. This chart shows how much of the total electricity from renewables is contributed by each source, and how much each is projected to contribute by the year 2030.

Biomass

Anything derived from recently living plants and animals and used as a fuel is known as biomass. Wood, plants, and chicken manure are used in developing countries to fuel cooking and heating in the home, while some crops, such as sugar cane, are fermented to make ethanol, a type of alcohol that can be used as a fuel.

FUELS MADE FROM BIOMASS ARE CALLED BIOFUELS

ONE WIND TURBINE CAN PRODUCE ENOUGH ELECTRICITY TO POWER UP TO 300 HOMES

CALIFORNIA, USA, HAS 34 GEOTHERMAL POWER PLANTS

Covering **4%** of deserts with solar panels would meet all the world's electricity needs

Wind power

Windmills have been used as a source of energy since ancient times. Modern wind turbines use the wind's power to generate electricity. The movement of the blades drives a generator on top of the tower. More than 70 countries use wind power and it is the fastest growing renewable energy source.

Geothermal energy

The Earth's natural store of heat, which radiates upwards from its core, can be harnessed to produce electricity. Water is piped from a geothermal energy plant to deep underground, where it heats up. The water then becomes steam that rises up a pipe to turn a generator, which converts the movement to electricity.

Hydroelectric power

Hydroelectric power uses the power of water that flows downhill to turn an electricity generator. It supplies about 15% of the world's electricity needs. The top five producers of hydropower are China, Canada, Brazil, USA, and Russia.

Electric future

By far the biggest contributor to renewable-sourced electricity is hydroelectricity. Solar and tidal power each contribute less than 1%. By 2030, improved technologies, such as solar panels and wind turbines, should allow solar and wind power to increase their share. This is reflected in the graph by the drop in hydroelectricity's share, as the other renewable energies grow in use.

WATER PROVIDES ELECTRIC POWER FOR 28.3 MILLION PEOPLE

BIOFUELS PROVIDE ABOUT 4% OF THE ENERGY USED IN THE USA

A WIND TURBINE CAN WORK WITH AN AVERAGE WIND SPEED OF JUST 22 KM/H (13.7 MPH)

THE ANCIENT ROMANS WERE THE FIRST PEOPLE TO HEAT HOUSES WITH GEOTHERMAL ENERGY

ENOUGH SUNLIGHT FALLS ON THE EARTH IN ONE HOUR TO SUPPLY THE WORLD WITH ENERGY FOR A YEAR

Solar radiation

Solar energy is captured in two main ways. Photovoltaic cells (solar panels) convert sunlight directly into electricity, while solar collectors use solar energy to heat air or water, which can then be transferred to where the heat is needed. Solar water heaters are used by about 50 million people worldwide, most of them in China.

Tidal and wave power

The energy in tides and waves can both be converted into electricity, but currently this is the least developed form of renewable energy. Several large, commercial tidal power plants are being developed, but only two are in operation – one in France and another in Canada. The world's first wave power plant opened in Portugal in 2008.

Nuclear Energy

Uranium-235 nucleus

Neutron

Nuclear fission
The process of splitting an atom's nucleus to release its energy is called nuclear fission. A Uranium-235 nucleus is struck by a particle called a neutron and splits in two. It also gives out two or three neutrons that in turn can split other nearby nuclei.

Nuclear energy is the energy stored inside the nucleus (central part) of an atom. Nuclear power stations release this energy by a process called nuclear fission, and use it to make electricity. Nuclear power is a cleaner way of generating electricity than burning fossil fuels, but it produces radioactive waste that remains hazardous for many years and cannot be allowed to escape into the environment.

Concrete dome stops radiation leaks if there is an accident

Inside a nuclear power station

Nuclear power stations convert nuclear energy into electricity. As the uranium fuel in the reactor undergoes fission, it heats up. The heat is used to boil water and produce steam. The force of the steam spins a turbine at high speeds, powering a generator that produces electricity.

Steam flows through the turbine, making it spin like a propeller

The spinning turbine powers a generator, which makes electricity

Atoms split in the reactor generate heat energy

Heat from the reactor boils water in the tank to make steam

The steam cools, changes back to water, and is piped back for reuse

Energy equivalents

A pellet of uranium is the size of your fingertip and weighs only 7 g (0.2 oz). But it can generate the same amount of energy as much larger quantities of fossil fuels.

1 URANIUM PELLET
(shown actual size)

=

3.5 BARRELS OF OIL
(556 litres/147 gallons)

=

807 KG COAL
(1,780 lbs)

=

481 M³ NATURAL GAS
(17,000 ft³)

10,000 m³ (350,000 ft³)   210,000 m³ (7.4 million ft³)

Hazardous waste

The world's nuclear power facilities produce 210,000 cubic metres of radioactive waste every year. Most of the waste is intermediate or low-level – only slightly radioactive. Less than 5% is classified as high-level waste. It must be carefully processed so as not to cause harm to people or the environment.

NUCLEAR ACCIDENTS

Chernobyl, Ukraine (1986)
Explosions at the Chernobyl Nuclear Powerplant released 400 times more radioactive fall-out than the atomic bombing of Hiroshima, Japan, in 1945. More than 330,000 local people had to be evacuated.

Three Mile Island, USA (1979)
When a nuclear reactor at the Three Mile Island Generating Station, in Pennsylvania, overheated, part of the core containing the fuel melted. Radioactive gas was released into the atmosphere.

Windscale, UK (1957)
The core of Britain's first nuclear reactor at Windscale (now known as Sellafield) overheated and caught fire. Radioactive gas and dust were released from the reactor's chimney.

FRANCE 76%

LITHUANIA 72.3%

SLOVAKIA 56.5%

BELGIUM 55%

UKRAINE 47.5%

SWEDEN 42%

SLOVENIA 42.7%

ARMENIA 39.5%

SWITZERLAND 39%

HUNGARY 37%

WORLD AVERAGE 15%

Relying on nuclear power

About 15% of all the electricity generated worldwide is produced by nuclear power stations. Some countries rely heavily on nuclear power. In France, nuclear power provides more than three-quarters of all the electricity produced.

There are **439** nuclear power stations in **31** countries

Clean and green

Nuclear power stations emit next to no greenhouse gases, though they do generate some preparing and transporting fuel. Their main environmental impact is the hazardous waste they produce.

0.1 0.2 0.3 0.4 0.5 0.6 0.7 0.8 0.9 1.0 1.1 1.2

GREENHOUSE GAS EMISSIONS (KG CO2-EQUIVALENT PER KILOWATT HOUR)

START

industry is the name for any business activity that processes raw materials, manufactures products, or provides a service. All the businesses dealing with the same type of raw material or product belong to the same industry. industries are interlinked. They supply products and services to each other as well as to the public.

Industry

ENERGY

Iron ore mine
Iron ore is iron-rich rock found in the Earth's crust. Like most industries, the mining business that extracts it from the ground requires large amounts of energy.

Making steel
Iron is used to make steel, a very strong, hard alloy (substance made by mixing a metal with another metal or non-metal).

Steel and oil
In order for motorists to fill up their tanks at a petrol station, a whole range of industries have played their part – from the ships that carried the crude oil across the world, to the mines where the raw materials to build the ships were extracted.

ENERGY

ELECTRONICS

ENGINE-BUILDING

Steel supply
Many different industries use steel, including the car manufacturing, construction, and shipbuilding industries.

CAR MANUFACTURING

CONSTRUCTION

Shipbuilding
Shipbuilders use thousands of tonnes of steel, as well as products from the electronics, plastics, and marine engineering industries to make ships.

Oil refineries produce **1 litre** (2 US pints) of petrol from **2 litres** (4 US pints) of crude oil

Shipping oil
An oil tanker made by the shipbuilding industry transports oil from the country where it is extracted to a refinery in another part of the world.

PORT

Refining oil
At the refinery, the oil is processed to make a variety of chemicals and fuel, including petrol.

REFINERY

Satellite
Oil tankers and other ships are guided across the oceans by products of the space and electronics industries – navigation satellites.

SATELLITE

TRUCK-BUILDING INDUSTRY

PETROL DEPOT

Petrol station
Motorists visit petrol stations and pay to fill up their cars with fuel.

Petrol supply
Petrol is trucked from the oil refinery to a depot, where tanker trucks fill up and haul it by road to petrol stations.

PETROL STATION

The meat business

The food we buy starts off on farms but many other industries contribute to getting it into the shops. Some of the food we buy comes from nearby farms, but much of it may have travelled long distances from other countries, using energy, materials and other inputs from many industries.

START

ENERGY   WATER   CHEMICALS   MACHINERY

Growing grain
Wheat is grown by farmers. Most is used to make bread, but some is processed into animal feed.

Cattle food
On another farm, cattle are reared. The cows mainly eat grass, but their diet is supplemented by the wheat-based feed.

Cattle slaughtered
At 1–2 years old, the cattle are taken to a nearby slaughterhouse, usually by road.

Farming inputs
Farming uses large amounts of energy and water. Many farmers use chemical sprays to protect crops from pests and diseases.

ROAD, BRIDGE, TUNNEL CONSTRUCTION

On the road
The construction industries that build and maintain the transport infrastructure allow goods from all industries to be transported by road from one place to another.

Road transport
The meat is transported from the slaughterhouse to a port by refrigerated truck.

Chilled to **−25°C** (-13°F), refrigerated shipping containers can keep meat frozen solid

Shipping meat
The meat can be transported across the world and arrive fresh, thanks to refrigerated containers. Like oil tankers, containerships are guided by satellite.

At the wholesaler
A wholesaler is a business that buys large quantities of meat and sells it on in smaller quantities to shops and food processors.

PORT

SATELLITE

Shop
Shoppers can buy the meat of their choice in their local supermarket or butcher's shop.

Food processors
Some of the meat goes to factories to be turned into processed food, such as burgers and pies. The rest goes directly to the retailer as cuts of meat.

SUPERMARKET

Land Use

Land covers 149 million sq km (57.5 million sq miles) of Earth. This may sound like a lot, but in reality it is less than one-third of the world's surface area, and it must support the housing, commercial, industrial, transport, farming, and other needs of 6.8 billion people. As the human population is growing, the need for land is increasing. By 2050, there will be 9 billion people on Earth. As there is no more land, it will be increasingly important to make the best use of the resources that we have through careful planning.

Agriculture
The area of agricultural land is nearly 60 times bigger than the area used by cities and suburbs. However, the expansion of towns and industry in growing economies such as Brazil and India is often at the expense of agricultural cropland.

Residential
Places where many people live are called residential areas. More than 50% of the world's population are now tightly packed into apartments and houses in towns and cities, which sprawl out across more and more land. Many countries now have laws to protect the countryside from being built on.

More than **35%**
of the world's ice-free land area has been cleared or converted for agriculture

Industry
Even in highly industrialized countries, things like factories and power stations take up very little land. In Japan, for example, one of the world's biggest manufacturers and exporters, only 0.4% of the land area is used by industry.

Infrastructure

The network of roads, bridges, railway lines, communications, electric power, and other services are collectively called infrastructure. They make life easier on a day-to-day basis.

There are **245** cars per km (392 cars per mile) on Hong Kong's crowded road network

The USA has paved more than **160,000 sq km** (61,000 sq miles) of land for roads and car parks

Unused land

Wildland, or wilderness, describes places that are mainly unchanged by human activities. Surprisingly, despite the billions of people on Earth and their cities, roads, and farms, nearly 50% of the world's land area is still wild.

Institutions

As well as housing, roads, shops, and businesses, communities need public buildings such as libraries and sports facilities. Hospitals and schools are also extremely important. Town planners must include these public buildings and institutions in plans for new communities.

95% of the people on Earth are concentrated on just **10%** of the land

55% of Bangladesh's land is suitable for growing crops, more than anywhere else on Earth

Reaching for the Sky

For most of the 20th century, the world's tallest buildings were American. Since 1998, the height charts have been topped by buildings in Malaysia, Taiwan, and, most recently, Dubai. As engineers defy the vertical challenge again and again with new and more innovative ways to build higher and higher, there seems to be no limit to a building's height.

Highest tower

The CN Tower in Toronto, Canada, stands 553.3 m (1,815 ft) tall. It was built as a communications tower with public areas, including a restaurant and observation gallery, near the top. It would be the world's second tallest building but because it does not have floors all the way up from the ground it is categorized as a tower, not a building.

East versus west

At 522 m (1,713 ft) high, the East Tower to the already standing West Tower is due to dwarf its neighbour after completion in 2015.

Empire State Building

Constructed in 1931 and rising 381 m (1,250 ft) tall, the Empire State Building in New York City was the world's tallest building for more than 40 years. Today, it is the 13th tallest building in the world.

381 m (1,250 ft)

391 m (1,282.8 ft)

415 m (1,361.5 ft)

415 m (1,361.5 ft)

421 m (1,381 ft)

438 m (1,437 ft)

EMPIRE STATE BUILDING
New York City, USA
Completed: 1931

CITIC PLAZA
Guangzhou, China
Completed: 1997

TRUMP INTERNATIONAL HOTEL AND TOWER
Chicago, USA
Completed: 2009

TWO INTERNATIONAL FINANCE CENTRE
Hong Kong, China
Completed: 2003

JIN MAO TOWER
Shanghai, China
Completed: 1999

GUANGZHOU WEST TOWER
Guangzhou, China
Completed: 2010

MEASURING HEIGHT

Each building's height is measured from the pavement level of the building's main entrance to its structural top. This includes spires on top of the building, but does not include antennae or flagpoles.

Green skyscrapers

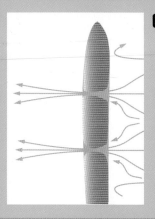

The 310-m- (1,017-ft-) high Pearl River Tower in Guangzhou, China, is the world's most environmentally friendly skyscraper. Wind turbines and solar panels built into its structure generate more than enough electricity to cover the entire building's energy needs.

Reaching new heights

A new building proposed for construction in Dubai, the Nakheel Tower could be the first skyscraper to be more than a kilometre (0.62 miles) high. As the design has evolved, the height it could reach is estimated to be about 1,400 m (4,593 ft) – almost double that of the current record holder, Burj Khalifa.

Petronas Towers

The Petronas Towers were the world's tallest buildings between 1998 and 2004. The two towers are linked 170 m (558 ft) above the ground by the world's highest two-storey "skybridge".

442 m (1,450 ft)

450 m (1,476 ft)

452 m (1,483 ft)

492 m (1,614 ft)

509 m (1,670 ft)

828 m (2,716.5 ft)

WILLIS TOWER
Chicago, USA
Completed: 1974

NANJING GREENLAND FINANCIAL CENTRE
Nanjing, China
Completed: 2010

PETRONAS TOWERS
Kuala Lumpur, Malaysia
Completed: 1998

SHANGHAI WORLD FINANCIAL CENTRE
Shanghai, China
Completed: 2008

TAIPEI 101
Taipei, Taiwan
Completed: 2004

BURJ KHALIFA
Dubai,
United Arab Emirates
Completed: 2010

The **first skyscraper** was the 10-storey Home Insurance Building, built in Chicago in 1885

Forest cover

The world's forests blanket 40 million sq km (15.4 million sq miles) of Earth, which is almost a third of its total land area. Two-thirds of Earth's forests are located in just 10 countries, and 45 countries have more than 50% of their land area covered by these woody environments.

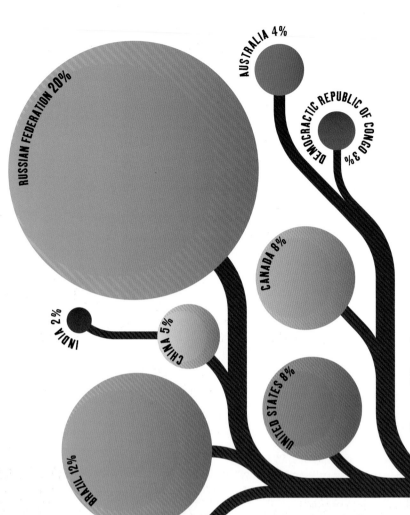

RUSSIAN FEDERATION 20%

AUSTRALIA 4%

DEMOCRACTIC REPUBLIC OF CONGO 3%

CANADA 8%

INDIA 2%

CHINA 5%

UNITED STATES 8%

BRAZIL 12%

INDONESIA 2%

PERU 2%

THE REST OF THE WORLD 34%

Types of forest

Some forests have grown naturally over the centuries, relatively untouched by people. Others have been planted by humans and the trees are comparatively young.

Primary forest
Also referred to as old-growth forest or ancient woodland, this native forest accounts for about a third of the planet's woodlands.

36.4%

Modified natural forest
Following damage by human interference, this type of forest has been regenerated with native tree species. It accounts for more than half of Earth's forest cover.

52.7%

Productive forest plantation
Planted to produce timber and other materials, the trees in this forest-type tend to be the same species and age.

3%

Semi-natural forest
These are forests that have been replanted by humans with native trees that would have grown there naturally.

7.1%

Protective forest plantation
Sometimes forests are planted in order to protect such things as soil, water resources, air quality, habitats, and biological diversity.

0.8%

forests

The world's forests are a precious resource that have evolved over millions of years, and we rely on trees for many things. They protect wildlife, land, and water. They bear many fruits, providing us with food, and their wood is used to build houses, as well as for the paper that this book is printed on. But forests are easily damaged; a wooded area the size of New Zealand is lost to fire each year, and human activity has led to many forests being damaged beyond repair.

Fruits of the forest

Nearly every part of a tree can be used in one way or another. The construction, energy, publishing, pharmaceutical, textile, and food industries all make use of goods from the woods.

Leaves
Leaves provide a variety of flavourings in food and are a source of the fibres used to make ropes and textiles.

Flowers
A quarter of all the medicines we use are made from parts of plants, including some found in tropical rainforests.

Bark
Tree bark products such as cork are used to make traditional bottle stoppers, notice boards, and wall tiles.

Fruits and nuts
Many fruits and nuts can be eaten as they are. Some are processed to make other foods, such as chocolate, which is made from cocoa beans.

WOOD
CELLULOSE
TREE GUM
TREE RESIN
SAP

Wood
The main product of forestry, timber is world's more than ($60 billion) a year worldwide, and is used in buildings and furniture.

Cellulose
Extracted from wood pulp, cellulose is used to make paper, cardboard. Cellophane (a type of fibre used in textiles), rayon, and some glues and pastes.

Tree gum
A useful thickening and stabilizing agent, gum is used to make many rubber products such as wellies, as well as chewing gum.

Tree resin
Resin is used to make some soaps, varnishes, and adhesives. It is also rubbed on dancing shoes and violin bows to increase friction.

Sap
The sugary sap of some trees is made into maple syrup and sweets such as marshmallows. Canada is the biggest maple syrup producer.

Deforestation

Primary forests are often cleared for farming, building, and to plant crops for making biofuels. Earth's total forest area decreases at a rate of 130,000 sq km (50,193 sq miles) every year. The destruction of forests, called deforestation, displaces people who live in the forests, destroys wildlife habitats, and contributes to global warming.

CAUSES OF DEFORESTATION

Over-logging   Agriculture   Plantations   Urban expansion   Natural disasters

EFFECTS OF DEFORESTATION

Cracked earth
Tree roots hold soil together and keep the nutrient-rich topsoil in place for new plants to grow in. When trees are felled, the exposed topsoil can be washed away by rain. The remaining soil dries out in the sun, leaving a dry, cracked, nutrient-poor soil that new plants struggle to grow in.

Forest species
Two-thirds of all plant and animal species on Earth are found in forest habitats. Tropical rainforests are especially rich in wildlife, and the deforestation of these areas could cause the extinction of many species.

Global warming
Trees take in large amounts of carbon dioxide – a greenhouse gas that contributes to global warming. Deforestation causes the release of up to 20% of all greenhouse gas emissions – more than the entire global transport sector.

Farming

The world's farms have to produce enough food to sustain the global population of 6.8 billion people. Just three crops (wheat, rice, and maize) provide nearly two-thirds of human food. With the population rising, farming will have to produce even more in future to feed everybody. However, global warming may make it even more difficult to increase farm production.

Farmland

Only 11% of Earth's land is suitable for growing crops. Even the areas that can be farmed are not equally productive. Farmers in the developing world may not have access to technology or techniques that would allow them to get the higher yields out of the land.

CLIMATE TOO DRY 28%

SOIL TOO SHALLOW 22%

CHEMICAL PROBLEMS 23%

CLIMATE TOO WET 10%

PERMAFROST 6%

SUITABLE FOR AGRICULTURE 11%

Top wheat producers

Wheat is an important food crop that is cultivated all over the world. It can be ground up into flour and used to make all sorts of foodstuffs, including bread and pasta. China is the world's leading wheat producer, producing more than the USA and Russia combined.

Producer	Millions of tonnes
CHINA	109.3
INDIA	75.8
USA	55.8
RUSSIA	49.4
FRANCE	32.8

WHEAT PRODUCED PER YEAR (MILLIONS OF TONNES)

Key crops

The most important food crops are wheat, rice, and coarse grains such as barley, oats, and maize. Oilseed crops include palm, soya bean, and sunflower, and are grown to provide oils for cooking, industry, and making fuel, while cotton is grown to make into textiles.

COTTON 120.5

OILSEEDS 391.6

MILLED RICE 433.4

WHEAT 610.7

COARSE GRAINS 1,078.6

AMOUNT PRODUCED PER YEAR (MILLIONS OF TONNES)

More than **1.3 billion** people work in farming worldwide

Top rice producers

Rice is the staple food for roughly half of the world's population. Milled (white) rice is the most common form eaten by people. China and India provide more than three-quarters of all the rice grown in the world.

RICE PRODUCED PER YEAR (MILLIONS OF TONNES)

CHINA — 187.4
INDIA — 144.6
INDONESIA — 57.1
BANGLADESH — 43
VIETNAM — 35.9

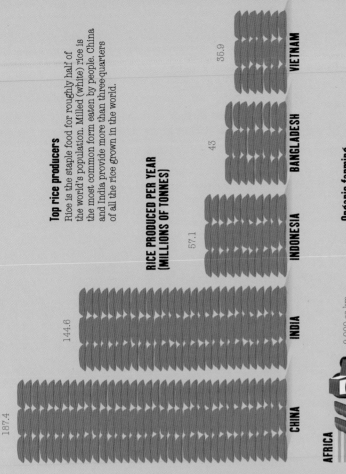

Organic farming

More than 300,000 sq km (115,830 sq miles) of land worldwide is managed organically. This is an area of land similar in size to the US state of New Mexico. Organic farmers use natural methods and materials to grow crops and raise livestock.

AFRICA — 9,000 sq km (3,475 sq miles)
ASIA — 29,000 sq km (11,197 sq miles)
EUROPE — 78,000 sq km (30,116 sq miles)
LATIN AMERICA — 64,000 sq km (24,711 sq miles)
NORTH AMERICA — 22,000 sq km (8,494 sq miles)
OCEANIA — 121,000 sq km (46,718 sq miles)

AREA USED FOR ORGANIC FARMING

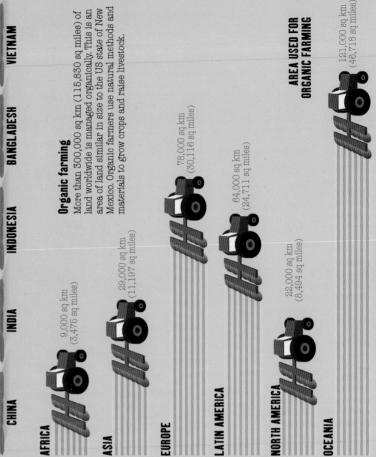

Livestock accounts for **18%** of all greenhouse gas emissions – more than all forms of transport put together

Poultry populations

The global poultry population numbers in the billions. The majority of birds are farmed using "intensive" methods, in which they are reared to be slaughtered as soon as possible.

Poultry icons sized proportionally

DUCKS: 1 BILLION

CHICKENS: 15.8 BILLION

Livestock populations

Hundreds of millions of animals are farmed for meat. Cows are the most numerous. Cattle ranching is the main cause of deforestation in the Amazon rainforest. The forest is cleared to make way for pasture to feed cattle. About 75% of Brazil's greenhouse gas emissions are due to deforestation.

1.34 BILLION
1.03 BILLION
743 MILLION
941 MILLION

LIVESTOCK NUMBERS

= 100 million cows
= 100 million goats
= 100 million sheep
= 100 million pigs

Cocoa and Chocolate

Chocolate is the world's favourite treat — more than 7 million tonnes of it is consumed worldwide annually and global sales are worth more than £64 billion ($100 billion) a year. Chocolate is made from cocoa beans, which come from the cacao tree, an evergreen plant found only near the equator. The beans have a strong, bitter taste, and must be fermented and roasted to bring out the chocolate flavour.

Cocoa crop

Cocoa is grown in more than 35 countries in a narrow belt around the equator. Nearly three-quarters of all cocoa is grown in Africa, most of it in West Africa, but only 10% of the beans go on to be processed there. Most are shipped to processors in Europe, Asia, and the Americas. The world's biggest cocoa handling port is Amsterdam in the Netherlands.

A cacao tree produces about **30** pods a year, and each pod holds up to **50** seeds

GROWING COCOA

THE AMERICAS 11%
ASIA 19%
AFRICA 70%

PROCESSING COCOA

EUROPE 41%
AFRICA 16.5%
ASIA 19.5%
THE AMERICAS 23%

Cocoa consumption

The USA consumes more cocoa in total than any other country. However, at 5 kg (11 lbs) per head, their per capita consumption is only about half that of the Swiss, who eat a massive 10 kg (22 lbs) a year each. This is not just because the Swiss have a sweet tooth: Swiss chocolate tends to contain much more cocoa than American chocolate, about 60% cocoa solids compared to as little as 10% in the US.

Belgium 68,000
Canada 69,000
Spain 70,000
Italy 72,000
UK 134,000
Brazil 212,000
France 224,000
Germany 235,000
Netherlands 500,000
USA 634,000

THE WORLD'S TOP COCOA CONSUMERS
(total consumed in tonnes)

Chocolate quality

Cocoa powder is used in different amounts to make different grades of chocolate. Sweet milk chocolate contains about 20% cocoa solids (cocoa powder), while dark chocolate contains at least 60% cocoa solids. White chocolate is made from cocoa butter and contains no cocoa powder.

FROM BEAN TO BAR: HOW CHOCOLATE IS PRODUCED

1. Harvesting
Cocoa pods are harvested by hand. Workers cut the pods off using machetes or knives on long poles.

2. Deshelling
The cocoa pods are split open and the beans are scooped out. The pod shells are thrown away.

3. Fermenting
For 2–8 days the beans are left in wooden boxes to ferment as sugars in the pulp change to acids.

4. Drying
The fermented beans are left to dry in the sun. In bad weather, hot-air blowers are used instead.

5. Shipping
When the beans are ready, they are shipped to a manufacturer to be made into chocolate.

6. Roasting
First the beans are roasted to bring out the distinctive flavour and aroma of chocolate.

Can you grow cocoa?

The cacao trees that produce cocoa beans only grow in certain very specific conditions. If the soil type, average temperature, humidity level, and amount of sunlight and rainfall are not all exactly right, the trees will not thrive.

YES You can grow cocoa!

NO Cocoa won't grow — Is the growing site protected from too much sun and wind?

YES

NO Cocoa won't grow — ...but less than 3 m (9.8 ft) of rainfall each year?

YES

NO Cocoa won't grow — Is there more than 1 m (3.2 ft) of rainfall a year...?

YES

NO Cocoa won't grow — Is the climate humid?

YES

NO Cocoa won't grow — Is the average annual temperature between 18°C and 20°C?

YES

NO Cocoa won't grow — Is the soil loose?

YES

NO Cocoa won't grow — Are you less than 400 m (1,300 ft) above sea level?

YES

NO Cocoa won't grow — Are you between 20° north and 20° south of the equator?

An estimated **3 million tonnes** of cocoa is produced every year

A ripe cocoa pod is **15–30 cm** (6–12 in) long – about the same size as a pineapple

Who profits?

For every £1 you spend on chocolate, the farmer who produces the cocoa beans earns just 8p. The chocolate manufacturer and the shop that sells the chocolate each receive more than a quarter of the total price of the bar.

GROWER: 8p

COCOA BUYER: 7p

IMPORTER: 14p

CHOCOLATE COMPANY: 28p

SHOP: 28p

GOVERNMENT TAX: 15p

---

7. Husks removed
The outer husks are removed and then the roasted beans are ground into a liquid.

8. Fat extracted
The liquid is pressed to remove the fat (cocoa butter), some of which is used to make cosmetics.

9. Mixing
The remaining powder is mixed with sugar, cocoa butter, vanilla, and, for milk chocolate, milk.

10. Rolling
This mixture is squeezed through a series of heavy rollers, changing it into a dry flake.

11. Stirring
Ingredients are added that help to bind the mixture, then it is stirred into a smooth paste.

12. Tempering
The chocolate is tempered (repeatedly heated and cooled) for a glossy finish, then left to set in a mould.

Fishy Business

Fish is an important part of the diet in many countries. More than one billion people rely on fish and other seafood as their main source of animal protein. The world's commercial fishing fleet has always met the growing demand for fish, but there are clear signs that too many fish are being taken from the wild, threatening the survival of many species. Farmed fish are having to make up more and more of global production.

13 million
people worldwide work in the fishing industry

One of the world's biggest trawl nets could encircle more than a dozen Boeing **747s**

Rich waters
The Pacific Ocean is the world's biggest ocean and the most productive. In 2007, Pacific fish and shellfish production amounted to 64.5 million tonnes – almost twice as much as the catches of all other oceans and seas added together.

- Pacific
- Atlantic
- Indian
- Mediterranean and black sea

Fish production
In 2007, the total world catch of fish and shellfish amounted to 90 million tonnes, while another 50 million tonnes were farmed. More than half of the world's total production is caught and farmed by just five nations (see below).

- Fish farmed
- Fish captured

10 times
In every catch of prawns, up to 10 times their weight in other species is also caught in the net and then discarded, often already dead.

Biggest fishers
China is the world's biggest fishing nation by a long way, catching more than three times as much, and farming almost nine times more than, the next biggest fishing nation, India. Even though 75% of China's fish is consumed by its domestic market, it is the largest exporter of fish in the world.

USA 4,767,306 tonnes
INDONESIA 4,936,629 tonnes
PERU 7,210,544 tonnes
INDIA 3,953,476 tonnes
CHINA

14,669,036 tonnes
51,420,276 tonnes
836,281 tonnes
1,392,304 tonnes
59,551 tonnes
3,364,754 tonnes

Deadly cuisine
Despite the fact that its liver and intestines contain a deadly poison, the spiny puffer fish is a great delicacy in Japan, where it is called fugu. Only specially trained "fugu-certified" chefs are allowed to prepare this potentially fatal fish dish.

174

70%
More than **70%** of the world's fish species are either fully exploited or depleted

What's the catch?
Fish stocks are in decline. Populations of firm food favourites, such as tuna, cod, swordfish, and marlin, have fallen by up to 90% in the past century. As the bigger, fully grown fish have disappeared, the fishing industry has reduced the mesh (hole) sizes of nets to catch smaller and younger fish. But if young fish continue to be caught before they are able to reproduce, then the remaining populations will soon die off.

Reeling them in
Advances in technology have led to more efficient fishing methods, but also to overfishing and environmental damage. Of the 3.5 million fishing boats in the world, only 1% are large, industrial vessels, but they reel in about 60% of all fish caught. In developing countries, fish caught using traditional fishing methods provide 80% of people's protein needs, and yet they represent only about 10% of the global catch.

How would you like your fish?
Worldwide, almost 39% of all the fish and shellfish that is both caught and farmed is sold fresh, while about 21% is frozen. Of the remaining 40%, 12% is canned, and 9% is cured by drying, salting, smoking, or pickling. The rest is processed to produce "non-foods", such as fishmeal and oil.

Fresh

Frozen

Cured

Canned

Non-food

Leftovers
Not all fish and fish-bits in a catch are suitable for human consumption. Instead, these leftovers are ground up: oil is extracted and used to make products like cod liver oil, while the rest is made into animal food called fishmeal.

Fresh or processed?
Much of the fish supplied for human consumption in developed countries is frozen so that it remains fresher for longer. In developing countries, where access to freezers and electricity is poor, consumers rely more on fresh fish, which are eaten straight away, as the fish deteriorate rapidly after they are caught.

Fish species
There are more than 31,000 species of fish, but very few of them are eaten by humans. The main food fish species include anchovy, carp, catfish, cod, eel, haddock, halibut, herring, mackerel, salmon, sardine, scad, snapper, tilapia, trout, and tuna.

Fish fingers are a popular and easy fish-fix in Britain, where about **350 million** are sold every year.

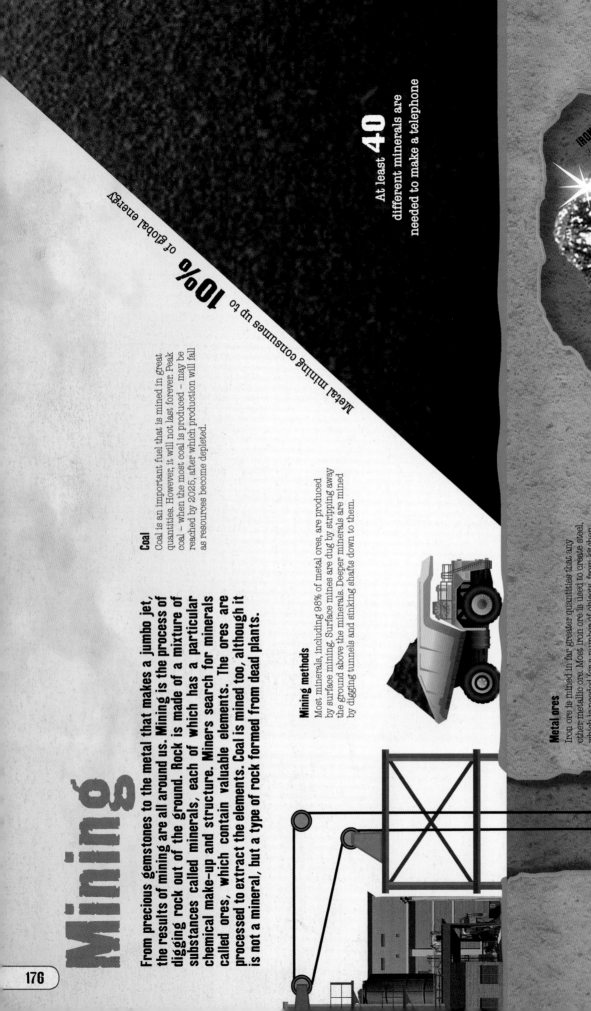

Mining

From precious gemstones to the metal that makes a jumbo jet, the results of mining are all around us. Mining is the process of digging rock out of the ground. Rock is made of a mixture of substances called minerals, each of which has a particular chemical make-up and structure. Miners search for minerals called ores, which contain valuable elements. The ores are processed to extract the elements. Coal is mined too, although it is not a mineral, but a type of rock formed from dead plants.

Coal

Coal is an important fuel that is mined in great quantities. However, it will not last forever. Peak coal – when the most coal is produced – may be reached by 2025, after which production will fall as resources become depleted.

Mining methods

Most minerals, including 98% of metal ores, are produced by surface mining. Surface mines are dug by stripping away the ground above the minerals. Deeper minerals are mined by digging tunnels and sinking shafts down to them.

Metal ores

Iron ore is mined in far greater quantities that any other metallic ore. Most iron ore is used to create steel, which is needed for a number of objects, from kitchen appliances to bridges. To a much lesser extent, iron is also an ingredient in medicine, paint, and fertilizer.

TOP 5 METAL ORES MINED IN 2007

IRON ORE
2,045 million tonnes

ALUMINIUM ORE (BAUXITE)
192 million tonnes

MANGANESE ORE
66 million tonnes

CHROMIUM ORE
24 million tonnes

MAGNESIUM ORE
5.6 million tonnes

Metal mining consumes up to **10%** of global energy

At least **40** different minerals are needed to make a telephone

Precious metals
Precious metals have a high value because of their rarity. Gold, silver, and platinum are examples of precious metals. They are used in industry and traded because of their value, but they are best known for their use in the production of jewellery.

TOP 5 PRECIOUS METALS MINED IN 2007

SILVER
20,883 tonnes

GOLD
2,340 tonnes

PLATINUM
239 tonnes

Gems
Gemstones, or gems, are mineral crystals mined for their beauty and rarity. Most gems are cut and polished, and then made into jewellery – except diamonds, which are used mostly in industry. There are about 40 popular gems, and the most precious are diamond, sapphire, ruby, and emerald.

TOP 5 GEMS MINED IN 2007

DIAMOND
27 tonnes

SAPPHIRE
28.6 tonnes

RUBY
11 tonnes

EMERALD
5.4 tonnes

Deepest mine
The world's deepest mine is the Tau Tona gold mine in West Wits, South Africa. When it opened in 1957, its main shaft was 2 km (1.2 miles) deep. Today, this mine is 3.9 km (2.4 miles) deep and contains 800 km (497 miles) of tunnels worked by 5,600 miners.

Negative effects of mining

Water pollution
Mineral-rich water leaking from mines, and chemicals used in mining processes, can pollute water in the ground and in nearby rivers.

Soil contamination
The ground around mines can be affected by acid produced by chemical reactions between water and mineral-rich rock in some mines.

Subsidence
If old mine shafts and tunnels collapse, the ground above them may subside (sink). Modern mines plan carefully to avoid subsidence.

Visual impact
Mines, especially surface mines, can cause ugly scars on the land. When mines close, the ground is landscaped and trees replanted.

Eco-damage
Deforestation, dust, noise, spoil (waste) heaps, and chemical pollution caused by mining can damage or destroy plant and animal habitats.

Greenhouse gas emissions
Methane, a powerful greenhouse gas, is produced when coal is formed. Mining releases methane, but it can be collected and used as fuel.

The temperature at the bottom of the world's deepest mine is **60°C** (140°F)

Diamonds

Diamond is the hardest material found in nature. It is made of carbon, the same substance that forms graphite (the lead in a pencil) — one of the world's softest materials. The difference between them is the way the carbon atoms are linked together. The rarity of large, gem-quality diamonds and their sparkling appearance increases their value. About £8 billion ($13 billion) of diamonds are produced each year, and the diamond industry employs about 10 million people.

FINDING THE DIAMONDS

Mining from the land

Diamonds form deep underground at high temperatures and great pressure. Most are more than one billion years old. Ancient volcanoes brought them to the surface in pipe-like rock structures, from which they are mined today.

Sifting from rivers

When water erodes diamond-bearing rock, the diamonds may be washed out into a river. These diamonds are called alluvial diamonds, because they are found by sifting the alluvium, the silt and sediment deposited by a river.

Sieving from the sea

Alluvial diamonds are sometimes carried all the way down rivers and into the sea. They are mined by boats that suck up the seabed sediments, which are then sieved to obtain the diamonds.

Pie chart values: 23.2%, 20.5%, 17.2%, 12%, 10.3%, 9%, 6%, 1.4%, 0.6%, 0.6%

TOP 10 DIAMOND PRODUCERS

- Russia
- Botswana
- Democratic Republic of Congo
- Australia
- Canada
- South Africa
- Angola
- Namibia
- Guinea
- China

Top diamond producers

The output of the top 10 diamond-producing countries amounted to 166 million carats, or just over 33 tonnes, in 2007. Russia was the top producer, with an output of more than 38 million carats, or about 7.6 tonnes. One carat is equal to 0.2 g (0.0004 lb). Diamonds with larger carats are more expensive than lower carat diamonds.

From the rough

Diamonds that are mined from the ground are rough and dull so they have to be cut and polished to transform them into sparkling gemstones. A diamond is cut to give it a new shape (shown here in blue) and to get rid of faults called inclusions (shown here in red). It is then polished and set in a ring, necklace, or other piece of jewellery.

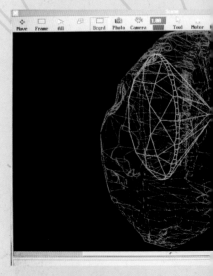

The biggest diamond ever found in the universe is the heart of an old star called BPM 37093 – the 10 billion trillion trillion carat diamond star has a diameter of **4,000 km** (2,485 miles)

Jewels in the crown

The largest rough diamond ever found is the Cullinan. It was discovered in South Africa in 1905, weighing 3,106 carats, or 621 g (1.4 lb). It was cut into nine large gemstones and 96 smaller stones. The nine largest stones of the Cullinan are in the British Crown Jewels and other jewellery worn by the British royal family.

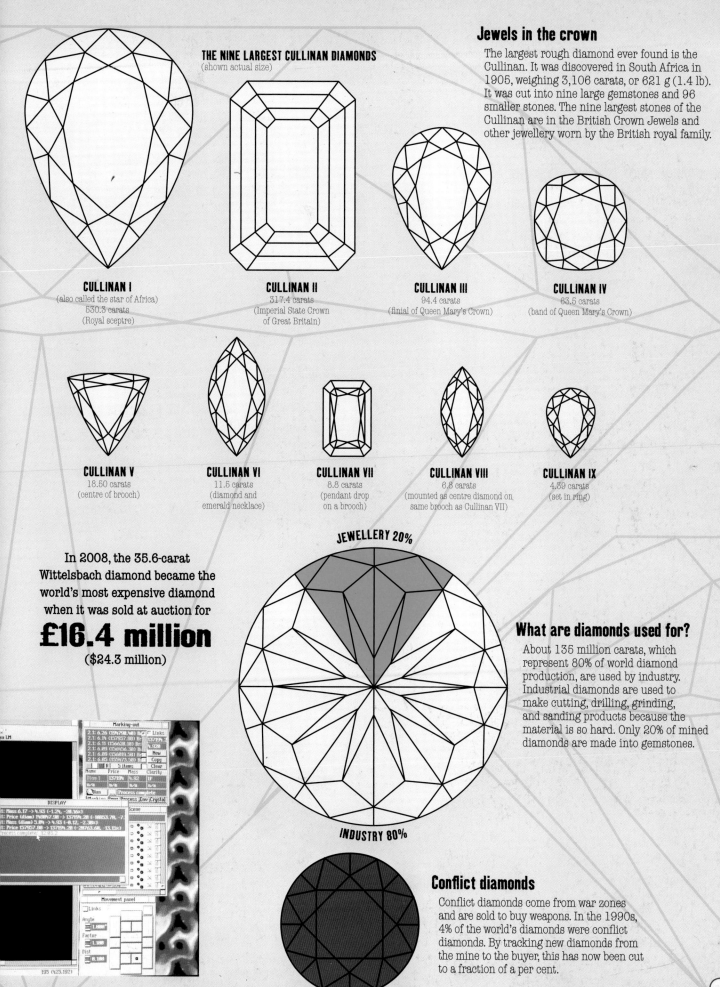

THE NINE LARGEST CULLINAN DIAMONDS
(shown actual size)

CULLINAN I
(also called the star of Africa)
530.3 carats
(Royal sceptre)

CULLINAN II
317.4 carats
(Imperial State Crown
of Great Britain)

CULLINAN III
94.4 carats
(finial of Queen Mary's Crown)

CULLINAN IV
63.5 carats
(band of Queen Mary's Crown)

CULLINAN V
18.50 carats
(centre of brooch)

CULLINAN VI
11.5 carats
(diamond and
emerald necklace)

CULLINAN VII
8.8 carats
(pendant drop
on a brooch)

CULLINAN VIII
6.8 carats
(mounted as centre diamond on
same brooch as Cullinan VII)

CULLINAN IX
4.39 carats
(set in ring)

In 2008, the 35.6-carat Wittelsbach diamond became the world's most expensive diamond when it was sold at auction for

£16.4 million
(\$24.3 million)

JEWELLERY 20%

INDUSTRY 80%

What are diamonds used for?

About 135 million carats, which represent 80% of world diamond production, are used by industry. Industrial diamonds are used to make cutting, drilling, grinding, and sanding products because the material is so hard. Only 20% of mined diamonds are made into gemstones.

Conflict diamonds

Conflict diamonds come from war zones and are sold to buy weapons. In the 1990s, 4% of the world's diamonds were conflict diamonds. By tracking new diamonds from the mine to the buyer, this has now been cut to a fraction of a per cent.

Making the Modern World

A global effort

We use manufactured products in every aspect of our lives. They range from machine parts, engines, toys, and cars to electronic components, mobile phones, TV sets, and computers. Follow the assembly line to see how the whole world is involved in creating, selling, and buying manufactured goods.

Manufactured goods are all around us, from the clothes we wear to the chairs we sit on. Most items are made in a handful of countries, but the parts they contain will often have been manufactured separately all over the world. The global market for manufactured products was worth more than £7 trillion ($11 trillion) in 2009, with developing countries such as China increasing their share every year.

CHEMICALS

MACHINERY

METALS

TELEPHONES

Auto top-up
Car production is one of the biggest manufacturing industries. More than 600 million cars are in use today, and another 50 million were manufactured in 2008. Japan alone produced nearly 10 million cars.

9.9 million

6.7 million

5.5 million

NUMBER OF CARS PRODUCED (2008)

GERMANY

CHINA

JAPAN

Toy exports
China is a leader in toy manufacturing, making almost three out of every five toys in the world. Electronic and stuffed toys are the most popular types.

SHARE OF TOY MANUFACTURING

Rest of the world 16%

Italy 3%

Turkey 5%

Hong Kong 7%

China 59%

Taiwan 10%

The biggest US manufacturing sector is **chemical** products, worth **$249 billion** in 2007

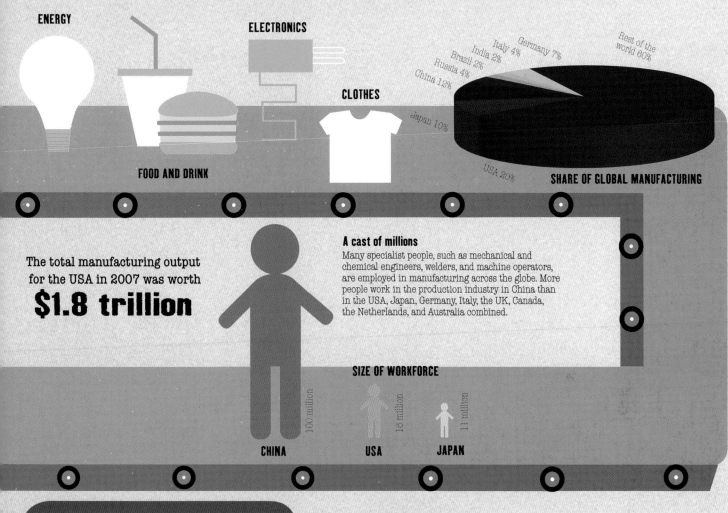

China has the fastest-growing manufacturing industry, increasing by **27%** in 2007

The leaders of tomorrow

Today, the top five manufacturing countries – USA, China, Japan, Germany, and Italy – account for more than half of all global manufacturing output. The world's leading emerging economies are known as BRIC (Brazil, Russia, India, and China). BRIC's total manufacturing output combined is equal to the world's largest manufacturing country, the USA. China alone is expected to overtake the USA in the next few years.

ENERGY

ELECTRONICS

CLOTHES

FOOD AND DRINK

Germany 7%
Italy 4%
India 2%
Brazil 2%
Russia 4%
China 12%
Japan 10%
Rest of the world 60%
USA 20%

SHARE OF GLOBAL MANUFACTURING

The total manufacturing output for the USA in 2007 was worth **$1.8 trillion**

A cast of millions

Many specialist people, such as mechanical and chemical engineers, welders, and machine operators, are employed in manufacturing across the globe. More people work in the production industry in China than in the USA, Japan, Germany, Italy, the UK, Canada, the Netherlands, and Australia combined.

SIZE OF WORKFORCE

100 million — **CHINA**

16 million — **USA**

11 million — **JAPAN**

The ones that got away

Not all manufactured goods prove popular with the public. An early Apple computer, Lisa, failed due to its high price. A clear cola called Tab was launched by Coca-Cola in 1992 but didn't prove popular with consumers.

APPLE LISA

TAB CLEAR

Sourcing parts

In order to build a complex product, individual parts must be sourced from many different companies across the globe to take advantage of the lowest costs for each component. To make a computer, for example, power adaptors may be supplied from Thailand, batteries from Mexico, power cords from India, and microprocessors from California, USA.

Robots

A robot is a machine that can be programmed to carry out tasks for humans. There are about 6.5 million of them in operation around the world today. Some robots are remotely controlled by a person, while others are programmed to carry out tasks automatically. Robots are commonly used for tasks that are either too dangerous, dirty, or dull for humans to do. Some robots are strong enough to move cars, while others have a touch delicate enough to carry out surgery.

Japan expects to have
1 million
robots by 2025

Robot density

The number of industrial robots in relation to workers in a country is called the robot density. Japan has the world's highest robot density, with almost 300 industrial robots for every 10,000 manufacturing workers.

Japan 295
Singapore 169
South Korea 164
Germany 163
Sweden 126
Italy 124
Finland 98
Belgium 89
US 86
Spain 84

NUMBER OF ROBOTS
PER 10,000 WORKERS

Service robots

Instead of making products, service robots help humans. Domestic service robots, like the Roomba vacuum cleaner, help out around the home. Professional service robots work in hospitals, offices, farms, transport, military forces, and space exploration.

Hoovering about

The Roomba is a robot vacuum cleaner that can steer itself around a room automatically, turning to avoid obstacles and walls. It even returns to its charging station to recharge its battery when it is finished.

Asimo

One of the world's most advanced robots, Asimo looks like a 1.3-m- (4-ft-) tall astronaut wearing a backpack. Its joints are moved by 34 electric motors. Asimo can walk, talk, understand spoken commands, and even dance.

Industrial robots

As the cost of using machines has fallen and the cost of employing people has risen, industrial robots have replaced workers in many factories. There are about one million of them in operation around the world. They can drill, cut, and weld parts, paint products, and move items from place to place.

Motor vehicles

Car-building robots assemble a car's body panels and weld them together. Painting robots, eight to a car, can paint 50 cars an hour. Each car can be a different colour, if required, and the robots can keep going 24 hours a day.

Robots by industry

This table shows which industries bought the most robots in 2008. About 40,500 robots were bought by vehicle and vehicle parts manufacturers. The food industry bought 3,000 robots, mainly for stacking and packing products.

INDUSTRIAL ROBOT SALES 2008

- Motor vehicle: 20,500
- Motor vehicle parts: 20,000
- Electrical machinery: 14,000
- Chemical, rubber, and plastics: 12,500
- Metal products: 10,500
- Machinery: 5,000
- Food: 3,000
- Communications: 1,000
- Non-metallic products: 750
- Medical, precision, and optical instruments: 750
- Other vehicles: 500

Food

Robots are just starting to be used in the food processing industry. They can load and unload workers. The latest robots have smooth, easy-to-clean bodies that meet the industry's strict hygiene standards for handling food.

Robots by service

There are 5.5 million service robots at work around the world, worth a combined £7 billion ($11.2 billion). About 30% of the service robots sold in 2008 were for defence, rescue, and security – doing dangerous jobs such as bomb disposal.

SERVICE ROBOT SALES 2008

- Defence, rescue, security: 20,000
- Farming: 14,950
- Logistic: 2,500
- Medical: 5,050
- Mobile robot platforms: 4,000
- Cleaning: 6,000
- Building and demolition: 4,950
- Underwater: 5,000
- Household robots: 4,200
- Entertainment and leisure: 2,950

Medical robots

In some hospitals, robots deliver packages such as patients' records. Other robots visit patients and let a doctor elsewhere see them and talk to them. The most advanced hospital robots are surgical robots, remotely controlled by surgeons to carry out operations.

Robot soccer

Designers are trying to build a team of robots good enough to play a team of human footballers. Until then, the robots play against each other at the Robot Soccer World Cup. In 2008, 373 teams of robots were entered.

At your Service!

Whether you need to buy a box of chocolates or book a flight, you will need the help of service industries. People who work in this sector do not produce any manufactured goods, but exist to serve the public. About 39% of the global workforce are employed in service industries, in a whole range of jobs, from retail sales to tourism.

Hotel check-in
The hotel industry encompasses a wide variety of services. From the moment you arrive and are greeted by reception, to eating a meal prepared by the hotel chef, the aim of most hotels is to provide a high level of service and comfort. But be careful how much you pay – a night in the best suite at the Atlantis Hotel in the Bahamas will cost you £16,000!

Money, money, money!
The banking industry deals with money, from setting up a personal savings account to more complex financial planning for businesses and governments. The types of jobs vary enormously, from administration to accounting and computer programming, to name just three. By 2008, this industry employed 1.8 million people in the USA.

Get up and go!
All over the world, transport is a major service industry and we would not get very far without it – literally! In India, the railways alone carry more than 6 billion passengers every year, and employ more than 1.4 million people.

Retail detail
Retailing is the selling of goods directly to the customer. In developed countries retail has moved away from traditional high street shops to out-of-town supermarkets. By 2005, supermarkets accounted for 73% of all grocery sales in the UK.

Changing times
As they develop, economies tend to move from agriculture towards manufacturing. As they become more prosperous, wages rise and manufacturers move elsewhere to find cheaper sources of labour. Most developed countries have economies dominated by the service industries. However, with a globalized economy and modern communications, service industries may be located anywhere. Many call centres have now been moved from Europe to India, where wages are lower.

In Cuba, there is
1 doctor
for every
170 patients

Read all about it!
The communications and media industries include newspapers, magazines, books, radio, television, and websites. The rise of electronic media is challenging traditional printed media – there are already 1.7 billion Internet users worldwide.

Take a holiday
Are you planning a holiday any time soon? If so, you can book your ticket at a travel agent – in person, via telephone, or online. The Internet is fast becoming the most popular way to research and book holidays. In 2007, 55% of Internet users booked a holiday online in the UK.

Care for your health
The level of healthcare depends on the experience and quality of the staff – from medical to administrative – and the condition of hospitals and equipment. The UK's National Health Service is the world's biggest healthcare employer, with a labour force of about 1.5 million.

School time
Education is a crucial public service because teachers help to shape the minds of future generations. The ability to read and write clearly is one of the most vital skills taught at school. Literacy rates vary widely, from 99.8% in Cuba to under 24% in Burkina Faso.

Shop till you Drop!

The sale of goods directly to the public is known as retail. Retail is big business, and it is getting bigger, but it is also changing. Today, an increasing number of small independent or family-run shops are losing out to chain stores and large supermarkets. The way people shop has also changed, with many consumers using the Internet to buy goods online.

Big spenders

The shopping bags identify the highest spending countries in the world. Between them, they account for about two-thirds of the world's retail sales. In 2008, the biggest spender of all, the USA, accounted for about one-quarter of these sales.

FRANCE $2.4 billion
RUSSIA $2.9 billion
ITALY $3.4 billion
UK $3.6 billion
MEXICO $4.4 billion
KOREA $7 billion
GERMANY $8.9 billion
BRAZIL $10.1 billion
JAPAN $22.8 billion
USA $29.6 billion

The world's biggest shopping malls

A shopping mall is like a town in itself. The top five largest malls in the world, listed below, bring together all sorts of different shops under a single roof, with covered walkways, escalators, dining areas, and even ice rinks, casinos, and swimming pools. The great shopping mall boom of the 1990s and 2000s created giants; however, economic recession has forced many malls around the world to downsize or rethink their future.

More than **40 million** people went to the Mall of America in Bloomington, USA, in 2006, making it the world's most visited shopping mall

Mall food

What is the secret to a successful shopping mall? Food, of course. The main activity in a mall is not actually shopping, but eating.

1) New South China Mall
Dongguan, China
2.2 million sq m
(7.1 million sq ft)
Special features: a theme park, but this has not been taking shoppers away from the shops

2) Golden Resources Mall
Beijing, China
557,400 sq m
(6 million sq ft)
Special features: more than 1,000 shops over five storeys

3) SM Mall of Asia
Pasay City, Philippines
390,200 sq m
(4.2 million sq ft)
Special features: swimming pool and cinema, and its very own tram system

4) Dubai Mall
Dubai, United Arab Emirates
353,000 sq m
(3.8 million sq ft)
Special features: ice rink, aquarium, and top fashion outlets

5) Cevahir Istanbul
Istanbul, Turkey
353,000 sq m
(3.8 million sq ft)
Special features: Europe's largest mall, with wavepool and rollercoaster

Market day

Many outdoor or covered markets date back to ancient times, and are often at the heart of community life. Chatuchak Weekend Market in Bangkok, Thailand, covers a huge 109,265 sq m (1,176,119 sq ft), with about 15,000 stalls and 200,000 visitors daily. Market vendors are generally small independent traders who are prepared to haggle over the price of goods.

Biggest retailers

With outlets often spread worldwide, shoppers spend an incredible amount of money at major retailers. The main retail sectors include food, personal and household goods, motor vehicles, and accessories. Above are the world's top 10 retailers in 2009 – most of them make the biggest bucks by selling groceries.

10. TARGET (US) $65 billion
9. ALDI (GERMANY) $66 billion
8. COSTCO (US) $70 billion
7. HOME DEPOT (US) $71 billion
6. KROGER (US) $78 billion
5. SCHWARZ (GERMANY) $80 billion
4. TESCO (UK) $96 billion
3. METRO (GERMANY) $99 billion
2. CARREFOUR (FRANCE) $128 billion
1. WAL-MART (US) $401 billion

The future of shopping?

The ultimate in-store electronic technology is being tried out at a Metro group shop in northern Germany. The Future Store has scales that recognize products visually, electronic price labelling, computer handsets to guide shoppers round the store, and electronic product information.

Shopping online

In 2007, online shopping accounted for under 7% of retail sales, but it is growing at a phenomenal rate. Today, 40% of the world's population have bought items on the Internet. In 2008, books were purchased by the most people online, with clothing and shoes just behind.

Top online purchases
(proportion bought online)

1 **Books** 41%
2 **Clothing and shoes** 36%
3 **Videos, DVDS, and games** 24%
3 **Airline tickets** 24%
4 **Electronic goods and gadgets** 23%
5 **Music** 19%
5 **Cosmetics and nutrition** 19%
6 **Computer hardware** 11%
7 **Hotel and tour reservations** 16%
8 **Tickets and events** 15%

Plastic fantastic

When you pay for goods with a debit card, the money is immediately transferred out of your bank account. When you pay with a credit card, you borrow the money from the bank and pay it back later with interest. The first credit cards were introduced by Diners Club in 1950. They are convenient, quick, and easy to use – but they can lead users into serious debt.

About **10,000** payment card transactions are made around the world every second

Advertising

Scaling the side of buildings, splashed across webpages, and coming through your letter box, advertising has increasingly become a feature of the modern world. Manufacturers and retailers spent a combined £306 billion ($487 billion) in 2008 to persuade the public to buy their products or services. Advertising has always existed, but since the 1950s, advertisers have made use of a growing understanding of human psychology to achieve success.

Getting the message across

Though the ways we see and hear advertising are constantly changing, they can be roughly divided into a few key areas: print, outdoor, Internet, and TV, cinema, and radio. The pie chart segments show how much of the worldwide advertising budget for 2008 was spent on each area. The best form of advertising is generally considered to be the one that money can't buy – word of mouth.

Logging on

The Internet has only existed since 1990, yet it has totally changed advertising. Internet promotion includes banner displays, spam messages, and virals, which rely on people to pass the ad on.

11%

Great outdoors

Whenever you step outside, you can rarely avoid seeing advertising and promotions. They appear on traditional billboards, but may also be moving, on screens, or on the side of lorries or buses.

7%

The printed word

Newspapers have been around for about 400 years, but the rise of the Internet has hit newspaper sales and their advertising income. Newspapers now have to seek a new readership and advertising revenue online.

36%

Word of mouth

Advice passed from one person to another is completely free. Studies have shown that 90% of people rate personal recommendation as the most effective form of advertising, even if they haven't met the person giving the advice.

Sound and vision

TV remains the most popular advertising medium on Earth. Ads on TV, radio, and film may include sponsorship and product placement, which means that certain brands are used during the course of the feature.

46%

Most advertised

Of the 100 companies that spend the most on advertising in the world, half are based in the United States. The advertising budgets of some of these companies can be larger than the GDP of a developing nation.

Wheels and deals
About £16 billion ($25 billion) is spent around the world promoting cars and vehicles, more than any other type of product. Two of the top five advertisers are car companies.

The big take away
Fast-food restaurants are major advertisers. McDonald's spends about £1.3 billion ($2 billion) per year advertising their food, helping them to serve 47 million customers every day.

Ring tones
The mobile phone is the must-have item of the modern age, and mobile phone companies are the ninth biggest advertisers. Mobiles are also increasingly being used as a way of selling other products.

Child's play
The toy company Mattel spent £268 million ($424.6 million) on advertising in 2008. Toy promotion increases around Christmas time, when people are more likely to spend a lot of money.

Food, glorious food
The third largest sector is food advertising. Some of the heavyweights in the field – such as Mars, Nestlé, and Kraft – spend about £1.3 billion ($2 billion) each on advertising per year.

Clean and fresh
Keeping you and your home clean and tidy is clearly of top importance. It is the second most advertised field, and the top three companies all promote personal care and beauty products.

Fizzy pop
The manufacturers of popular soft drinks are the eighth biggest advertisers around the world, and the leader of the field is Coca-Cola, which is the sixth biggest spender on advertising.

Human Impact

Nearly everything we do creates some kind of waste. Land, water, and even the atmosphere have become our dumping grounds. The planet is running out of room. With one US rubbish dump already visible from space, the world's most wasteful nation may have just 18 years of landfill capacity left. We need to reuse and recycle more and, most importantly, reduce the amount we consume. When millions of people take small steps, the effects can be huge.

Water pollution

Every day humans dump 2 million tonnes of waste into lakes, rivers, and streams. Inland, agricultural and industrial chemicals devastate whole ecosystems. The ultimate destination of most water pollution is the sea. The Pacific Ocean is home to an estimated 3 million tonnes of floating plastic, carried by ocean currents to converge on an area twice the size of the USA. Plastic litter kills a million seabirds and 100,000 marine mammals each year.

The great Pacific garbage patch

Of the massive amount of plastic that floats in the Pacific Ocean, 80% was probably dropped on land. Toothbrushes, bottles, and plastic bags bob on the surface, while a "soup" of tiny plastic particles extends up to 10 m (33 ft) below. Some larger bits can sink to more than 30 m (100 ft) below the surface.

Oil spills

Humans ship more than 2 billion tonnes of oil around the world every year, but sometimes disaster strikes. The Exxon Valdez spill – compared to other major oil spills, below – killed at least 1,000 sea otters, 151 bald eagles, and 35,000 other birds. Today, toxic crude oil still lurks under the affected shores.

Exxon Valdez (1989, USA) 37,000 tonnes

Sea Empress (1996, UK) 72,000 tonnes

Torrey Canyon (1967, UK) 119,000 tonnes

Amoco Cadiz (1978, France) 220,000 tonnes

Atlantic Empress (1979, Tobago) 287,000 tonnes

Space junk

About 17,000 unused satellites and large pieces of space junk orbit the Earth. Collisions can damage or destroy the active satellites that support our communications, television, and weather networks, creating even more debris.

Air pollution

Toxic gases and tiny particles released by power plants, industry, and vehicle engines cause 800,000 deaths every year, of which 65% are in Asia. Many cities that were once heavily polluted have made their air safer by adopting cleaner technologies and stricter rules.

SOUTH KOREA	INDIA	RUSSIA	USA	CHINA
4,285,000	7,920,000	9,793,000	17,866,000	34,205,000

Sulphur dioxide emissions

The chimneys show, in tonnes, the greatest emitters of sulphur dioxide in 2000. This damaging air pollutant is released by burning fossil fuels and particularly coal, which provides 70% of China's energy. The gas causes lung and heart diseases, and is also the main cause of acid rain, damaging lakes and forests.

Car exhaust

Every year the average US passenger car emits 5,194 kg (11,450 lb) of the global-warming gas carbon dioxide, plus a deadly cocktail of ground level pollutants: suffocating nitrogen oxides, cancer-causing particles, toxic carbon monoxide, and smog-forming hydrocarbons.

Land pollution

We produce up to 50 million tonnes of electronic waste every year by upgrading to the latest televisions, computers, and mobile phones. When it ends up in landfill, toxic chemicals leach into the soil. To get around this, developed countries ship much of their "e-waste" to Asia and Africa, where there is a market for reusable parts. With far fewer controls, much of the waste is buried or burned, transferring our pollution to someone else's backyard.

Waste per capita

With each person contributing 760 kg (1,653 lb) of waste every year – and recycling only one-tenth of household rubbish – the USA is the world's most wasteful country. In Japan, about 25 billion pairs of disposable chopsticks are thrown away each year, equivalent to 14 million trees.

JAPAN	ITALY	UK	SPAIN	DENMARK	USA
415 kg (915 lb)	550 kg (1,213 lb)	585 kg (1,290 lb)	600 kg (1,323 lb)	740 kg (1,631 lb)	760 kg (1,676 lb)

THE World IN ONE Day

INDUSTRY

Most people have to work to earn a living, and all jobs produce something. What's on the planet's production line today?

Hens lay **189 million eggs**, the combined weight is heavier than 110 passenger aeroplanes

550,000 robots work on **car assembly** worldwide

If all **142,387 cars** made were in one long **traffic jam**, they would stretch the length of the United Kingdom

483 robots are sold around the world – **310** of them will work in **industry**, and **173** of them are **service** robots

270 million cotton **shirts** could be made with the **61,370 tonnes** of **cotton** picked

513,500 tonnes of **rice** are produced in **China**, the same weight as five cruise ships

6.4 tonnes of **gold** is mined, enough to make **853,300** gold **rings**

288,800 tonnes of **fish** is turned into **food**, the same weight as **18,750** articulated trucks

Enough **oil** is pumped to fill **5,343** Olympic-sized swimming pools

450,000 carats of diamonds are mined

811,072 cows are turned into beef products

2,351 rabbits are used for rabbit meat

6.3 million ducks are slaughtered

12,671 horses are slain for horse meat, considered a delicacy in parts of Asia and Europe

128.8 million chickens are killed for meat

783,561 laptop and desktop **computers** are sold, a figure that is steadily rising

298,944 bicycles are produced

A **solar energy** cell can generate **360 watt hours** of electricity, enough to power a **laptop** computer for **8 hours**

Brazil is the top producer of coffee with **5,930 tonnes** – enough to give everyone in the country **3.5** cups of coffee

Coca-Cola spends **£4.5 million** ($7.3 million) worldwide on **advertisement**, the same cost as **6.5 million** cans of Coke

1.7 million tonnes of **fruits** are harvested, the same weight as **876,245** cars

If laid side by side from New York City, the **75 million** disposable **nappies** used in the US would reach to Mexico City and back

The UK produces enough **rubbish** to fill **Trafalgar square** to the top of Nelson's column

93,150 tonnes of **aluminium** are produced, with **43,835 tonnes** recycled

Connections

The world is shrinking. Transport is getting quicker and more people are travelling, but those who stay at home are more connected, too. Modern telecommunications means data can travel around the world far quicker than humans ever could – we can watch events unfolding, even if they are happening on the other side of the world. Our interests connect us too, as sporting events and films attract an ever-increasing global audience.

Taking flight

Every day, tens of thousands of aircraft take off for destinations all over the world. They range from the smallest business jets to the biggest airliners. In 2007, the world's 240 airlines scheduled 25 million flights. US aircraft travelled the furthest, clocking up a staggering 11 billion km (6.9 billion miles) in 2009.

AIR 1.6%

TRANSPORT 13%

ROAD 10%

In the driving seat

There are more than 600 million cars on Earth – one car for every 10 people. Roughly 250 million of the world's cars are in the USA. Another 50 million new cars are added to the world total every year.

Stretching a total of

6,465,799 km

(4,017,661 miles), the USA's road network is the longest in the world

Car ownership

Luxembourg leads the world with 647 cars for every 1,000 people. In China, however, there are only 18 cars per 1,000 people, though car use there is increasing rapidly.

LUXEMBOURG 647

CHINA 18

On the road

Up to 40% of a country's road traffic is carried on high-speed routes called motorways. The maximum speeds allowed on these long, wide, and, where possible, straight routes are much higher than on other roads.

On the Move

A vast network of transport routes extends across the world, keeping people and cargo moving along roads, railways, air routes, and sea lanes. Transport of all types is getting faster and more frequent, but concerns about global warming are leading to a change to less polluting engines and fuels. No cars at all will be allowed in a new city called Masdar being built in Abu Dhabi. Instead, citizens will rely on the world's most advanced public transport network.

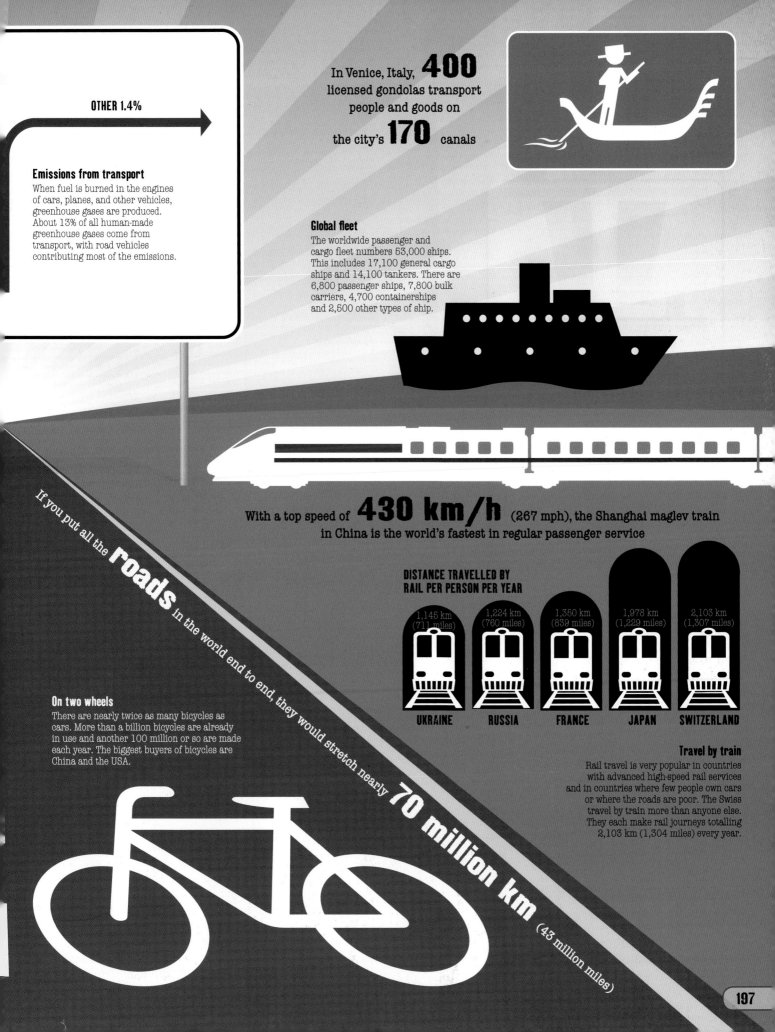

OTHER 1.4%

Emissions from transport
When fuel is burned in the engines of cars, planes, and other vehicles, greenhouse gases are produced. About 13% of all human-made greenhouse gases come from transport, with road vehicles contributing most of the emissions.

In Venice, Italy, **400** licensed gondolas transport people and goods on the city's **170** canals

Global fleet
The worldwide passenger and cargo fleet numbers 53,000 ships. This includes 17,100 general cargo ships and 14,100 tankers. There are 6,800 passenger ships, 7,800 bulk carriers, 4,700 containerships and 2,500 other types of ship.

With a top speed of **430 km/h** (267 mph), the Shanghai maglev train in China is the world's fastest in regular passenger service

If you put all the **roads** in the world end to end, they would stretch nearly **70 million km** (43 million miles)

On two wheels
There are nearly twice as many bicycles as cars. More than a billion bicycles are already in use and another 100 million or so are made each year. The biggest buyers of bicycles are China and the USA.

DISTANCE TRAVELLED BY RAIL PER PERSON PER YEAR

UKRAINE	RUSSIA	FRANCE	JAPAN	SWITZERLAND
1,145 km (711 miles)	1,224 km (760 miles)	1,350 km (839 miles)	1,978 km (1,229 miles)	2,103 km (1,307 miles)

Travel by train
Rail travel is very popular in countries with advanced high-speed rail services and in countries where few people own cars or where the roads are poor. The Swiss travel by train more than anyone else. They each make rail journeys totalling 2,103 km (1,304 miles) every year.

Up and Away!

Air travel is big business. Almost 2.3 billion people – a third of all the people in the world – travelled by aeroplane in 2007. About 40% of all goods by value are also transported by air. Aviation produces 2% of global carbon emissions, one of the causes of global warming. This figure has not changed much in 20 years, even though air traffic is increasing, because today's aircraft engines are more efficient and burn less fuel.

Longest passenger flight

The world's longest scheduled non-stop passenger flight is the Singapore Airlines service from Newark, USA, to Singapore. The flight covers a distance of 15,345 km (9,535 miles) and takes about 19 hours.

Largest planes

The largest airliner in service today is the Airbus A380. This giant double-deck airliner can carry up to 840 passengers. Fully loaded, it can weigh up to 560 tonnes.

The world's busiest airline, Southwest Airlines of the US, carried

101.9 million

passengers in 2008

Sick bags

There are air sickness bags in the seat-back pockets of every airliner, in case of emergencies. The bags are made in huge numbers. One company, Jinan Horizon International in China, can supply up to 300,000 a day.

1: AIRBUS A380
Wingspan 79.8 m
(261 ft 8 in)

2: BOEING 747-400
Wingspan 64.4 m
(211 ft 5 in)

3: AIRBUS A340-600
Wingspan 63.4 m
(208 ft 2 in)

4: BOEING 777-300
Wingspan 60.9 m
(199 ft 11 in)

Strange cargo

Airlines have very strict rules about what items can be taken on board an aeroplane. But that hasn't stopped people trying to smuggle on some very strange items indeed. All the things in the list on the right have been seized by airport security.

1 **Baby alligator**
2 **Suitcase full of cockroaches**
3 **Two live pigeons**
4 **Dead cat**
5 **Full set of tyres**
6 **Frozen monkey head**

CONCORDE
Mach 2.04
2,172 km/h (1,360 mph)

LARGE JET AIRLINER
Mach 0.85
913 km/h (567 mph)

SMALL REGIONAL AIRLINER
Mach 0.43
460 km/h (285 mph)

5. MILAN–ROME: 1,518,767 PASSENGERS

4. MELBOURNE–SYDNEY: 1,563,106 PASSENGERS

3. LONDON–NEW YORK: 1,609,337 PASSENGERS

2. LOS ANGELES–NEW YORK: 1,697,593 PASSENGERS

1. HONG KONG–TAPEI: 2,138,484 PASSENGERS

Busiest routes by passenger numbers
Some air routes are more popular with passengers than others. The Hong Kong–Taipei route is the busiest of all, with more than 2 million passengers every year.

Cruising speeds
Sound travels at 1,236 km/h (768 mph), known as Mach 1. Small regional airliners cruise at about half the speed of sound. Concorde, a supersonic jet that retired in 2003, flew at twice the speed of sound.

HARTSFIELD-JACKSON ATLANTA
90,039,280
(Atlanta, Georgia, USA)

HEATHROW
67,056,379
(London, U.K.)

TOKYO INTERNATIONAL
66,754,829
(Tokyo, Japan)

KINGFORD SMITH
32,900,000
(Sydney, Australia)

SÃO PAULO/GARULHOS
20,400,504
(São Paulo, Brazil)

TAMBO AIRPORT
18,400,000
(Jo'burg, S. Africa)

BUSIEST AIRPORT ON EACH CONTINENT

AIRBUS A380
$190 million+
($300 million+)

BOEING 747-8
$187–197 million
($295–308 million)

BOEING 767
$81–110 million
($127.5–173 million)

BOEING BUSINESS JET 3
$47–54 million
($74.5–84.5 million)

Priciest planes
Large passenger jets cost hundreds of millions of dollars to buy. The Airbus A380 and Boeing 747-8 are the priciest, each costing around $190 million ($300 million), twice as much as the next most expensive, the Boeing 767.

Busiest airport by passenger numbers
The world's busiest airport is Hartsfield-Jackson in Atlanta, USA. More than 90 million passengers passed through it in 2008. In contrast, the busiest airport in Africa, Johannesburg's Tambo Airport, saw only around 18 million fliers.

DAY 1: ROTTERDAM, THE NETHERLANDS

The ship carries tulip bulbs, machinery parts, and furniture as it makes its way to New York, USA.

DAY 7: NEW YORK, USA

A week later, the Rotterdam cargo is unloaded in New York, and is replaced with aircraft parts, cars, and computers.

DAY 18: SANTOS, BRAZIL

In Santos, footwear, coffee, and timber are loaded onto the ship after the New York load is delivered.

Trip around the world

Above is a typical journey around the world for an average containership. They can cruise at 46 km/h (29 mph) – fast enough to cross an ocean in less than two weeks – and can carry 2,500 containers.

Shipping and Ports

About 80% of goods by weight are transported by sea. At the end of 2009, the world's shipping fleet had a carrying capacity of almost 2 billion tonnes. The fleet includes more than 4,700 containerships, carrying 13 million standard shipping containers. People travel by sea, too. About 12 million go on a cruise each year and millions more travel short distances by ferry.

Global seaborne trade in 2008 was about

8 billion tonnes

New York, USA
Los Angeles, USA
New Orleans, USA
Cartagena, Colombia
Santos, Brazil

PACIFIC OCEAN

ATLANTIC OCEAN

Busiest ports

Singapore is the world's busiest container port. It handled nearly 30 million standard shipping containers in 2008. The port of Shanghai was just behind with 28 million containers handled.

Numbers of containers handled in a year (in millions)

SINGAPORE
SHANGHAI, CHINA
HONG KONG, CHINA
SHENZHEN, CHINA
BUSAN, SOUTH KOREA
DUBAI, UNITED ARAB EMIRATES
GUANGZHOU, CHINA
ZHOUSHAN, CHINA
ROTTERDAM, NETHERLANDS
QINGDAO, CHINA

Types of ship

Cargo ships include containerships, which carry cargo in shipping containers, and bulk carriers, which carry unpackaged cargo such as coal. Passenger ships include cruise ships and ferries.

Knock Nevis

The biggest oil tanker ever built is the Knock Nevis. It is 458 m (1,503 ft) long, and can carry more than 564,000 tonnes of oil. It is now coming to the end of its working life, and will be scrapped.

MSC Danit

At 365 m (1,200 ft) long and 51 m (167 ft) wide, the MSC Danit is the world's biggest container ship. It can carry 14,000 shipping containers, weighing up to 165,000 tonnes.

DAY 38:
SHANGHAI, CHINA

It takes almost three weeks to reach China, where the Santos cargo is replaced with toys, clothes, and optical equipment.

DAY 42:
YOKOHAMA, JAPAN

The Shanghai cargo is delivered in Yokohama, where games consoles, cars, and office machinery are loaded.

DAY 57: LOS ANGELES, USA

The Japanese goods are delivered to Los Angeles, where paper, animal food, and scrap metal are loaded as the ship continues its journey back to Rotterdam.

Containerships usually have a crew of about
30 people

Rotterdam, the Netherlands

Marseilles, France

Dubai, UAE

Vladivostok, Russia

Qingdao, China

Busan, South Korea

Shanghai, China
Zhoushan, China

Yokohama, Japan

Guangzhou, China

Hong Kong, China

Shenzhen, China

Singapore

PACIFIC OCEAN

INDIAN OCEAN

Port Hedland, Australia

Sydney, Australia

Pirates of the oceans

Piracy is a growing problem, particularly in the waters around Somalia in Africa. In 2008, 49 ships – including a supertanker – were hijacked and 889 crew members were taken hostage by pirates worldwide.

Lost property

Lost containers

About 10,000 shipping containers fall off ships every year. When nearly 29,000 floating toys spilled out of a container in the Pacific Ocean in 1992, their movements helped scientists to study ocean currents.

WARNING! HEAVY LOAD

Alternative container uses

The average life of a shipping container is about 10–15 years. Containers taken out of circulation have been converted into offices, homes, storage units, hotels, and museums. One was even used as a travelling home for an elephant!

SHIPPING FROM MAJOR PORTS
(Traffic in millions of tonnes)

400+	20–100
300–400	10–20
200–300	5–10
100–200	

World shipping routes

The busiest shipping routes in the world carry goods and materials between Europe, the Middle East, the Far East, and North America. The busiest routes of all carry more than 400 million tonnes of cargo a year.

MS Berge Stahl

The largest bulk carrier ship in the world is the MS Berge Stahl. It carries iron ore between Brazil and Rotterdam. A full load weighs about 364,000 tonnes.

Oasis of the Seas

The 100,000-tonne Oasis of the Seas is the biggest cruise ship. It carries up to 5,400 passengers, who are looked after by a crew of 2,165.

MV Ulysses

The world's largest car ferry is the MV Ulysses. It can carry 1,342 cars and 1,875 passengers.

Tourism and Travel

Tourism on a mass international scale began in the 1950s, and people have been travelling in ever greater numbers since then. Today, most tourists travel between countries within their own region of the world. Only about one in five tourists choose to venture any further and visit another continent. The most adventurous tourists are always looking for new places to go. A handful of wealthy travellers became the first space tourists in the early 2000s.

1.6 BILLION

2020

1.05 BILLION

2010

On the rise

The number of international tourists travelling every year has more than doubled since 1990. The number is predicted to continue growing at more than 4% a year, reaching 1.6 billion by 2020.

Top destinations

More tourists visit European countries than visit Asia, the Pacific, the Americas, Africa, and the Middle East added together. France is the world's favourite holiday destination, with nearly 82 million tourists in 2007.

FRANCE — 81.9 MILLION

USA — 56 MILLION

SPAIN — 59.2 MILLION

GERMANY — 24.4 MILLION

CHINA — 54.7 MILLION

ITALY — 43.7 MILLION

UNITED KINGDOM — 30.7 MILLION

MEXICO — 21.4 MILLION

TURKEY — 22.2 MILLION

UKRAINE — 23.1 MILLION

NUMBER OF VISITORS PER YEAR

A massive **16.64 million** people every year visit Disney World, Florida, USA, the most popular amusement park in the world

The biggest earners

International tourism generated a global revenue of £600 million ($944 million) in 2008. It is the main source of income for some developing countries and island nations. The biggest earner is the USA, even though it is not the most popular destination.

MONEY EARNED FROM TOURISM IN 2008
(in millions)

$96.7	$57.8	$54.2	$42.7	$41.9	$37.6	$36	$22.2	$18.9	$18.5
USA	SPAIN	FRANCE	ITALY	CHINA	UK	GERMANY	AUSTRALIA	AUSTRIA	TURKEY

MOST FREQUENT TRAVELLERS IN 2005

POLAND — 40.8 MILLION

RUSSIA — 28.4 MILLION

FRANCE — 22.3 MILLION

UNITED STATES OF AMERICA — 63.5 MILLION

MALAYSIA — 30 MILLION

ITALY — 23.3 MILLION

UNITED KINGDOM — 66.5 MILLION

CHINA — 31 MILLION

CZECH REPUBLIC — 36.7 MILLION

GERMANY — 77.4 MILLION

Keenest travellers

More than half of the world's tourists are Europeans. Germans top the list, followed by the British and Americans. The numbers of tourists from growing economies are rising fast. Chinese tourists, who numbered only 720,000 in 1993, grew to 31 million by 2005.

With **35.2 million**

visitors each year, Times Square is the most popular attraction in the world

687 MILLION 2000

439.5 MILLION 1990

278.1 MILLION 1980

1970...165.8 MILLION

1960...69.3 MILLION

1950...25.3 MILLION

Space cadet

Dennis Tito became the first space tourist in 2001, when he paid £13 million ($20 million) to visit the International Space Station.

In the Post

Millions of people take letters to post offices or drop them into post boxes every day. The mail is handled by more than 5.5 million postal workers worldwide, processing a staggering 445 billion individual pieces of mail every year. The mail is delivered using all sorts of vehicles, from bicycles and trucks to aircraft. There were even unsuccessful attempts in the 1930s to see if mail could be carried long distances by rocket.

Letters: 66%

Just under 300 billion letters are posted worldwide every year. Most are posted to addresses within the same country, but almost 5.5 billion are international mail, going from one country to another. Four billion of these are transported by aircraft (and are called airmail).

Advertising mail: 32%

You may have noticed the volume of advertising mail in your post. More than 143 billion pieces of mail, selling everything from pizza to phones, are sent every year. In most cases, this type of mail is not requested by the receiver, and is often called junk mail.

Parcels: 2%

Usually taking longer to deliver than the other kinds of mail, parcels make up more than 6.5 billion of the total worldwide post. They take longer to process due to their different shapes, sizes, and weights.

Postal percentages

These three boxes are sized to show the division of the three kinds of postal item. The majority of the mail is letter and postcards, just under a third are advertising items, and only 2% are parcels.

AD mail 32%

Environmental impact

More than 100 million trees are felled every year to make the junk mail delivered in the US alone. The amount of trees needed to make the paper would cover 3,000 sq km (1,158 sq miles).

Why do you get it?

When you buy a product or service, the seller may ask for your name and address. If you're not careful, the details you give may be added to databases and used by companies sending out direct advertising information, or junk mail.

Parcels 2%

Letters to God

More than 1,000 letters arrive every year in Jerusalem, Israel, addressed to God. They are blessed before being stuffed into the cracks of the Western Wall, of the Temple of Jerusalem. They are sent by people of all faiths from all over the world.

Letters to Santa

Children have been writing messages to Santa Claus for 800 years. Children post 6 million Christmas letters every year. These special letters are collected and answered by Santa's postal elves in the North Pole.

Machine help

So many letters are sent every day that it is impossible to sort them all by hand. Machines sort mail wherever possible, using scanners and barcodes. The fastest machines can sort 50,000 letters per hour.

Letters
66%

Lost letters

Thousands of letters are delivered to the wrong addresses every day. Sometimes, the addressee is known to the receiver, who then delivers the letter, and there is no record of the error. However, some letters never reach the correct address and are lost forever.

A letter sent from Queensland, Australia, in 1889 to Aberdeen, Scotland, took a record **112 years** to arrive

12.4 million
letters are lost in the
UK every year

Dead letters

Post that cannot be delivered or returned to their senders are called dead letters. They are taken to mail recovery centres (often called "dead letter offices"), where staff open them and try to find a sender or addressee. If none can be found, the paper is destroyed to protect privacy and any valuable items are sold at a special postal auction.

The United States Postal Service handles **46%** of the world's total letter post

Internet

Although the Internet is only 20 years old, for its 1.7 billion users it has become indispensable for communication, shopping, work, and entertainment. By linking computer networks across the globe into one huge global network, it gives easy access to information and allows nearly any type of data to be exchanged in an instant.

Online access

The number of people using the Internet varies enormously around the world. Each of these pie charts shows the percentage of people who have access to the Internet in a given region. In North America, more than 70% of the population is online, whereas in Africa the figure is just 7%. However, the number of Internet users in Africa is growing faster than anywhere else, except the Middle East.

ASIA 19%

AFRICA 7%

MIDDLE EAST 24%

WORLDWIDE 25%

EUROPE 50%

LATIN AMERICA/ CARIBBEAN 30%

AUSTRALIA 60%

NORTH AMERICA 74%

More than **14 billion** images have been uploaded onto Facebook, a social networking site that currently has more than **300 million** users

There are currently **150** webpages to every person in the world

28% of all webpages are written in English...

...22% are in Chinese

The average American spends **68 hours** a month online

Internet speed

At first, Internet users connected their computers via an ordinary telephone line and a device called a modem. The modem changes data into sounds that can be sent down a telephone line. At most, dial-up access transfers 57,344 bits of data per second. Broadband Internet connections provided by digital telephone lines, satellites, or fibre-optic cables are much faster. They carry digital data without having to change it into sounds. Japanese Internet users enjoy the world's fastest broadband service, with an average download speed of 64 million bits per second.

GREECE 1.0

NEW ZEALAND 2.5

UK 2.6

USA 4.9

GERMANY 6.0

CANADA 7.6

FRANCE 17.6

FINLAND 21.7

SOUTH KOREA 49.5

JAPAN 63.6

AVERAGE BROADBAND SPEEDS
(million bits per second)

File sharing

One of the most popular online activities is file sharing – uploading music, images, and video files onto websites for other people to download and enjoy. The most popular video sharing site, YouTube, exceeded 10 billion views in a single month for the first time in August 2009.

Piracy

The music industry loses billions of pounds a year because of Internet piracy – downloading music without paying for it. Up to 95% of all the music available online is downloaded from an illegal source, often websites set up to allow people to upload files for other people to download for free. A survey of 16 countries found that about 40 billion music files were shared illegally in 2008. It's not just music – films and software are also commonly shared illegally. Since 2003, there have been an estimated 30,000 lawsuits filed against pirates, often resulting in heavy fines.

Confidence tricks

Fraud is a crime that involves deceiving people, usually to steal money. A third of all online fraud involves persuading people to pay for goods that are never delivered. A further quarter sees fraudsters sell goods at auction that don't to live up to their description. But there is a whole range of more elaborate scams. Identity theft involves stealing someone else's personal details. Confidence fraud means conning someone into giving you money by pretending to be someone you're not. Advance-fee fraudsters send emails that offer huge sums of money in return for use of the recipient's bank details. Phishing scams try to con Internet users into giving out their bank details by posing as a financial institution.

- 33% Non-delivery of goods
- 25.5% Misrepresenting goods at auction
- 9% Fraudulent use of a debit/credit card
- 8% Confidence fraud
- 6% Altering data without permission, e.g., on a social networking profile
- 5% Buying goods with a cheque that is rejected by the seller's bank
- 3% Advance-fee fraud
- 2.5% Identity theft
- 2% Phishing
- 2% Conning users into installing malicious software
- 4% Other

Viruses and malware

In 2008, one Internet security company claimed to have discovered 1,656,227 online threats – viruses and other harmful software. This was more than double the number discovered in 2007.
Malware is the name for all malicious computer codes that damage unprotected machines. Viruses are a specific type of malware that infect computers and then create new versions of themselves to infect even more computers. Unlike real viruses, which occur naturally, Internet viruses are created by people and released deliberately onto the Internet.

Online fraud: the culprits

More than half of all online fraudsters operate from the USA. More than 90% of the people who report online crimes are in the USA too, mainly in California, Texas, and Florida. But online crime is truly international, so co-operation between countries is essential to deal with it. Police forces in many countries now have dedicated cyber crime units.

- 66% United States
- 11% United Kingdom
- 7.5% Nigeria
- 3% Canada
- 3% China
- <1% South Africa
- <1% Ghana
- <1% Spain
- <1% Italy
- <1% Romania
- 8% Other

Who sends the spam?

Roughly 65% of spam emails originate from just 10 countries. The USA tops the list of spam-producing countries, accounting for 25% of the nuisance emails sent at the beginning of 2009. The USA is having some success in reducing the numbers of spam emails originating from within its borders, but the numbers coming from some other countries are increasing. Spammers often hijack unprotected home computers, using them to send out millions of emails without their owners suspecting anything is wrong. Just one response per 10 million emails is enough to make the venture profitable.

COUNTRIES OF ORIGIN

- United States
- Brazil
- Turkey
- India
- Poland
- South Korea
- Russia
- Romania
- Spain
- Czech Republic
- Rest of the world

25% — 10% — 6% — 5.5% — 5% — 4.5% — 2.5% — 2.5% — 2% — 2% — 35%

Online Crime

Online crime, also called cyber crime, is one of the fastest-growing types of criminal activity. It costs businesses an estimated £640 billion ($1 trillion) a year. Cyber criminals steal money and valuable information, such as bank and credit card details, spread damaging software, or send nuisance emails without even having to leave home.

The **electricity** used to send all the spam emails sent worldwide in one year is equivalent to the yearly output of **four** large power stations

Spam

Spam is electronic junk mail – unwanted emails sent out in large numbers to advertise products or dupe people into falling for money-making scams. Spammers send millions of emails at a time to computers all over the world. In a bad month, up to 97% of all emails sent worldwide are spam. Over the course of 2008, a whopping 62 trillion spam emails were sent.

Sport Watch

Sport has always been entertaining, and watching the strongest, fastest, most skilful athletes on the planet compete can be exhilarating. Although nothing compares with watching sport live amongst the cheering fans, television allows audiences of millions to watch their favourite teams play around the world. Sport is also big business in the 21st century, and global brands clamour to sponsor the best players.

Most watched sports on TV

Soccer and Formula One events always attract a global audience. However, an enormous home audience and a tense match propelled one of China's most popular sports – volleyball – to the top of the 2008 chart with 184 million viewers. Meanwhile, the 2008 Super Bowl was the most watched sporting event ever in the USA.

SPORTING EVENTS WITH BIGGEST TV AUDIENCES, 2008

Volleyball
Summer Olympics match between China and Cuba (184 million viewers)

Athletics
Men's 100 m final at the Summer Olympics (178 million viewers)

Soccer
European Championship final between Germany and Spain (166 million viewers)

£70 million
($110 million)

1972 – VALERI BORZOV

1984 – CARL LEWIS

1992 – LINFORD CHRISTIE

|95 m

|96 m

|97 m

AMOUNT EARNED IN 2009

£30 million
($45 million)

£30 million
($45 million)

£30 million
($45 million)

£27 million
($42 million)

TIGER WOODS   **KOBE BRYANT**   **MICHAEL JORDAN**   **KIMI RAIKKONEN**   **DAVID BECKHAM**

Show me the money!

Modern sports stars earn megabucks, but not all of the money is from their regular jobs alone. The huge amounts shown to the left combine salaries, endorsements, prize money, bonuses, and licensing income in just one year. Tiger Woods has earned almost £585 million ($900 million) during his 13-year golf career. Branding helps Michael Jordan earn £55 ($85) per minute, seven years after his last professional basketball game.

American football
Super Bowl; New England Patriots vs New York Giants (104 million viewers)

Soccer
Champions League final between Manchester United and Chelsea (98 million viewers)

Formula One
World Championships; Brazillian Grand Prix (80 million viewers)

Tennis
Wimbledon men's finals between Roger Federer and Rafael Nadal (23 million viewers)

Ice hockey
World Championship final between Canada and Russia (23 million viewers)

Basketball
NBA finals between Boston Celtics and Los Angeles Lakers (20 million viewers)

Motor cycling
MotoGP World Championship in Catalunya, Spain (19 million viewers)

Golf
US Masters final day in Augusta, USA (19 million viewers)

NASCAR
Daytona 500 car race, located at Daytona Beach, Florida, USA (18 million viewers)

Baseball
Final between Philadephia Phillies and Tampa Bay Rays (17 million viewers)

Cycling
Stage 9 of the gruelling Tour de France (14 million viewers)

Cricket
Indian Premier League final between Rajasthan and Chennai (12 million viewers)

 = 1 million viewers

Fast, faster, fastest
Jamaica's Usain Bolt proved his incredible speed and strength when he won gold in three events at the 2008 Olympics. His record-breaking time of 9.69 seconds in the 100 m final would leave past Olympic sprinting champions trailing three or more metres behind. This diagram shows where some others sprinting greats would be as Bolt crossed the finish line.

2008 -- USAIN BOLT

98 m   99 m   100 m

Mr Strong
Many sports stars are also national heroes. The Iranian weightlifter Hossein Rezazadeh smashed world records at the Sydney Olympics in 2000, lifting a total of 472.5 kg (1,042 lb) – the equivalent of a large cow! He is so popular in Iran that his wedding was broadcast live on state television.

Surf's up!
Bad weather is usually bad news for sports fans, but the world's ultimate surfing competition at Oahu, Hawaii, only takes place when a hurricane or tropical storm strikes, generating waves more than 6 m (20 ft) tall. The biggest wave ever surfed was a bone-crushing 26 m (85 ft) high by American Ken Bradshaw in 1998.

- 27 M (90 ft)
- 24 M (80 ft)
- 21 M (70 ft)
- 18 M (60 ft)
- 15 M (50 ft)
- 12 M (40 ft)
- 9 M (30 ft)
- 6 M (20 ft)
- 3 M (10 ft)
- 0 M (0 ft)

Movie Magic

The global film industry is dominated by the film studios in Hollywood and Bollywood. Big-budget Hollywood movies top the box office charts around the world and generate billions in total revenue. Bollywood produces the most films and has an enormous home audience. The world's largest potential audience lies in China where moviegoing is becoming more popular and the film industry is thriving.

Avatar, the highest-grossing film of all time, made **£1.4 billion** ($2.2 billion) in its opening eight weeks

The big three

HOLLYWOOD, USA

The US film industry has been based in Hollywood, California, since the very first silent movies of the 1910s and 1920s, and made the world's first "talkie" (talking movie) in 1927. It still leads the world in developing new filmmaking techniques and has produced some of the most expensive films in history.

BOLLYWOOD, INDIA

The most famous part of the Indian film industry based its name on its American equivalent, changing the "H" for a "B" after Bombay (Mumbai), the industry's home city. As in Hollywood, the first Indian films were silent, but today's Bollywood films are famous for their singing, dancing, colours, and costume changes.

CHINA

The first Chinese movie, called *The Difficult Couple*, was filmed in 1913. During the 1920s, US filmmakers trained Chinese filmmakers in Shanghai, and the industry grew slowly for most of the 20th century. More recently, government control over the industry has relaxed, making it easier to make films.

Production costs per film

Hollywood has the highest average production costs, but the salaries of actors and technical staff can make up as much as 75% of a Bollywood film's production budget. In China, filmmakers typically receive about 7% of a film's budget from the Chinese government, but they sometimes struggle to secure the rest to make big-budget films.

HOLLYWOOD £8.7 MILLION ($13.6 MILLION)

CHINA £4.5 MILLION ($7 MILLION)

BOLLYWOOD £0.8 MILLION ($1.3 MILLION)

Nollywood

Nigeria's booming film industry – known as "Nollywood" – produces more than 17 movies every week. Although the country has just four cinemas, a huge DVD and home video market in Nigeria and neighbouring countries generates about £160 million ($250 million) in revenue every year.

Top moviegoing nations

About a quarter of New Zealand's population visits the cinema once a month or more, and the average person visits the cinema almost nine times a year. Contrast this with China, where the average person visits the cinema only once every six years. The US boasts 39,476 screens (one for every 7,700 people), which is more than the whole of the European Union put together.

CINEMA TRIPS PER PERSON PER YEAR

NEW ZEALAND: 8.9 TRIPS

AUSTRALIA: 7 TRIPS

ICELAND: 4.6 TRIPS

CANADA/IRELAND: 4.2 TRIPS (each)

Marketing costs per film

Hollywood film studios often spend enormous amounts to attract audiences, usually about half the cost of making the film. Television, print, poster, radio, and online advertising usually take 75% of the marketing budget.

CHINA
£1.5 MILLION
($2.3 MILLION)

BOLLYWOOD, INDIA
£321,000
($500,000)

HOLLYWOOD, US
£21 MILLION
($32.7 MILLION)

Revenues

Beyond the box office, films make money through home viewing, licensing, and merchandising. Although DVD sales are falling, online DVD rental and film downloads are growing. These revenue sources are threatened by piracy, particularly in China and India, where pirate DVDs are much cheaper than cinema tickets. Piracy is thought to cost the Indian film industry £600 million ($1 billion) every year.

And the winner is...

No film industry would be complete without its own awards show – and the global audiences of millions watching them. The winners may be chosen by past victors, expert panels, or the fans themselves.

The Oscars

The Academy Awards, popularly called "the Oscars", began in 1929. Since then, more than 2,700 awards have been handed out. The gold-plated Oscar trophy – a knight holding a sword, standing on a reel of film – weighs as much as a newborn baby. The films *Ben Hur*, *Titanic*, and *Lord of the Rings: the Return of the King* share the record of 11 Oscars each.

IIFA trophy

The International Indian Film Awards (IIFA) take place in a different country every year. Despite being held for the first time in 2000, the IIFA already attracts a total global audience of 350 million. The fans decide who get the trophies, which display a Sun-influenced design. The 2003 film *Kal No Naaa Ho* (*Tomorrow May Not Come*) broke records with 14 IFAA awards.

Golden Horse

The Taiwanese Golden Horse Awards are the most prestigious of the Chinese-language film industry. The horse-shaped statuettes are awarded to films from Taiwan, Malaysia, Singapore, Hong Kong, and China. The record haul goes to *Gun Gun Hong Chen* (*Red Dust*), with eight wins at the 1990 awards show.

Tickets sold

The world spends almost £19.2 billion ($30 billion) on cinema tickets every year. China leads the way with 1,497 million tickets, but the US (1,446 million) and India (1,341 million) are not far behind. The growing number of 3D films is expected to keep sales rising by about 5% annually, as more people pay higher ticket prices for an experience they can't have at home.

Films produced

Films are made so fast in Bollywood that actors may shoot as many as four different films at a time using the same sets. The Chinese film industry is growing rapidly, and now makes double the amount of films it did in 2004.

CHINA
456 FILMS
PER YEAR

HOLLYWOOD
485 FILMS
PER YEAR

BOLLYWOOD
1,091 FILMS
PER YEAR

El Mariachi, made in 1992 in Mexico is the most profitable film ever – it cost just £4,500 ($7,000) to make, but took more than

£1.3 million

($2 million) in sales worldwide

Media

In the past, it could take hours or days for news to travel, but now we can read about events straight away or even watch them happening. The various means of mass communication are referred to collectively as the media, and include television, radio, newspapers, and the Internet. The media is dominated by a small number of massive international companies, who each own a variety of publishers, broadcasting companies, and news websites.

1. Walt Disney

$59.1 billion

The world's biggest media and entertainment organization, the Walt Disney Company was founded in 1923 by brothers Roy and Walt Disney. The company's wide-ranging activities include films, television, publishing, and the world-famous Disney theme parks.

4. Time Warner

$50.1 billion

The Time Warner media group was formed in the 1990s when the magazine publisher Time Inc merged with the film studio and music producer Warner Communications. The AOL Internet service provider was also part of the organization until it was sold in 2009.

Newspapers

The best-selling newspapers sell millions of copies every day. The world's most avid newspaper readers are the Japanese. Three times more newspapers are delivered to the average Japanese home than in the USA, and nearly 10 times more than in France.

Top 10 newspapers by circulation (in millions):
1 **Yomiuri Shimbun** (Japan) 14.1
2 **The Asahi Shimbun** (Japan) 12.1
3 **Mainichi Shimbun** (Japan) 5.6
4 **Nihon Keizai Shimbun** (Japan) 4.6
5 **Chunichi Shimbun** (Japan) 4.5
6 **Das Bild** (Germany) 3.5
7 **Reference News** (China) 3.2
8 **The Times of India** (India) 3.1
9 **The Sun** (UK) 3.0
10 **The People's Daily** (China) 2.8

TOP FIVE MEDIA COMPANIES' INTERESTS

- Theme parks
- TV
- Radio
- Films
- Telecoms
- Sports
- Magazines
- Music
- Online
- Print media

Magazines

A more glossy type of print media, magazines are usually published weekly or monthly. News magazines concentrate on issues in the news, often dealing with them in greater depth than a newspaper can. Special interest magazines deal with one particular subject, such as sport, entertainment, or fashion.

Top 10 magazines by circulation (in millions):
1 **National Geographic** (USA) 6.7
2 **Time** (USA) 3.3
3 **Newsweek** (USA/UK) 2.7
4 **US News & World Report** (USA) 1.7
5 **The Economist** (UK) 1.4
6 **India Today** (India) 1.1
7 **Veja** (Brazil) 1.08
8 **The New Yorker** (USA) 1.05
9 **Der Spiegel** (Germany) 1.03

Media through time

The first news sheets were published in China in the 8th century. They were handwritten on silk. Over time, the world gradually developed into the multimedia society that we live in today.

Radio

Radio was the first of the broadcast media. Today, it is the most popular news medium in developing countries. Radio is going digital, with the introduction of Digital Audio Broadcasting (DAB), which is growing in popularity, especially in Europe.

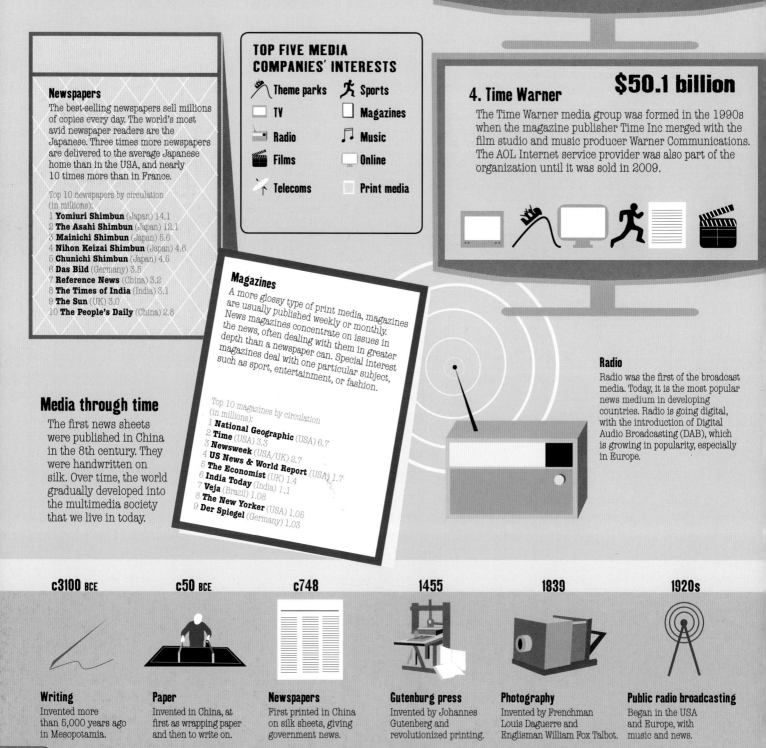

c3100 BCE	c50 BCE	c748	1455	1839	1920s
Writing	**Paper**	**Newspapers**	**Gutenburg press**	**Photography**	**Public radio broadcasting**
Invented more than 5,000 years ago in Mesopotamia.	Invented in China, at first as wrapping paper and then to write on.	First printed in China on silk sheets, giving government news.	Invented by Johannes Gutenberg and revolutionized printing.	Invented by Frenchman Louis Daguerre and Englisman William Fox Talbot.	Began in the USA and Europe, with music and news.

2. News Corp

$58.9 billion

This massive global corporation owns scores of television channels, book publishers, newspapers, magazines, sports organizations, film studios, record labels, and digital media. It was created in 1980 by Australian business tycoon Rupert Murdoch.

3. Comcast

$57.7 billion

The Comcast name amalgamates "communication" and "broadcast" – its main activities – into one word. Comcast began in cable television in the USA in the 1960s, before branching out to supply telephone and broadband Internet services to its US subscribers.

5. Vivendi

$45.7 billion

This French media group operates worldwide in television, film, telecommunications, music publishing, and video games. It was formed in 1998 from a company with interests in water, energy, transport, and construction, which then moved into media activities.

Television

Many TV news channels reach huge audiences. The most popular is BBC World News – a 24-hour news and information channel that broadcasts to 292 million households in more than 200 countries. In second place, US channel CNN reaches 200 million households, while Qatar-based Al Jazeera broadcasts to 150 million.

Online

The Web is an increasingly popular and convenient source of news. One measure of the success of news websites is the number of people who look at a site for the first time each month. These numbers are called monthly uniques.

Top 10 news sites by monthly uniques:
1 **Yahoo News** 42 million
2 **CNN Digital** 38 million
3 **MSNBC Digital** 36 million
4 **AOL News** 25 million
5 **NYTimes** 21 million
6 **Fox News Digital** 17 million
7 **Tribune** 16 million
8 **ABCNews Digital** 14 million
9 **Google news** 14 million
10 **Gannett News** 12 million

Today's **mobiles** enable users to access up-to-the-minute news coverage, and to submit news and photographs taken with, and sent via, their phones

1936

TV broadcasting
Began with programmes broadcast by the BBC in London.

1962

Telstar
Launched into Earth's orbit as the first communications satellite.

1977

Personal computers
Invented with the introduction of the Commodore PET.

1979

Cellular phones
Developed in the 1980s, allowing people to make phone calls on the move.

1990

World Wide Web
Invented by Tim Berners-Lee and made available to the public.

1991

Mobiles go digital
Second-generation cellular phones introduced.

Telephone Networks

When you make an international telephone call, whether from a landline or a mobile phone, the signal travels through a vast network of cables, radio links, and satellites to reach its destination. It may travel thousands of kilometres, but it gets there — and is relayed back — in the blink of an eye. Here are the main stages in that journey.

Calling from a landline

The telephone network can connect any telephone line to any other. There are so many phones over such a wide area that calls must travel through a series of exchanges – hubs that electronically connect one telephone line to another.

Local telephone exchange

The call first goes to a local telephone exchange. It is carried there as an electronic signal along copper wires underground or strung between telephone poles overhead, or as pulses of light along underground fibre-optic cables.

Main exchange

Calls are relayed from the local exchange to a main exchange located in a nearby town or city. If the call is destined for a nearby city, it is forwarded from one main exchange to another.

System of cells

Each cell has a radio antenna, called a base station, that picks up signals from nearby mobiles and sends them to the mobile switching centre.

Mobile switching centre

The mobile switching centre is a type of exchange. If the call is for a nearby mobile, it will be directed back to the relevant base station. If the call needs to go further afield or to a landline, it is sent to the main exchange.

Calling from a mobile phone

A mobile phone call uses the same main exchange as a landline, but to get there it is routed through the mobile network. The mobile network divides the land into areas called cells. The size of each cell depends on the type of terrain and the number of people it contains.

Communications satellite

Orbiting 36,000 km (22,370 miles) above the equator, a satellite receives the radio signal and transmits it to a different location. Communications satellites follow a geostationary orbit, meaning they always stay over the same spot on the ground. This is so dishes on Earth can be fixed in one position.

Satellite earth station

A telephone call going a very long distance, especially over land, may be sent to a satellite earth station. From here, the signal is sent via a satellite dish to a communications satellite orbiting the Earth.

Satellite earth station

In the destination country, a satellite earth station receives the radio signal. It is changed back into an electronic signal and sent along wires, or into pulses of light and sent down optical fibres.

Telecommunications tower

International calls are sent from the main exchange to a dish antenna at the top of a tall telecommunications tower. The antenna sends a microwave radio signal to a satellite earth station or an exchange near the coast.

Satellite or submarine signal?

Telephone calls for overseas are most often connected by submarine cable because it is cheaper and more reliable than using a satellite. A call from Europe to the USA, for example, might travel 6,000 km (3,700 miles) end to end if linked by submarine cable. The same call connected by satellite has to travel 12 times further – 36,000 km (22,370 miles) up and then the same distance back down.

CONNECTIONS

Overhead cable

Underground optical fibre

Microwaves

Submarine cable

Coastal exchange

A coastal exchange on the other side of the sea receives the call from the submarine cable and sends it on through a chain of telephone exchanges, as before.

Coastal exchange

A telephone call going overseas may be sent by submarine (underwater) cable – a fibre-optic cable laid on the seabed. A telephone exchange located near the coast sends the signal on its way.

By the end of 2009, **4.6 billion** mobile phones were in use worldwide.

Satellites

Anything that orbits a planet is known as a satellite. The Moon is a natural satellite of Earth. Thousands of artifical satellites also circle the Earth, doing all sorts of jobs. Some photograph clouds and storms to help with weather forecasting, others relay telephone calls, Internet traffic, and television programmes from place to place. The US space agency NASA uses a fleet of satellites to keep in touch with its spacecraft, while orbiting telescopes such as Hubble use the clear view above Earth's atmosphere to study distant galaxies.

Rocket power

Satellites are launched on rockets. When a satellite reaches orbit, it is travelling at the speed its rocket boosted it to. In space, there is nothing to stop it, so it just keeps going. Gravity pulls the satellite towards Earth, but the satellite is moving forwards, so its falling path matches the curve of Earth's surface. The satellite stays in orbit because its forward speed balances the pull of Earth's gravity.

3. Old satellites

Satellites in low orbits are gradually slowed by the faint wisps of atmosphere that they fly through. As they slow down they orbit lower and lower and eventually spiral into the atmosphere and burn up. Satellites at higher altitudes may remain in orbit, but most only function for around 15 years.

With a fleet of about **1,400**, Russia owns nearly half of all the satellites in orbit

2. Into orbit

A satellite takes about 8 minutes to go from the launch-pad into orbit. To get a satellite into space a large amount of fuel is needed – the weight of a rocket on launch is mostly made up of the fuel it will burn on its journey.

4% satellite
6% rocket structure

90% fuel

WEIGHT OF THE ROCKET

1. Ready for liftoff

Putting a satellite into orbit is a costly affair. Tens of millions of dollars are spent on the launch, and on insuring the mission against the risk of accidents. These costs are dwarfed by that of the satellite itself, which may run into hundreds of millions of dollars.

LAUNCH COSTS

- **Insurance** $50 million
- **Launch** $80 million
- **Satellite itself** $250 million

A satellite in low Earth orbit moves through space at **28,000 km/h** (17,400 mph)

Geostationary orbit

A satellite 30,000 km (22,370 miles) above the equator goes as fast as the Earth turns. This means it stays above the same spot on the ground all the time, but because it is far away, its signal can reach a wide area. Communications satellites often use this orbit.

Highly elliptical orbit

Countries near the poles use this orbit for communications satellites. While a satellite in this orbit is far from Earth, it travels slowly over the polar regions. Then it swoops round the Earth fast and starts the long, slow part of its next orbit.

Medium Earth orbit

Medium Earth orbit extends from a height of about 1,000 km (620 miles) to 20,000 km (12,430 miles). Medium Earth orbits are used mainly by navigation satellites, such as GPS (see below).

Polar orbit

Some satellites orbit from pole to pole. Polar orbits are used by satellites observing the Earth, including some weather satellites, because this orbit takes satellites over the Earth's entire surface.

Low Earth orbit

Satellites in low Earth orbit are between 300 km (186 miles) and 1,000 km (620 miles) above the ground. The International Space Station and the Hubble Space Telescope both use this orbit.

Orbits

Satellites can be placed in a number of different orbits ranging from hundreds to tens of thousands of kilometres above the ground. The choice of orbit depends on the job a satellite will do. On its orbit, a satellite can follow a path over the quator, or between the poles, or anywhere in between.

GPS satellites

The Global Positioning System (GPS) uses a network of 24 satellites in six circular orbits to give global coverage. Each satellite sends out radio signals with their exact location and the time. A GPS receiver anywhere on Earth will always be in range of at least three of these satellites. The receiver calculates the distance between itself and each of the satellites, and uses this information to work out its own position and directions to the desired destination.

International Space Station

The International Space Station (ISS) is the biggest structure ever built in space. Orbiting the Earth at an altitude of about 340 km (211 miles), it is the ongoing work of 16 countries, all working together to complete this ambitious project. Construction began in 1998 and is expected to be completed by 2011. It is assembled from dozens of parts that are launched separately and then linked together by astronauts.

Completion

After more than 80 flights of US Space Shuttles and Russian rockets, the International Space Station will be completed in 2011. It will measure 74 m (243 ft) by 108.5 m (356 ft), with as much space inside as a Boeing 747 passenger cabin.

ISS structure

When the International Space Station is complete, it will consist of about a dozen cylindrical modules, where the crew live and work, connected to a main beam called the truss structure. Solar panels and radiators, which keep the space station cool, are fixed to the ends of the same beam.

Zarya

The Zarya (Sunrise) Module, also known as the Functional Cargo Block, was built by Russia and was the first piece of this massive feat to be launched into space, in November 1998.

Truss structure

Truss structure

Quest airlock

Astronauts will have made 1,705 hours of spacewalks from the Space Shuttle and airlocks like Quest to complete the station.

Solar panels

Electrical power is provided by solar panels. They contain an impressive 262,400 individual solar cells and cover a total area of about 2,500 sq m (26,910 sq ft). Together, they generate more than 100 kilowatts from sunlight.

Radiator

Node 3

Tranquillity, or Node 3, is attached to Node 1 and houses a seven-window dome called a cupola. From here, the robotic arm Canadarm 2 will be operated.

A total of **52 computers** control all the systems on board the International Space Station

Docking at the ISS

Docking ports allow spacecraft such as the Space Shuttle and European ATV supply craft to link up with the space station. A Russian Soyuz spacecraft is always docked with the station to serve as a lifeboat in an emergency.

Life on board

The crew's daily activities at the ISS are planned in detail before they leave Earth. Life on board is split between scientific experiments, maintenance work, and exercise – essential to stop muscles from wasting away in the weightlessness of space.

Space clothing

Everyday wear in the space station is a casual affair of T-shirt and shorts or trousers. To make spacewalks, astronauts don a 127-kg (280-lb) spacesuit that feels as light as a feather in micro-gravity, and comes with its own special underwear.

Space food

The crew on board the ISS eat three meals a day. Today's astronauts can pick and choose what they eat, from cereal and fresh fruit to meat and vegetables. Some food is fresh, some packaged in foil or cans, and some is dehydrated and so has to be mixed with water.

Robotic arm

Canadarm 2 is a mobile robotic arm that moves along the length of the space station on rails. It is 17.6 m (57.7 ft) long and can move large loads of up to 116,000 kg (256,000 lb), making it a key worker in the construction and maintenance of the space station.

The International Space Station orbits Earth every

91 minutes

Destiny Laboratory

This US science research laboratory has rack upon rack of equipment to carry out different experiments in its stellar environment. Fitted with a large window for photographing Earth, the laboratory provides the scientists on board with an excellent view.

Node 1

Also known as the Unity Module, Node 1 was the first major US-built part of the space station. The 5.5-m- (18-ft-) long module connects the Destiny Laboratory to the Zarya Module.

Node 2

The Harmony Module (Node 2) was supplied by the European Space Agency. It provides a passageway between the US Destiny, Japanese Kibo, and European Columbus laboratories.

BUILDING THE ISS

United States
The driving force behind the ISS, the USA supplies most of the hardware and funding.

Russia
The USA's main partner, Russia launches some of the hardware and crews.

Japan
Japan supplied the Kibo science research module and experiment platform.

Europe
The European Space Agency (ESA) is providing a module and supply craft.

Canada
Canada's contribution is a robotic arm, which was installed in 2001.

Italy
As well as contributing to ESA, Italy supplies cargo modules.

Brazil
An experiment pallet and research facilities were supplied by Brazil.

About **80%** of the world's land is directly opposite an ocean

The only continents that are

opposite

each other are South America and Asia

London

Getafe

Journey through the Earth

These coloured lines represent what would happen if you drilled a hole through the centre of the Earth from different points on the surface. The most obvious antipodal points are the North and South poles, which are both cold zones, but other antipodal points are complete opposites in many ways. Follow each coloured line and discover its global opposite on the facing page.

to get to the other side

5 days

Machu Picchu

Atacama Desert

Amazon

Botswana

Perito Merino

Punta Arenas

If you travelled through the centre of Earth at 100 km/h (62 mph), it would take you more than

Hainan Island, China
Atacama Desert, Chile

Hainan Island in the South China Sea is abundantly green. The tropical climate provides long, hot, rainy summers, with as much as 2 m (80 in) of rain falling per year. Its global opposite, the Atacama Desert, is the driest place on Earth.

Getafe, Spain
North Island, New Zealand

Getafe is a bustling industrial city where fighter jets zoom from the headquarters of the Spanish air force. Across the globe, the rolling pastures of North Island are home to millions of quietly grazing sheep; exporting sheep meat is one of New Zealand's largest industries.

Global Opposites

It is possible to trace the exact global opposite of any location on our planet by drawing a line from the location and running it through the centre of the Earth to the other side. Any two places on diametrically opposite sides of the globe are called antipodes. Every location on Earth has an antipodal point.

Russian border
Lake Baikal
Hainan Island
Vietnam
Manila
Mauna Kea
North Island
Pacific Ocean
South Pole

Mauna Kea, Hawaii / **Botswana**

The summit of Mauna Kea on Hawaii hosts the world's largest astronomical observatory. Across the world, the Nxai Pan National Park in Botswana is full of zebra, impala, and springbok.

Russian border / **Perito Merino, Argentina**

The Yenisey river basin in Russia is a green and fertile land where many animals live. By contrast, the icy and vast Perito Merino Glacier is located amongst rugged mountains and glacial lakes.

Lake Baikal, Russia / **Punta Arenas, Chile**

Mini submarines explore the world's deepest freshwater lake. Across the globe – near the very tip of South America – Punta Arenas is a starting point for explorers to Antarctica.

Manila, Philippines / **Amazon, Brazil**

Manila in the Philippines is one of the most densely populated cities in the world. Shoot across the globe and you are in the Amazon rainforest where you will find lush green trees and a huge diversity of animal life.

Dak Lak, Vietnam / **Machu Picchu, Peru**

The coffee-growing regions of Vietnam are thriving, producing up to one million tonnes a year. The ancient ruins of Machu Picchu lie atop a steep Andean mountain, 2,430 m (8,000 ft) high.

North Pole / **South Pole**

Though they share a cold climate, the poles have their differences. The North Pole is home to polar bears, while penguins live in the South Pole. The South Pole is much colder than the North because it sits on land.

London, UK / **Pacific Ocean**

London's busy streets are packed with commuters and tourists, and are miles from the sea. Its global opposite is the immense Pacific Ocean – a habitat for humpback whales and giant tube worms.

THE World IN ONE Day

CONNECTIONS

Whether you're a globe trotter or sofa surfer, technology has made the planet a smaller place, and information travels fast.

30 new **extrasolar planets** were announced in one day on October 2009, the most ever

There are **5 people** in **space,** all on the **International Space Station**

Actor Harrison Ford earned **£345,099** ($550, 847) a day on the fourth *Indiana Jones* film

About **10.7 million** people visit the **cinema** in India, more people than the population of **Paris**

4 official international **football matches** are contested somewhere around the world

63,000 sea travellers journey to and from UK **ports**

545,780,360 newspapers are circulated

Popstar Madonna earned **£189,041** ($301,370) per day in 2009

81,096 passenger **flights** are made very day, with about **200 million** airline **meals** served

9,589 people spend **30 minutes** each on the **London Eye** in London, England – it can carry **800** people at a time

76,712 people go to **Niagra Falls** to see the most powerful waterfall in North America

3.4 million people buy **mobile phones** – in the US, **3 billion** phone calls are made every day

2,753 books – enough to fill a small library – are published

The average Japanese household has at least one **TV** on for about **9 hours**

573,687 people buy **TV sets**

People make **1.2 billion** Internet searches through the **Google** search engine website

1,656,131,715 people have **Internet** access, **317 million** more than there are people in **China**

1.2 billion mail items are sorted worldwide

Twitter users clock up **39.5 million** tweets per day

209,996,664,788 email messages are sent, **163,797,398,535** of which are **spam**

28,800 hours of footage is uploaded to **YouTube**

Mickey Mouse and Donald Duck see **41,917** people at Paris **Disneyland**

53,000 visitors walk along the Great Wall of **China**

Only **300** people are allowed to visit the **Great Pyramid** of Khufu in Giza, Egypt for preservation reasons

Our World in the Future

it's 2050, and people are on average bigger, older, and fatter than now. Computers are smaller, faster, and virtually everywhere – from your clothes to the cells in your body. They think for themselves, and are connected to each other in countless ways, acting and reacting to help you through life. No classrooms, no washing, and no nasty surprises from overhead birds. . .This is a snapshot of what the future may bring.

Medicine

The human genome is mapped – leading the way to cures for diseases such as cancer and AIDS. In 2050, patients are diagnosed and treated according to their unique genetic profile, with doctors able to see exactly where disease and infections lie, making it possible to live even longer. Research into special cells called "stem cells" offer new ways to treat common ailments.

Economics

China overtook the US to become the world's largest economy in 2030. India is now catching up, at 90% the size of the US economy. However, the populations of India and China are so big that their per capita incomes are still 40% lower than that of the US.

LARGEST ECONOMIES IN 2050

China US India Japan Brazil

SPRAY'N'GO STORE

Future clothing

Washing and ironing is dead: spray-on fibres create disposable fashion with a perfect fit. Nanotechnology fabrics have brains as well as beauty, alerting you to changes in your body and even using the energy from your movements to power gadgets.

Hydrogen fuel

About 1.5 billion vehicles are zipping around in 2050, but there are diminishing fossil fuels left to power them. Hydrogen fuel is the clean, green, and renewable source of power that is used. It can be generated on huge solar farms and used to top up fuel cells in electrical devices of all sizes, from cars to computers.

School classroom

Classrooms are a thing of the past, along with textbooks, pens, and paper. Pupils interact with teachers online, while avatars – the pupils' identities in cyberspace – manage their personal learning plans. Despite your school being virtual, your homework is still a reality.

Robot helpers

One in five people are over the age of 60. Robots help them to zip around, "smart" slippers monitor their health, and their false teeth remind them to take their pills on time.

Nanotechnology

Microscopic computers are tucked inside your cells, nanorobots navigate your bloodstream, and all send signals to let doctors know exactly what is going on inside you. They even tell your cells how to make their own medicine, in exactly the right doses.

Population: 9 billion

The world's population is 9 billion, with less developed nations showing the most growth. In 2050, these five countries are home to almost half the world's people, with nearly 20% living in India alone. Roughly 70% of people live in towns and cities.

India: 1.7 billion
China: 1.4 billion
US: 439 million
Indonesia: 343 million
Pakistan: 335 million

LARGEST POPULATIONS IN 2050

Super-computers

Can't live without your mobile phone? Imagine if you'd downloaded the entire contents of your brain onto it. The handheld computers of 2050 are 100,000 times more powerful than those of 2010, processing data so quickly that your phone alerts you to falling bird poop before it splatters your nanotech jacket!

Animal cloning

In the last 40 years, one in 10 animals have become extinct. However, advances in cloning offer a lifeline to the most threatened species. But no need to stop there, when you can clone a dinosaur to carry your shopping and help you beat the rush-hour traffic!

Reference

This section contains a handy reference guide to the world's countries. Use the world map to locate them geographically and look up key statistics in the alphabetical chart. The sources pages list the agencies, reports, and websites that are the original sources for the data in this book.

World Map

The seven continents that make up the world's landmasses are, from largest to smallest, Asia, Africa, North America, South America, Antarctica, Europe, and Australia. Oceania is not a continent but a name for the region that includes Australia, New Zealand, and the Pacific islands.

Political map

This map is called a political map, because it shows country borders rather than physical features. Like many of the maps in this book, it uses an Eckert IV projection.

MAP KEY

————	Full international border
————	Disputed border
·········	Maritime border
FRANCE	Independent state
Gibraltar (to UK)	Self-governing dependent territory
Johnston Atoll (to US)	Non self-governing dependent territory

Squaring a circle

The only really accurate way to show the world is using a globe. Flat maps always involve distortions. The choice of how to portray the curve of the Earth on a flat surface is called a projection. Different projections distort different things depending on their purpose – some show area correctly, others show compass direction correctly.

Eckert IV

The projection used for the maps in this book is called the Eckert IV projection. It distorts area and direction as little as possible. This strikes a balance between the Peters' and the Mercator projections.

Map labels

ARCTIC OCEAN
Arctic Circle
Alaska (to US)
Great Bear Lake
Great Slave Lake
Baffin Bay
60°N
Aleutian Islands (to US)
PACIFIC OCEAN
C A N A D A
Lake Winnipeg
Great Lakes
Hudson Bay
St Pierre & Miquelon (to France)
NORTH AMERICA
UNITED STATES OF AMERICA
ATLANTIC OCEAN
30°N
Midway Islands (to US)
Tropic of Cancer
Guadalupe (to Mexico)
Gulf of Mexico
Bermuda (to UK)
MEXICO
BAHAMAS
Hawaii (to US)
Cayman Islands (to UK)
Turks & Caicos Islands (to UK)
British Virgin Islands (to UK)
Virgin Islands (to US)
Anguilla (to UK)
Johnston Atoll (to US)
Revillagigedo Islands (to Mexico)
CUBA
DOMINICAN REPUBLIC
ST KITTS & NEVIS
JAMAICA
HAITI
BELIZE
Caribbean
Puerto Rico (to US)
ANTIGUA & BARBUDA
Montserrat (to UK)
Guadeloupe (to France)
DOMINICA
Martinique (to France)
GUATEMALA
HONDURAS
Sea
Aruba (to Neth.)
Neth. Ant. (to Neth.)
ST LUCIA
BARBADOS
EL SALVADOR
NICARAGUA
ST VINCENT & THE GREN
GRENADA
Clipperton Island (to France)
COSTA RICA
VENEZUELA
TRINIDAD & TOBAGO
PANAMA
GUYANA
Kingman Reef (to US)
COLOMBIA
French Guiana (to France)
SURINAM
Palmyra Atoll (to US)
Equator
Galapagos Islands (to Ecuador)
ECUADOR
Baker & Howland Islands (to US)
Jarvis Island (to US)
K I R I B A T I
B R A Z I L
PACIFIC OCEAN
PERU
SOUTH AMERICA
Tokelau (to NZ)
Cook Islands (to NZ)
BOLIVIA
Wallis & Futuna (to France)
SAMOA
American Samoa (to US)
PARAGUAY
TONGA
Niue (to NZ)
French Polynesia (to France)
Tropic of Capricorn
Pitcairn Islands (to UK)
Sala y Gomez (to Chile)
Easter Island (to Chile)
San Felix Island (to Chile)
San Ambrosio Island (to Chile)
CHILE
30°S
Kermadec Islands (to NZ)
Juan Fernandez Islands (to Chile)
ARGENTINA
URUGUAY
Chatham Islands (to NZ)
Falkland Islands (to UK)
60°S
South Shetland Islands (to UK)
Antarctic Circle
150°W 120°W 90°W 60°W

Peters'

This projection shows the continents according to their actual area but distorts their shape. Africa and South Africa appear stretched lengthwise, Antarctica and Greenland are stretched sideways.

Mercator

Used for navigation, Mercator maps are accurate in terms of compass direction, but distort area, especially in polar regions. Greenland looks bigger than South America when it is actually about one-ninth of the size.

COUNTRY	CAPITAL CITY	CURRENCY	GDP	GDP PER CAPITA
Afghanistan	Kabul	Afghani	$12,061,000,000	$416
Albania	Tirane	Lek	$12,964,000,000	$4,090
Algeria	Algiers	Algerian Dinar	$159,669,000,000	$4,588
Andorra	Andorra la Vella	Euro	–	–
Angola	Luanda	Kwanza	$83,384,000,000	$5,054
Antigua and Barbuda	Saint John's	East Caribbean Dollar	$1,256,000,000	$14,556
Argentina	Buenos Aires	Argentine Peso	$324,767,000,000	$8,171
Armenia	Yerevan	Dram	$11,928,000,000	$3,685
Australia	Canberra	Australian Dollar	$1,013,461,000,000	$46,824
Austria	Vienna	Euro	$414,828,000,000	$50,039
Azerbaijan	Baku	Azerbaijani Manat	$46,378,000,000	$5,349
Bahamas	Nassau	Bahamian Dollar	$7,463,000,000	$22,359
Bahrain	Manama	Bahraini Dinar	$21,236,000,000	$27,248
Bangladesh	Dhaka	Taka	$81,938,000,000	$521
Barbados	Bridgetown	Barbadian Dollar	$3,682,000,000	$13,314
Belarus	Minsk	Belarussian Rouble	$60,288,000,000	$6,235
Belgium	Brussels	Euro	$506,183,000,000	$47,289
Belize	Belmopan	Belize Dollar	$1,381,000,000	$4,241
Benin	Porto-Novo	CFA Franc	$6,940,000,000	$828
Bhutan	Thimphu	Ngultrum	$1,368,000,000	$2,114
Bolivia	La Paz	Boliviano; Bolivian Peso	$17,413,000,000	$1,656
Bosnia and Herzegovina	Sarajevo	Convertible Mark	$18,469,000,000	$4,625
Botswana	Gaborone	Pula	$13,461,000,000	$7,554
Brazil	Brasilia	Real	$1,572,839,000,000	$8,295
Brunei	Bandar Seri Begawan	Brunei Dollar	$14,553,000,000	$37,053

LAND AREA	POPULATION	LIFE EXPECTANCY	LITERACY RATE
652,230 sq km (251,827 sq miles)	28,396,000	43	28.0%
28,748 sq km (11,099 sq miles)	3,196,000	75	99.0%
2,381,741 sq km (919,595 sq miles)	35,370,000	72	69.9%
468 sq km (180 sq miles)	86,000	–	–
1,246,700 sq km (481,353 sq miles)	17,074,000	43	67.4%
443 sq km (171 sq miles)	88,000	73	99.0%
2,780,400 sq km (1,073,518 sq miles)	40,276,000	75	97.6%
29,743 sq km (11,483 sq miles)	3,097,000	71	99.5%
7,741,220 sq km (2,988,901 sq miles)	21,852,000	81	99.0%
83,871 sq km (32,382 sq miles)	8,374,000	80	99.0%
86,600 sq km (33,436 sq miles)	8,781,000	72	99.5%
13,880 sq km (5,359 sq miles)	341,000	72	95.8%
741 sq km (286 sq miles)	1,217,000	75	88.8%
143,998 sq km (55,597 sq miles)	162,221,000	63	47.5%
430 sq km (166 sq miles)	281,000	76	99.7%
207,600 sq km (80,154 sq miles)	9,662,000	70	99.7%
30,528 sq km (11,786 sq miles)	10,792,000	80	99.0%
22,966 sq km (8,867 sq miles)	329,000	73	75.1%
112,622 sq km (43,483 sq miles)	8,935,000	56	34.7%
38,394 sq km (14,824 sq miles)	683,000	66	47.0%
1,098,581 sq km (424,164 sq miles)	9,863,000	65	90.7%
51,197 sq km (19,767 sq miles)	3,843,000	74	96.7%
581,730 sq km (224,607 sq miles)	1,991,000	49	81.2%
8,514,877 sq km (3,287,612 sq miles)	191,481,000	72	90.0%
5,765 sq km (2,225 sq miles)	383,000	75	94.9%

COUNTRY	CAPITAL CITY	CURRENCY	GDP	GDP PER CAPITA
Bulgaria	Sofia	Lev	$51,989,000,000	$6,561
Burkina Faso	Ouagadougou	CFA Franc	$8,103,000,000	$578
Burundi	Bujumbura	Burundi Franc	$1,097,000,000	$138
Cambodia	Phnom Penh	Riel	$11,182,000,000	$823
Cameroon	Yaounde	CFA Franc	$23,243,000,000	$1,224
Canada	Ottawa	Canadian Dollar	$1,499,551,000,000	$45,085
Cape Verde	Praia	Escudo Caboverdiano	$1,723,000,000	$3,464
Central African Republic	Bangui	CFA Franc	$1,997,000,000	$459
Chad	N'Djamena	CFA Franc	$8,390,000,000	$863
Chile	Santiago	Chilean Peso	$169,458,000,000	$10,117
China	Beijing	Chinese Yuan	$4,327,448,000,000	$3,259
Colombia	Bogota	Colombian Peso	$240,832,000,000	$4,989
Comoros	Moroni	Comorian Franc	$532,000,000	$816
Congo	Brazzaville	CFA Franc	$10,774,000,000	$2,952
Cote d'Ivoire	Yamoussoukro	CFA Franc	$23,508,000,000	$1,132
Dem. Rep. Congo	Kinshasa	Congolese Franc	$11,589,000,000	$185
Costa Rica	San Jose	Costa Rican Colón	$29,828,000,000	$6,544
Croatia	Zagreb	Croatian Kuna	$69,332,000,000	$15,634
Cuba	Havana	Cuban Peso	–	–
Cyprus	Nicosia	Euro	$24,943,000,000	$32,745
Czech Republic	Prague	Czech Koruna	$216,354,000,000	$20,760
Denmark	Copenhagen	Danish Krone	$340,029,000,000	$62,097
Djibouti	Djibouti	Djiboutian Franc	$982,000,000	$1,252
Dominica	Roseau	East Caribbean Dollar	$364,000,000	$5,082
Dominican Republic	Santo Domingo	Dominican Republic Peso	$45,597,000,000	$4,992

LAND AREA	POPULATION	LIFE EXPECTANCY	LITERACY RATE
110,879 sq km (42,810 sq miles)	7,590,000	73	98.3%
274,200 sq km (105,869 sq miles)	15,757,000	51	23.6%
27,830 sq km (10,745 sq miles)	8,303,000	49	59.3%
181,035 sq km (69,898 sq miles)	14,805,000	62	73.6%
475,440 sq km (183,568 sq miles)	18,879,000	52	67.9%
9,984,670 sq km (3,855,102 sq miles)	33,707,000	80	99.0%
4,033 sq km (1,557 sq miles)	509,000	71	81.2%
622,984 sq km (240,535 sq miles)	4,511,000	47	48.6%
1,284,000 sq km (495,755 sq miles)	10,329,000	78	25.7%
756,102 sq km (291,932 sq miles)	16,970,000	78	96.5%
9,596,961 sq km (3,705,407 sq miles)	1,331,398,000	73	93.3%
1,138,914 sq km (439,737 sq miles)	45,065,000	72	92.7%
2,235 sq km (862 sq miles)	676,000	64	56.8%
342,000 sq km (132,046 sq miles)	3,683,000	53	84.7%
322,463 sq km (124,503 sq miles)	21,395,000	52	48.7%
2,344,858 sq km (905,350 sq miles)	68,693,000	53	67.2%
51,100 sq km (19,729 sq miles)	4,509,000	78	95.9%
56,594 sq km (21,851 sq miles)	4,433,000	76	98.7%
110,860 sq km (42,803 sq miles)	11,225,000	77	99.8%
9,251 sq km (3,571 sq miles)	1,072,000	78	97.7%
78,867 sq km (30,450 sq miles)	10,511,000	77	99.0%
43,094 sq km (16,638 sq miles)	5,529,000	78	99.0%
23,200 sq km (8,957 sq miles)	864,000	54	70.3%
751 sq km (289 sq miles)	72,000	75	88.0%
48,670 sq km (18,791 sq miles)	10,090,000	72	89.1%

COUNTRY	CAPITAL CITY	CURRENCY	GDP	GDP PER CAPITA
East Timor	Dili	US Dollar	$499,000,000	$469
Ecuador	Quito	US Dollar	$52,572,000,000	$3,928
Egypt	Cairo	Egytian Pound	$162,617,000,000	$2,162
El Salvador	San Salvador	US Dollar	$22,115,000,000	$3,824
Equatorial Guinea	Malabo	CFA Franc	$18,525,000,000	$14,941
Eritrea	Asmara	Eritreian Nakfa; Ethiopian Birr	$1,476,000,000	$295
Estonia	Tallinn	Kroon	$23,232,000,000	$17,532
Ethiopia	Addis Ababa	Birr	$25,658,000,000	$333
Fiji	Suva	Fijian Dollar	$3,590,000,000	$4,094
Finland	Helsinki	Euro	$271,867,000,000	$51,588
France	Paris	Euro	$2,866,951,000,000	$46,037
Gabon	Libreville	CFA Franc	$14,519,000,000	$9,998
Gambia	Banjul	Dalasi	$808,000,000	$497
Georgia	Tbilisi	Lari	$12,870,000,000	$2,924
Germany	Berlin	Euro	$3,673,105,000,000	$44,729
Ghana	Accra	Cedi	$16,124,000,000	$739
Greece	Athens	Euro	$357,548,000,000	$32,105
Grenada	Saint George's	East Caribbean Dollar	$639,000,000	$6,587
Guatemala	Guatemala City	Quetzal	$38,956,000,000	$2,850
Guinea	Conakry	Guinean Franc	$4,542,000,000	$439
Guinea-Bissau	Bissau	CFA Franc	$461,000,000	$264
Guyana	Georgetown	Guyanese Dollar	$1,130,000,000	$1,509
Haiti	Port-au-Prince	Gourde	$6,952,000,000	$790
Honduras	Tegucigalpa	Lempira	$14,126,000,000	$1,826
Hungary	Budapest	Forint	$155,930,000,000	$15,523

LAND AREA	POPULATION	LIFE EXPECTANCY	LITERACY RATE
14,874 sq km (5,742 sq miles)	1,134,000	60	50.1%
283,561 sq km (109,483 sq miles)	13,625,000	75	91.0%
1,001,450 sq km (386,662 sq miles)	78,629,000	72	71.4%
21,041 sq km (8,123 sq miles)	7,339,000	71	80.5%
28,051 sq km (10,830 sq miles)	676,000	59	87.0%
117,600 sq km (45,405 sq miles)	5,073,000	57	60.5%
45,228 sq km (17,462 sq miles)	1,340,000	73	99.8%
1,104,300 sq km (426,372 sq miles)	82,825,000	49	35.9%
18,274 sq km (7,055 sq miles)	844,000	68	94.4%
338,145 sq km (130,558 sq miles)	5,339,000	79	99.0%
643,427 sq km (248,428 sq miles)	62,621,000	81	99.0%
267,667 sq km (103,346 sq miles)	1,475,000	57	84.0%
11,295 sq km (4,361 sq miles)	1,609,000	58	42.5%
69,700 sq km (26,911 sq miles)	4,611,000	74	–
357,022 sq km (137,846 sq miles)	81,980,000	79	99.0%
238,533 sq km (92,098 sq miles)	23,837,000	59	57.9%
131,957 sq km (50,948 sq miles)	11,277,000	79	97.1%
344 sq km (132 sq miles)	106,000	79	96.0%
108,889 sq km (42,042 sq miles)	14,027,000	78	69.1%
245,857 sq km (94,925 sq miles)	10,058,000	54	29.5%
36,125 sq km (13,947 sq miles)	1,611,000	45	44.8%
214969 sq km (82,999 sq miles)	773,000	65	99.0%
27,750 sq km (10,714 sq miles)	9,242,000	58	54.8%
112,090 sq km (43,278 sq miles)	7,466,000	72	80.0%
93,028 sq km (35,918 sq miles)	10,024,000	73	99.4%

COUNTRY	CAPITAL CITY	CURRENCY	GDP	GDP PER CAPITA
Iceland	Reykjavik	Icelandic Króna	$17,549,000,000	$53,058
India	New Delhi	Indian Rupee	$1,206,684,000,000	$1,017
Indonesia	Jakarta	Rupiah	$511,765,000,000	$2,239
Iran	Tehran	Iranian Rial	$335,233,000,000	$4,600
Iraq	Baghdad	Iraqi Dinar	$91,453,000,000	$3,007
Ireland	Dublin	Euro	$267,579,000,000	$60,510
Israel	Tel-Aviv	Israeli New Shekel	$202,101,000,000	$28,409
Italy	Rome	Euro	$2,313,893,000,000	$38,996
Jamaica	Kingston	Jamaican Dollar	$14,397,000,000	$5,199
Japan	Tokyo	Yen	$4,910,692,000,000	$38,457
Jordan	Amman	Jordanian Dinar	$20,030,000,000	$3,626
Kazakhstan	Astana	Tenge	$135,601,000,000	$8,719
Kenya	Nairobi	Kenyan Shilling	$30,236,000,000	$838
Kiribati	Tarawa Atoll	Australian Dollar	$137,000,000	$1,372
Kosovo	Pristina	Euro	–	–
Kuwait	Kuwait City	Kuwaiti Dinar	$158,089,000,000	$45,920
Kyrgyzstan	Bishkek	Kyrgyzstani Som	$5,049,000,000	$951
Laos	Vientiane	Kip	$5,260,000,000	$859
Latvia	Riga	Lats	$34,054,000,000	$14,964
Lebanon	Beirut	Lebanese Pound	$28,939,000,000	$7,708
Lesotho	Maseru	Loti, Maloti; South African Rand	$1,620,000,000	$660
Liberia	Monrovia	Liberian Dollar	$836,000,000	$216
Libya	Tripoli	Libyan Dinar	$89,916,000,000	$14,479
Liechtenstein	Vaduz	Swiss Franc	–	–
Lithuania	Vilnius	Litas	$47,304,000,000	$14,086

LAND AREA	POPULATION	LIFE EXPECTANCY	LITERACY RATE
103,000 sq km (39,768 sq miles)	321,000	81	99.0%
3,287,263 sq km (1,269,219 sq miles)	1,171,029,000	65	61.0%
1,904,569 sq km (735,358 sq miles)	243,306,000	70	92.0%
1,648,195 sq km (636,371 sq miles)	73,244,000	71	82.4%
438,317 sq km (169,235 sq miles)	30,047,000	58	–
70,273 sq km (27,132 sq miles)	4,528,000	79	99.0%
22,072 sq km (8,522 sq miles)	7,634,000	80	97.1%
301,340 sq km (116,348 sq miles)	60,274,000	81	98.9%
10,991 sq km (4,243 sq miles)	2,702,000	72	79.9%
377,915 sq km (145,913 sq miles)	127,568,000	82	99.0%
89,342 sq km (34,495 sq miles)	5,915,000	72	91.1%
2,724,900 sq km (1,052,089 sq miles)	15,880,000	66	99.6%
580,367 sq km (224,080 sq miles)	39,070,000	53	73.6%
811 sq km (313 sq miles)	99,000	61	–
10,887 sq km (4,203 sq miles)	2,222,000	69	–
17,818 sq km (6,879 sq miles)	2,985,000	78	94.5%
199,951 sq km (77,201 sq miles)	5,304,000	66	99.3%
236,800 sq km (91,428 sq miles)	6,320,000	61	68.7%
64,589 sq km (24,937 sq miles)	2,256,000	72	99.8%
10,400 sq km (4,015 sq miles)	3,876,000	72	89.6%
30,355 sq km (11,720 sq miles)	2,135,000	36	82.2%
111,369 sq km (42,999 sq miles)	3,955,000	46	–
1,759,540 sq km (679,362 sq miles)	6,283,000	73	84.2%
160 sq km (61 sq miles)	36,000	80	–
65,300 sq km (25,212 sq miles)	3,339,000	71	99.7%

COUNTRY	CAPITAL CITY	CURRENCY	GDP	GDP PER CAPITA
Luxembourg	Luxembourg	Euro	$54,973,000,000	$113,044
Macedonia	Skopje	Macedonian Denars	$9,569,000,000	$4,657
Madagascar	Antananarivo	Malagasy Ariary	$9,254,000,000	$468
Malawi	Lilongwe	Malawian Kwacha	$4,268,000,000	$313
Malaysia	Kuala Lumpur	Ringgit	$221,606,000,000	$8,118
Maldives	Male	Rufiyaa	$1,259,000,000	$3,654
Mali	Bamako	CFA Franc	$8,783,000,000	$657
Malta	Valletta	Euro	$8,338,000,000	$20,281
Marshall Islands	Majuro	US Dollar	–	–
Mauritania	Nouakchott	Ouguiya	$3,161,000,000	$1,042
Mauritius	Port Louis	Mauritian Rupee	$8,738,000,000	$6,872
Mexico	Mexico City	Mexican Peso	$1,088,128,000,000	$10,200
Micronesia	Palikir	US Dollar	–	–
Moldova	Chisinau	Moldovian Leu	$6,124,000,000	$1,693
Monaco	Monaco	Euro	–	–
Mongolia	Ulaanbaatar	Tugrik	$5,258,000,000	$1,975
Montenegro	Podgorica	Euro	$4,822,000,000	–
Morocco	Rabat	Moroccan Dirham	$88,879,000,000	$2,827
Mozambique	Maputo	Metical	$9,654,000,000	$477
Myanmar (Burma)	Rangoon	Kyat	$27,182,000,000	$446
Namibia	Windhoek	Namibia Dollar; South African Rand	$8,456,000,000	$4,278
Nauru	No official capital	Australian Dollar	–	–
Nepal	Kathmandu	Nepalese Rupee	$12,698,000,000	$444
Netherlands	Amsterdam	Euro	$876,970,000,000	$52,500
New Zealand	Wellington	New Zealand Dollar	$128,409,000,000	$30,030

LAND AREA	POPULATION	LIFE EXPECTANCY	LITERACY RATE
2,586 sq km (998 sq miles)	498,000	80	99.0%
25,713 sq km (9,927 sq miles)	2,049,000	74	97.0%
587,041 sq km (226,657 sq miles)	19,464,000	58	70.7%
118,484 sq km (45,746 sq miles)	14,214,000	46	64.1%
329,847 sq km (127,354 sq miles)	28,295,000	74	91.9%
298 sq km (115 sq miles)	315,000	73	97.0%
1,240,192 sq km (478,840 sq miles)	13,010,000	56	24.0%
316 sq km (122 sq miles)	414,000	79	92.4%
181 sq km (69 sq miles)	54,000	66	–
1,030,700 sq km (397,955 sq miles)	3,291,000	60	51.2%
2,040 sq km (787 sq miles)	1,276,000	72	84.3%
1,964,375 sq km (758,449 sq miles)	109,610,000	75	92.8%
702 sq km (271 sq miles)	111,000	67	–
33,851 sq km (13,069 sq miles)	4,133,000	69	99.2%
2 sq km (0.7 sq miles)	35,000	–	–
1,564,116 sq km (603,908 sq miles)	2,708,000	64	97.3%
13,812 sq km (5,332 sq miles)	628,000	73	–
446,550 sq km (172,413 sq miles)	31,495,000	70	52.3%
799,380 sq km (308,642 sq miles)	21,971,000	43	38.7%
676,578 sq km (261,228 sq miles)	50,020,000	61	89.9%
824,292 sq km (318,260 sq miles)	2,171,000	47	85.0%
21 sq km (8 sq miles)	10,000	55	–
147,181 sq km (56,826 sq miles)	27,504,000	64	48.6%
41,543 sq km (16,039 sq miles)	16,527,000	80	99.0%
267,710 sq km (103,363 sq miles)	4,317,000	80	99.0%

COUNTRY	CAPITAL CITY	CURRENCY	GDP	GDP PER CAPITA
Nicaragua	Managua	Córdoba	$6,350,000,000	$1,028
Niger	Niamey	CFA Franc	$5,379,000,000	$391
Nigeria	Abuja	Naira	$207,116,000,000	$1,401
North Korea	Pyongyang	North Korean Won	–	–
Norway	Oslo	Norwegian Krone	$451,830,000,000	$94,387
Oman	Muscat	Omani Rial	$52,584,000,000	$21,646
Pakistan	Islamabad	Pakistani Rupee	$164,557,000,000	$1,022
Palau	Melekeok	US Dollar	–	–
Panama	Panama City	Panamanian Balboa	$23,088,000,000	$6,784
Papua New Guinea	Port Moresby	Kina	$8,092,000,000	$1,306
Paraguay	Asuncion	Guarani	$16,006,000,000	$2,601
Peru	Lima	Peruvian Nuevo Sol	$127,462,000,000	$4,448
Philippines	Manila	Philippine Peso	$166,909,000,000	$1,845
Poland	Warsaw	Zloty	$527,866,000,000	$13,846
Portugal	Lisbon	Euro	$244,640,000,000	$23,041
Qatar	Doha	Qatari Riyal	$102,302,000,000	$93,204
Romania	Bucharest	Romanian Leu	$200,074,000,000	$9,310
Russia	Moscow	Rouble	$1,676,586,000,000	$11,807
Rwanda	Kigali	Rwandan Franc	$4,459,000,000	$465
Saint Kitts and Nevis	Basseterre	East Caribbean Dollar	$555,000,000	$10,310
Saint Lucia	Castries	East Caribbean Dollar	$1,025,000,000	$5,806
Saint Vincent and the Grenadines	Kingstown	East Caribbean Dollar	$601,000,000	$5,615
Samoa	Apia	Tala	$537,000,000	$2,608
San Marino	San Marino	Euro	–	–
São Tomé and Príncipe	Sao Tome	Dobra	$176,000,000	$1,094

LAND AREA	POPULATION	LIFE EXPECTANCY	LITERACY RATE
130,370 sq km (50,336 sq miles)	5,669,000	71	76.7%
1,267,000 sq km (489,191 sq miles)	15,290,000	57	28.7%
923,768 sq km (356,668 sq miles)	152,616,000	47	69.1%
120,538 sq km (46,539 sq miles)	22,665,000	71	99.0%
323,802 sq km (125,020 sq miles)	4,827,000	80	99.0%
309,500 sq km (119,498 sq miles)	3,108,000	74	81.4%
796,095 sq km (307,373 sq miles)	180,808,000	63	49.9%
459 sq km (177 sq miles)	21,000	71	–
75,420 sq km (29,119 sq miles)	3,454,000	75	93.4%
462,840 sq km (178,703 sq miles)	6,610,000	57	57.3%
406,752 sq km (157,047 sq miles)	6,349,000	71	94.6%
1,285,216 sq km (496,224 sq miles)	29,165,000	71	89.6%
300,000 sq km (115,830 sq miles)	92,227,000	69	93.4%
312,685 sq km (120,728 sq miles)	38,146,000	75	99.3%
92,090 sq km (35,556 sq miles)	10,639,000	79	94.9%
11,586 sq km (4,473 sq miles)	1,409,000	75	93.1%
238,391 sq km (92,043 sq miles)	21,474,000	71	97.6%
17,098,242 sq km (6,601,668 sq miles)	141,839,000	67	99.5%
26,338 sq km (10,169 sq miles)	9,877,000	47	64.9%
261 sq km (100 sq miles)	50,000	70	97.8%
616 sq km (237 sq miles)	172,000	73	94.8%
389 sq km (150 sq miles)	110,000	72	88.1%
2,831 sq km (1,093 sq miles)	190,000	73	98.7%
61 sq km (23 sq miles)	31,000	82	–
964 sq km (374 sq miles)	163,000	64	84.9%

COUNTRY	CAPITAL CITY	CURRENCY	GDP	GDP PER CAPITA
Saudi Arabia	Riyadh	Saudi Riyal	$469,462,000,000	$18,855
Senegal	Dakar	West African Franc; CFA Franc	$13,350,000,000	$1,066
Serbia	Belgrade	Serbian Dinar	$50,061,000,000	$6,782
Seychelles	Victoria	Seychelles Rupee	$834,000,000	$9,640
Sierra Leone	Freetown	Leone	$1,955,000,000	$332
Singapore	Singapore	Singapore Dollar	$181,939,000,000	$38,972
Slovakia	Bratislava	Euro	$95,404,000,000	$17,646
Slovenia	Lkubljana	Euro	$54,639,000,000	$27,149
Solomon Islands	Honiara	Solomon Islands Dollar	$473,000,000	$1,228
Somalia	Mogadishu	Somali Shilling	–	–
South Africa	Cape Town	Rand	$276,764,000,000	$5,685
South Korea	Seoul	South Korean Won	$929,124,000,000	$19,136
Spain	Madrid	Euro	$1,601,964,000,000	$35,117
Sri Lanka	Colombo	Sri Lankan Rupee	$39,604,000,000	$1,972
Sudan	Khartoum	Sudanese Pound	$57,911,000,000	$1,522
Surinam	Paramaribo	Surinamese Dollar	$2,415,000,000	$5,504
Swaziland	Mbabane	Lilangeni	$2,843,000,000	$2,778
Sweden	Stockholm	Swedish Krona	$478,961,000,000	$52,181
Switzerland	Bern	Swiss Franc	$500,260,000,000	$68,433
Syria	Damascus	Syrian Pound	$54,803,000,000	$2,768
Taiwan	Taipei	New Taiwan Dollar	$391,351,000,000	$16,987
Tajikistan	Dushanbe	Tajikistani Somoni	$5,135,000,000	$795
Tanzania	Dodoma	Tanzanian Shilling	$20,721,000,000	$520
Thailand	Bangkok	Baht	$273,313,000,000	$4,116
Togo	Lome	CFA Franc	$2,890,000,000	$436

LAND AREA	POPULATION	LIFE EXPECTANCY	LITERACY RATE
2,149,690 sq km (829,999 sq miles)	28,687,000	76	82.9%
196,722 sq km (75,954 sq miles)	12,534,000	62	39.3%
77,474 sq km (29,912 sq miles)	7,322,000	73	96.4%
455 sq km (175 sq miles)	87,000	72	91.8%
71,740 sq km (27,698 sq miles)	5,696,000	48	34.8%
697 sq km (269 sq miles)	5,113,000	81	94.4%
49,035 sq km (18,932 sq miles)	5,417,000	74	99.0%
20,273 sq km (7,827 sq miles)	2,043,000	78	99.7%
28,896 sq km (11,156 sq miles)	519,000	62	76.6%
637,657 sq km (246,200 sq miles)	9,133,000	48	–
1,219,090 sq km (468,376 sq miles)	50,674,000	50	82.4%
99,720 sq km (38,502 sq miles)	48,747,000	79	99.0%
505,370 sq km (195,124 sq miles)	46,916,000	80	97.9%
65,610 sq km (24,173 sq miles)	20,502,000	71	90.8%
2,505,813 sq km (967,499 sq miles)	42,272,000	58	60.9%
163,820 sq km (63,251 sq miles)	502,000	69	90.4%
17,364 sq km (6,704 sq miles)	1,185,000	33	79.6%
450,295 sq km (173,859 sq miles)	9,288,000	81	99.0%
41,277 sq km (15,937 sq miles)	7,754,000	82	99.0%
185,180 sq km (71,498 sq miles)	21,906,000	73	80.8%
35,980 sq km (13,891 sq miles)	23,079,000	78	–
143,100 sq km (55,251 sq miles)	7,450,000	67	99.6%
947,300 sq km (365,754 sq miles)	43,739,000	51	69.4%
513,120 sq km (198,116 sq miles)	67,764,000	72	94.1%
56,785 sq km (21,924 sq miles)	6,619,000	58	53.2%

COUNTRY	CAPITAL CITY	CURRENCY	GDP	GDP PER CAPITA
Tonga	Nuku'alofa	Pa'anga	$258,000,000	$2,510
Trinidad and Tobago	Port-of-Spain	Trinidad; Tobago Dollar	$24,806,000,000	$19,870
Tunisia	Tunis	Tunisian Dinar	$40,348,000,000	$3,955
Turkey	Ankara	New Turkish Lira	$729,983,000,000	$10,479
Turkmenistan	Ashgabat	Turkmen Manat	–	$3,606
Tuvalu	Funafuti	Australian Dollar	–	–
Uganda	Kampala	Ugandan Shilling	$14,529,000,000	$455
Ukraine	Kyiv	Hyrvnia	$179,604,000,000	$3,910
United Arab Emirates	Abu Dhabi	UAE Dirham	$262,150,000,000	$55,028
United Kingdom	London	Pound Sterling	$2,680,000,000,000	$43,734
United States of America	Washington D.C.	US Dollar	$14,441,425,000,000	$47,440
Uruguay	Montevideo	Uruguayan Peso	$32,262,000,000	$9,654
Uzbekistan	Tashkent	Uzbekistani Som	$27,918,000,000	$1,027
Vanuatu	Port-Vila	Vatu	$573,000,000	$2,442
Vatican City	Vatican City	Euro	–	–
Venezuela	Caracas	Bolivar	$319,443,000,000	$11,388
Vietnam	Hanoi	Dong	$89,829,000,000	$1,042
Yemen	Sanaa	Yemeni Rial	$27,151,000,000	$1,171
Zambia	Lusaka	Zambian Kwacha	$14,323,000,000	$1,248
Zimbabwe	Harare	Zimbabwe Dollar	$3,145,000,000	$268

LAND AREA	POPULATION	LIFE EXPECTANCY	LITERACY RATE
747 sq km (288 sq miles)	103,000	71	99.2%
5,128 sq km (1,979 sq miles)	1,333,000	69	98.7%
163,610 sq km (63,170 sq miles)	10,429,000	74	74.3%
783,562 sq km (302,534 sq miles)	74,816,000	72	88.7%
488,100 sq km (188,456 sq miles)	5,110,000	62	99.5%
26 sq km (10 sq miles)	11,000	64	–
241,038 sq km (93,065 sq miles)	30,700,000	48	66.8%
603,550 sq km (233,031 sq miles)	46,030,000	68	99.7%
83,600 sq km (32,278 sq miles)	5,066,000	78	90.0%
243,610 sq km (94,058 sq miles)	61,823,000	79	99.0%
9,826,675 sq km (3,794,100 sq miles)	306,805,000	78	99.0%
176,215 sq km (68,036 sq miles)	3,364,000	76	97.9%
447,400 sq km (172,742 sq miles)	27,562,000	67	96.9%
12,189 sq km (4,706 sq miles)	239,000	67	74.0%
0.44 sq km (0.16 sq miles)	826	77	100.0%
912,050 sq km (352,144 sq miles)	28,368,000	73	95.2%
331,210 sq km (127,996 sq miles)	87,263,000	73	90.3%
527,968 sq km (203,849 sq miles)	22,880,000	61	54.1%
752,618 sq km (290,587 sq miles)	12,555,000	38	68.0%
390,757 sq km (150,872 sq miles)	12,523,000	40	91.2%

Data sources

The statistical information throughout the book has been taken from the following sources:

Earth

18–19 Quakes and Shakes
Earthquake frequency:
British Columbia Institute of Technology
Measuring Earthquakes: Magnitude and Intensity
http://www.bcit.ca

30–31 Island Formation
Islands types: United Nations Environment Programme Islands directory
www.islands.unep.ch

36–37 Life on the Land
Earth's terrestrial biomes:
Bradshaw, M., Weaver, R. *Physical Geography* (Mosby, 1992)

42–43 Under Threat
Total number of species and number of threatened species figures: International Union for Conservation of Nature Redlist
www.iucnredlist.com

44–45 Six Degrees of Change
Rising sea levels and global warming figures:
IPCC Fourth Assessment Report: Climate Change 2007
www.ipcc.ch

Information on degree-by-degree temperature rises: *What will climate change do to our planet?*
http://www.timesonline.co.uk

People

50–51 How many People on the Planet?
Population figures:
PRB Datafinder,
Population Reference Bureau
www.prb.org

Population growth: *The World at Six Billion*, United Nations Population Division
www.un.org/esa/population

52–53 City Populations
World's most populous urban areas (agglomerations):
The Principal Agglomerations of the World
www.citypopulation.de

The rise of city living:
United Nations World Urbanization Prospects (New York, 2007)

54–55 Changing Populations
Fertility, birth, and death rates:*World Population prospects: The 2008 revision*
www.data.un.com

56–57 How Long have you Got?
Population pyramids: *Midyear Population, by Age and Sex*
www.census.gov

Life expectancy figures:
PRB Datafinder,
Population Reference Bureau
www.prb.org

58–59 Ways to Go
What are the chances?:
The global burden of disease: 2004 update,
World Health Organization
www.who.int

Different ways to die:
Roper, M., *101 Crazy Ways to Die* (Penguin, 2008)

60–61 Disease and Healthcare
Across continents: *The global burden of disease: 2004 update*,
World Health Organization
www.who.int

Doctors and patients and Cost of care figures: *Population, Health and Well-Being database*, Earthtrends
www.wri.org

62–63 Water
Global usage: *SIWI Statistics*,

Stockholm International Water Institute
www.siwi.org

Domestic usage:
Facts and Figures.
World Water Council,
www.worldwatercouncil.org

Stressed resources:
AQUASTAT main country database, AQUASTAT
www.fao.org

Water for the people:
AQUASTAT main country database, AQUASTAT
www.fao.org;

PRB Datafinder,
Population Reference Bureau
www.prb.org

64–65 Hunger
Where hunger hits the hardest:
The State of Food Insecurity in the World 2008, Food and Agriculture Organization;

The United Nations World Food Programme
www.wfp.org

Food aid: *Aid targets slipping out of reach?* (OECD, 2008)

66–67 Food Waste
Worst offenders: Quested, T., Johnson, H., *Household Food and Drink Waste in the UK* (WRAP, 2009)

What's in the bin?:
Quested, T., Johnson, H., *Household Food and Drink Waste in the UK* (WRAP, 2009)

Rotten rubbish:
Quested, T., Johnson, H., *Household Food and Drink Waste in the UK* (WRAP, 2009)

Waste at every stage:
Stuart, T., *Waste* (Penguin, 2009)

68–69 Globesity
Portion sizes: *Portion Distortion Interactive Quiz*, National

Institutes of Health
www.nih.gov

Weight across the nations:
BMI adults % obese,
World Health Organization
www.apps.who.int/bmi

Health issues:
WHO Global Infobase,
World Health Organization
www.who.int

Diabetes Atlas 2006,
International Diabetes Federation
www.diabetesatlas.org

70–71 Daily Diets
What's in the fridge?:
FAOSTAT: Food consumption pattern of main food groups,
Food and Agriculture Organization
www.fao.org

Cost of consumption:
International Food Consumption Patterns,
United States Department of Agriculture
www.ers.usda.gov

Counting the calories:
FAOSTAT: Kcals per day,
Food and Agriculture Organization
www.fao.org

72–73 Look who's Talking
Top 25 languages: *Summary by language size*, Ethnologue
www.ethnologue.com

76–77 Tribal Peoples
Indigenous inhabitants:
Tribes & campaigns,
Survival International
www.survivalinternational.org

78–79 Beliefs and Believers
Religions of the world:
Major Religions of the World
www.adherents.com

80–81 The Big Six
Figures on faiths and adherents: *Major Religions*

of the World
www.adherents.com

82–83 The Gender Gap
Heads of state:
*CIA Chiefs of
State & Cabinet
Members directory*
www.cia.gov

Mapping inequality:
Hausmann, R., Tyson,
L. & Zahidi, S., *The Global
Gender Gap Report*
(World Economic
Forum, 2007)

Nobel Prize winners:
Nobel Laureates Facts
www.nobelprize.org

Percentage of females enrolled in
primary education: *The State of
the World's Children 2009*
www.unicef.org

84–85 Happy Families
Family statistics:
UNECE Statistical
Division Database
www.unece.org;

Brown, S. et al.,
*Economist Pocket World in
Figures*, (Profile Books Ltd,
2009); UNESCO Insitute
for Statistics
www.uis.unesco.org;

86–87 Childhood
Figures from: *The State of
the World's Children 2009*
www.unicef.org

88–89 School Days
UNESCO Insitute for Statistics
www.uis.unesco.org;

*The State of the
World's Children 2009*
www.unicef.org

90–91 Work
Annual hours at work:
OECD Employment Outlook
(OECD, 2008)

Size of workforces:
CIA World Factbook
www.cia.gov

iPod index: *Ranking: The richest
cities in the world*
www.citymayors.com;

Prices and Earnings
www.ubs.com

92–93 The Teenage Day
Figures on time spent on various
activities: *How high school
students use time: a visual essay*
www.bls.gov

Teen TV viewing around the
world: *How Teens Use Media*
www.nielsen.com

96–97 Who's Happiest?
Life satisfaction chart:
Gallup Well-Being Index
www.worldview.gallup.com

GNI Per capita figures:
CIA World Factbook
www.cia.gov

98–99 People and their Pets
Pets in the USA: The American
Pet Product Association
www.americanpetproducts.org

Pet ownership figures:
American Society for the
Prevention of Cruelty to Animals
www.aspca.org;

The Humane Society of the
United States
www.humanesociety.org;

The American Pet
Product Association
www.americanpetproducts.org

Power

104–105 Countries and Flags
Population figures:
*PRB Datafinder,
Population Reference Bureau*
www.prb.org

116–117 International Alliances
Organizations information:
North Atlantic Treaty
Organization
www.nato.int;

Organization for
Economic Development
www.oecd.org;

Organization of
American States
www.oas.org;
Association of Southeast

Asian Nations
www.aseansec.org;

Organisation of the Islamic
Conference
www.oic-oci.org;

African Union
www.africa-union.org;

League of Arab States
www.arableagueonline.org;

Organization of Petroleum
Exporting Countries
www.opec.org;

Gulf Cooperation Council
www.gcc-sg.org/eng

118–119 European Union
EU Parliment:
The European Parliament
www.europa.eu

Money matters: *The 2008
EU budget Financial Report*
www.europa.eu

120–121 United Nations
Information from:
The United Nations
www.un.org

122–123 War and Terrorism
Definition of conflicts
and other information:
Uppsala Conflict Data Program
www.pcr.uu.se

124–125 Explosive Budgets
SIPRI Yearbook. *Armaments,
Disarmament and International
Security.* (SIPRI, 2009)

126–127 Far From Home
Refugees and asylum seeker
numbers: *UNHCR. Refugees,
Asylum-seekers, Returnees,
Internally Displaced and
Stateless Persons*
(United Nations, 2008)

128–129 Human Rights
Child labour: *Child labour*
www.childinfo.org

Press freedom: *Press Freedom
In the World 2009*
www.freedomhouse.org

Freedom of religion:
Global Restrictions on Religion
www.pewforum.org

130–131 Crime
Crime and police figures:
*The Tenth United Nations Survey
of Crime Trends and Operations
of Criminal Justice Systems*
(United Nations, 2006)

132–133 Punishment
Under lock and key and Prison
population rate: Walmsley, R.,
World Prison Population List
(Kings College London, 2008)

134–135 Surveillance
Smart cards: *Prime Numbers:
The Plastic Revolution*
www.foreignpolicy.com

136–137 Big Business
Powerhouses: *List of the top
100 multinational corporations*
www.money.cnn.com;

Wal-mart
www.walmartstores.com

Biggest employers:
Biggest employers
www.money.cnn.com

Investment in developing
countries figures: Miroux, et al.,
World Investment Report 2008.

*Transnational Corporations and
the Infrastructure Challenge*
(United Nations, 2008)

138–139 Making Money
Global currencies:
Currency in Circulation
www.dollardaze.org

Who's got the gold?: *Who Owns
Most of the World's Gold?*
www.goldworld.com

140–141 Wealth of Nations
Figures from: *World Economic
Outlook Database: 2008
International Monetary Fund*
www.imf.org

142–143 Inequality
Less than $1.25 a day:
*Population living on less
than $1.25 a day*
www.unicef.org

Haves and have nots: *The World
Distribution of Household
Wealth.* World Institute for
Development Economics
Research of the United

Nations University
www.wider.unu.edu

Who wants to be a billionaire?:
Billionaires by country of origin.
www.forbes.com

World's richest people:
Forbes Billionaire list 2009
www.forbes.com

Wealth within countries: *World Development Indicators 2007*
www.web.worldbank.org

144–145 Balancing the Books
A helping hand: *UNDP Human Development Report 2007-2008* (Palgrave Macmillan, 2007)

Indebted countries: *Total debt service as a percent of export earnings: Economics, Business and the Environment database,* Earthtrends
www.wri.org

Aid as a percentage of income: *Aid as a percent of GNI: Economics, Business and the Environment database,* Earthtrends
www.wri.org

Top recipients:
Top Ten Recipients of Gross ODA
www.oecd.org

Industry

150–151 World Market
Imported commodities and Balancing the scales: *International Trade Centre statistics*
www.trademap.org

Balance of trade figures: *Trading Economics*
www.tradingeconomics.com/

Raw materials and finished goods: *Nigerian National Petroleum Corporation 2008 ASB 1st Edition Web*
www.nnpcgroup.com/

152–153 Japanomics
GDP and Economy figures:
CIA World Factbook
www.cia.gov

154–155 Energy Resources
Different sources: International Energy Agency. *Key World Energy Statistics* (OECD, 2009)

Energy use by sector: *International Energy Agency data services*
www.iea.org

Per capita energy consumption: International Energy Agency. *Key World Energy Statistics.* (OECD, 2009)

Increase in energy consumption: *International Energy Outlook 2009*
www.eia.doe.gov

How long will supplies last?: BP: *World oil and gas reserves still growing at healthy pace*
www.energybulletin.net;

Supply of Uranium
www.world-nuclear.org;

International Energy Outlook 2009
www.eia.doe.gov

156–157 Fossil Fuels
Oil, gas, and coal reserves figures: *International Energy Outlook 2009*
www.eia.doe.gov

Coal consumption: *British Petroleum Statistical Review of World Energy* (BP, 2009)

158–159 Renewable Energy
Power for the people: International Energy Agency. *World Energy Outlook.* (OECD, 2004)

160–161 Nuclear Energy
Energy equivalents: Mitchell, M., *A prospector's guide to uranium deposits in Newfoundland and Labrador* (Prospectors Resource Room, 2007)

Hazardous waste: *Waste Management in the Nuclear Fuel Cycle*
www.world-nuclear.org

Relying on nuclear power: *Nuclear share of generation*
www.world-nuclear.org

Clean and green: *Risks and Benefits of Nuclear Energy* (OECD, 2007)

168–169 Forestry
Figures from: *Global Forest Resources Assessment* (FAO, 2005)

170–171 Farming
Rice and wheat figures: FAOSTAT: Food and Agricultural commodities production, Food and Agriculture Organization
www.fao.org

Key crops: Williams, et al., *World Agricultural Production* (USDA, 2009)

Livestock populations: FAOSTAT: *Selected Indicators of Food and Agriculture Development,* Food and Agriculture Organization
www.fao.org

Organic farming: Willer, et al., *The World of Organic Agriculture. Statistics and Emerging Trends.* FiBL-IFOAM Report (ITC, 2009)

172–173 Cocoa and chocolate
Cocoa consumption: *Cocoa: actual and projected consumption* www.fao.org

Who profits?: *All children have the right to nutritious food*
www.unicef.org.uk/teacherzone

Cocoa production information: FAOSTAT: Major Food and Agricultural Commodities and Producers, Food and Agriculture Organization
www.fao.org

174–175 Fishy business
Fish production: *World Fisheries production, by capture and country*
www.fao.org

Fish species: *The State of World Fisheries and Aquaculture* (FAO, 2009)

176–177 Mining
Metal ore, precious metals,

and gem figures: Brown, T. J. et al., *World Mineral Production 2003-07* (British Geological Survey, 2009)

178–179 Diamonds
Diamond production figures: Brown, T. J. et al., *World Mineral Production 2003-07* (British Geological Survey, 2009)

180–181 Making the Modern World
The leaders of tomorrow: *Manufacturng output as a percent of world manufacturing output* www.bls.gov

A cast of millions: *Employment in manufacturing*
www.bls.gov

Auto top-up: *2008 production statistics*
www.oica.net

Toy exports: *Top 20 Exporter Activity Statistics*
www.exportbureau.com

182–183 Robots
Robot density: *Top 10 Countries by Robot Density*
www.asia.cnet.com

Robots by industry and service figures: *World Robotics 2009*
www.ifr.org

186–187 Shop till you drop
Big spenders: World Federation of Direct Selling Associations
www.wfdsa.org

The world's biggest shopping malls: *The World's Largest Malls*
www.forbes.com

Biggest retailers: *Global Powers of Retailing*
www.deloitte.com
Shopping online: *Trends in online shopping*
www.nielsen.com

188–189 Advertising
Global advertising budget figures: *Global advertising expenditure by medium*
www.zenithoptimedia.com

Most advertised figures:
Advertising Age
www.adage.com

190–191 Human Impact
Oil spills:
Case histories.
The International
Tanker Owners
Pollution Federation
www.itopf.com

Sulphur dioxide and carbon
emissions figures:
Sulfur dioxide emissions.
Energy and Resources
database, Earthtrends
www.wri.org

Waste per capita:
Municipal waste generation
per capita (OECD, 2009)

Connections

196–197 On the Move
Car ownership:
Brown, S. et al., *Economist*
Pocket World in Figures
(Profile Books Ltd, 2009)

Emissions from transport:
World Greenhouse Gas
Emissions. Energy and
Resources database,
Earthtrends
www.wri.org

Distance travelled by rail:
Economist Pocket World in
Figures (Profile Books Ltd,
2009)

198–199 Up and Away!
Aircraft sizes and speeds figures:
Aircraft Data
www.airliners.net;

Commercial Airplanes
www.boeing.com;
Aircraft families
www.airbus.com

Priciest planes:
www.forbes.com

Busiest routes by
passenger numbers:
Why the plane in Spain
continues to reign
www.oag.com

Busiest airports by
passenger numbers:
The ACI World Airport
Traffic Report 2008
www.aci.aero

200–201 Shipping and Ports
Busiest ports:
Port of Rotterdam Authority.
Port Statistics. Rotterdam
(Port of Rotterdam
Authority, 2009)

202–203 Tourism
Top destinations:
World's Top 10 Tourism
Destinations, 2007
www.unwto.org

On the rise:
International tourism,
expenditures (current US$),
World Development Indicators
Database
www.web.worldbank.org

The biggest earners:
World's Top 10 Tourism
Earners 2007, World
Tourism Organization
www.unwto.org

Keenest travellers:
International tourism,
receipts (current US$),
World Development I
ndicators Database
www.web.worldbank.org

204–205 In the Post
Mail figures:
The Universal Postal Union
www.upu.int

206–207 Internet
Online access:
World Internet Users
www.internetworldstats.com

Internet speed:
The 2008 ITIF Broadband
Rankings
www.itif.org

208–209 Online Crime
Confidence tricks
and Online fraud:
the culprits: *Internet*
Crime Complaint Center
www.consumerfraudreporting.org

Who sends the spam?:
McAfee Threats Report: Second

Quarter 2009
www.mcafee.com

210–211 Sport Watch
Worldwide TV viewing figures:
Alavy, K., Mison, S. & Salazar,
V., *Viewer Track. The most*
watched TV sporting events
of 2008
(Futures sport +
entertainment, 2009)

Show me the money!:
The World's Highest-Paid Athletes
www.forbes.com

212–213 Movie Magic
Production costs per film:
Bollywood vs. Hollywood
www.mpaa.com;

Outlook for the Chinese
Film Industry
www.midlinc.net

Films produced:
Number of feature
films produced
www.data.un.org

Marketing costs per film:
Entertainment Industry Market
Statistics 2007
www.mpaa.com;

Bollywood vs. Hollywood
www.mpaa.com

Top moviegoing nations:
Brown, S. et al., *Economist*
Pocket World in Figures
(Profile Books Ltd, 2009)

214–215 Media
Biggest media organizations:
Global 500 by sector
www.ft.com

Magazines:
National Geographic
www.ngm.nationalgeographic.
com;

TIME
www.timemediakit.com;
Newsweek
www.magazine.org;

U.S. News & World Report
www.magazine.org;

The Economist
www.economist-circulation.com;

India Today
www.indiatodaygroup.com;

Veja
www.publicidade.abril.com.br;

New Yorker
www.magazine.org;

Der Spiegel
www.media.spiegel.de

Online:
Largest Online News
Websites Globally
www.techcrunchies.com

Television:
CNN25
www.edition.cnn.com;

BBC Press Office
www.bbc.co.uk/pressoffice;

al-Jazeera Reaches
100m English-Speaking Homes
www.warc.com

218–219 Satellites
Launch cost figures:
Big Growth in World Satellite
Market Over The Next Ten Years
www.spacemart.com

220–221 International
Space Station
Space station, NASA
www.nasa.gov

226–227 Our World
in the Future
Largest economies in 2050:
Hawksworth, J,. Cookson, G.
The World in 2050.
(PricewaterhouseCoopers
LLP, 2008)

Largest populations in 2050:
PRB Datafinder,
Population Reference Bureau
www.prb.org

Index

Acknowledgements

DK would like to thank:
Additional designers: Spencer Holbrook, Johnny Pau, Owen Peyton Jones, Smiljka Surla, and Jacqui Swan.
Additonal editors: Carron Brown and Caitlin Doyle.
Additional writing: Philip Steele.
Proofread by Caitlin Doyle.
Indexer: Jackie Brind.

Happiness data p96: copyright © 2010 Gallup, Inc.
Viewing figures p210: thanks to futures sport + entertainment.

The publisher would like to thank the following for their kind permission to reproduce their photographs:
Key: a-above; b-below/bottom; c-centre; f-far; l-left; r-right; t-top

21 Corbis: Arctic-Images (tr); Roger Ressmeyer (cra); Jim Sugar (crb); Tony Waltham / Robert Harding World Imagery (br). Getty Images: Arlan Naeg / AFP (cr/ Mount Pinatubo). Photolibrary: Dani / Jeske N/A (cr/Krakatau). **27** Corbis: (cra) (br); Hervé Collart (crb); Ilya Naymushin / Reuters (tr); Wen Zhenxiao / XinHua / Xinhua Press (cr). **28** Corbis: Stuart Westmorland / Science Faction (bl). FLPA: Norbert Wu / Minden Pictures (br). **29** Corbis: Bettmann (br). Science Photo Library: Dr Ken Macdonald (bl). **38** iStockphoto.com: Laurence Dean (cra) (cr) (crb); Paul Pantazescu (tr); Clee Villasor (br). **39** iStockphoto.com: Laurence Dean (tl); Cihan Demirok (r); fajean (fbr); Jamie Farrant (bc); grimgram (tc); Paul Pantazescu (br); penfold (c); Yevgeniy Il\'yin (cb). **40** iStockphoto.com: Oscar Fernandez Chuyn (crb); Josef Prchal (cr) (cb); Panagiota Vorgia (br). **40-41** iStockphoto.com: Mark Stay (t). **41** iStockphoto.com: David Crooks (br/bee); cyfrogclone (bl); Jim Snyder (cl); Michael Travers (br/fly); Yevgeniy Il\'yin (br/ant). **42** Getty Images: AFP (br). iStockphoto. com: Laurent Renault (tl). **43** Alamy Images: blickwinkel (tl). Corbis: Alberto Aparicio/Xinhua Press (bc); Keren Su (bl). iStockphoto.com: Tanveer Ali (clb); alle12 (cla); Ivan Bajic (cb); Ermin Gutenberger

(cra); Jun Yan Loke (tr); Carlos Santa Maria (crb); John Woodworth (tc). NHPA / Photoshot: Joe Blossom (br). **44** iStockphoto. com: creatingmore (r). **57** Corbis: Jean Pierre Fizet / Sygma (tc). **62** iStockphoto. com: Gürsel Devrim Çelik (br/footprints); Igor Djurovic (cr); fckuen (tl); Dave Stevens (c/house & factory). **63** iStockphoto.com: breckeni (br/microchips); julichka (bc/ paper); Leontura (tr); Spauln (br/gun). **64** iStockphoto.com: song_mi (bl). **66** iStockphoto.com: Stephen Dumayne (tc); Julien Grondin (b); Alison Hess (c) (bc); sorbetto (cb). **67** iStockphoto.com: Roman Dekan (bc); Paul Fleet (fbl); grimgram (fcla); Alison Hess (c); Giovanni Meroni (fbr); Mark Stay (cl); Hogne Botnen Totland (cla). **68** iStockphoto.com: (fbr); Dmitriy Osminskiy (br); Edyta Pawłowska (c); Stockphoto4u (cr); Kristina Velickovic (bc). **69** Corbis: E.M.Pasieka / Science Photo Library (bc). **80** Alamy Images: JTB Photo Communications, Inc. (br). Getty Images: Paul Beinssen (bl); Richard Nowitz (bc). **81** Corbis: Herbert Spichtinger (bl). Getty Images: Martin Gray (br); Nabeel Turner (bc). **86** iStockphoto.com: song_mi (bl). **91** iStockphoto.com: Brendon De Suza (br); Kathy Konkle (cra). **93** iStockphoto.com: bubaone (ca); Qizhi He (cla); Paul Pantazescu (tr). **98** Corbis: DLILLC (cra); Pat Doyle (cl); Martin Harvey (fcra) (cr/rabbit); Jakob Helbig / cultura (c); Mark Mawson / Robert Harding World Imagery (ca); Hans Reinhard (cla). **99** Getty Images: John W Banagan (c). **110** iStockphoto.com: James Steidl (br). **114-115** iStockphoto.com: Illustrious (b). **116** NATO: (tl). OAS: (bl). OECD: (l). **117** OPEC: (clb). **118** iStockphoto.com: Brandon Laufenberg (tr). **119** iStockphoto. com: Brandon Laufenberg (tl). **120** UN/DPI Photo: (cla). **121** UN/DPI Photo: (br). USPS: (tr). **122** iStockphoto.com: creatingmore (cl); Karlkotas Inc (cla); Karl Kotas (clb). **125** iStockphoto.com: 4x6 (cr); apatrimonio (tr). **134** iStockphoto.com: Marc Brown (cla) (br) (c); Sander Kamp (tr); Frank Ramspott (ca). **135** iStockphoto.com: Marc Brown (tl); bubaone (bl); David Foreman (cr). **138** iStockphoto.com: Er Ten Hong (cla); -Mosquito- (ca). **138-139** iStockphoto.com: imgendesign (banks / wallet). **139** Getty

Images: Thomas Northcut (tr). iStockphoto. com: Er Ten Hong (ca/bank note); -Mosquito- (br) (ca/cakes); roccomontoya (br/ wheelbarrow). **143** Corbis: Peter Turnley (tr). **151** The Fairtrade Foundation: (crb/ logo). **155** iStockphoto.com: Peter Garbet (br); Nicky Laatz (t/lightbulbs); pialhovik (bl); Russell Tate (c). **156** iStockphoto. com: andres (tr/flames); Goce Risteski (tr/ oil rigs). **157** iStockphoto.com: (tr/power stations); Pavel Khorenyan (tl/oil rig). **160** iStockphoto.com: Todd Harrison (bc/ oil) (bc); Aleksandr Volodin (br). **166** Getty Images: gulfimages (tr). **166-167** iStockphoto.com: Teun van den Dries (b). **167** Getty Images: (tr). **174** Alamy Images: Markus Redmann / imagebroker (c). **175** Corbis: Bloomimage (br); Image Source (cra). **178** Corbis: Reuters (tl); Tugela Ridley/epa (cl). Getty Images: Richard du Toit (bl). **178-179** Science Photo Library: Christophe Vander Eecken / Reporters (b). **182** Corbis: James Leynse (bc); Julian Martin/epa (bl). **183** iStockphoto. com: AtomA (br). **190** iStockphoto.com: Christopher Hudson (bl). **191** iStockphoto. com: Giovanni Banfi (tr); Philip Barker (cr); Bob Vidler (br). **202** iStockphoto.com: Albert Campbell (bc) (cl) (clb) (crb). **203** iStockphoto.com: renatorena (tl); Jeffrey Thompson (cb). **206** iStockphoto.com: _zak (tr). **207** iStockphoto.com: Dave Hopkins (bc); _zak (tr). **208** Science Photo Library: Laguna Design (br). **210** iStockphoto.com: Nicolas Hansen (fbl) (bc) (bl) (br) (fbr). **212** iStockphoto.com: addan (clb); Petr Stepanov (cl). **213** iStockphoto.com: Petr Stepanov (b); _zak (tc). **218** iStockphoto. com: rdiraimo (cb). **220** Science Photo Library: Friedrich Saurer (tl). **221** Corbis: NASA/Reuters (tr). NASA: (tl) (ftl). Science Photo Library: NASA (ftr)

All other images © Dorling Kindersley
For further information see:
www.dkimages.com